Group Work
With Sexually
Abused Children

D1710167

Group Work With Sexually Abused Children

A Practitioner's Guide

Lynn Grotsky • Carel Camerer • Lynn Damiano

Sage Publications, Inc.

International Educational and Professional Publisher

Thousand Oaks ▪ London ▪ New Delhi

For information:

Sage Publications, Inc.
2455 Teller Road
Thousand Oaks, California 91320
E-mail: order@sagepub.com

Sage Publications Ltd.
6 Bonhill Street
London EC2A 4PU
United Kingdom

Sage Publications India Pvt. Ltd.
M-32 Market
Greater Kailash I
New Delhi 110048 India

Printed in the United States of America

Library of Congress Cataloging-in-Publication Data

Grotsky, Lynn.
  Group work with sexually abused children : A practitioner's guide / by
Lynn Grotsky, Carel Camerer, Lynn Damiano.
     p. cm. — (Interpersonal violence)
Includes bibliographical references.
ISBN 0-7619-2079-X (pbk: acid-free paper)
  I. Title. II. Series. III. Camerer, Carel. IV. Damiano, Lynn.
1. Sexually abused children—Rehabilitation. 2. Group psychotherapy for
children—Problems, exercises, etc.
  RJ507.S49 G76 2000
    618.92′858360651—dc21   99-006835

00 01 02 03 04 05 06 8 7 6 5 4 3 2 1

Acquiring Editor:	Kassie Gavrilis
Production Editor:	Denise Santoyo
Typesetter/Designer:	Danielle Dillahunt

CONTENTS

PREFACE

We believe it is important for you, the reader, to understand our theoretical framework. This framework is based on our philosophy, which has formed how we work with sexually abused children and their families and is the foundation for the goals and objectives of our groups. The suppositions we are working under are as follows:

- Child abuse exists.
- It is atypical for young children to lie about being sexually abused. In fact, children are more apt to omit rather than commit information to avoid negative consequences.
- In order to treat the symptoms of sexual abuse, the therapist must treat the whole person: the intellectual, emotional, physical, sexual, and spiritual selves.
- The entire family is affected when a member is sexually abused. Therefore, the entire family needs and deserves treatment.
- There are no effective quick, short-term treatments for victims of ongoing sexual abuse, and a combination of modalities is needed for treatment to be effective.
- Society is in various stages of denial about sexual abuse. Society is limited to the discovery and assertion of only that which it sanctions.
- Abuse is perpetuated by a society that encourages people to be competitive, judgmental, and controlling and where one or more groups of people are considered to be inferior to another. Victims need to be educated about society's imbalance of power to minimize future victimization.
- Sexual abuse is a socially communicable disease that, if left untreated, is passed from one generation to the next.

ACKNOWLEDGMENTS

This book, like many good things in life, is the result of a team effort. There are many people we have learned from and been inspired by, and who have greatly influenced us. The first of these, of course, are the incredible children and their families with whom we have worked over the years. To them we extend our gratitude and dedicate this book. May your wounds be transformed into wisdom and the causes of your pain into compassion.

A special thanks to all the staff and interns at the Center for Individual and Family Counseling who challenged us, developed many of the exercises in this book, and had and continue to have a major influence on our work with children. Our heartfelt thanks to the following staff members: Patricia Godleman, Karen Farber, Gabrielle Clayton, Dawn Larsen, Sandra Hurd, Katy Murray, and Jody Ferguson. We deeply appreciate and admire your creativity, passionate dedication to your work, and impeccable clinical skills. A specific thank-you to the following interns: Margaret Vest, Kendall Wark, Susan Kravit, Sara Vanucci, Mike Holly, Linda Lunow, Christine Auvil, Jesalyn Greenwald, Heather Brown, Elizabeth Marcus, Beth Rogers, and Marsha Zaritsky. Your questioning and wonderment kept us on our toes and forced us to articulate how and why we use the techniques we do. Thank you to Karen McQuivey, Lucy Berliner, Faye Adams, Bev Emery, Melissa Allen, Jill Cooper, St. Peter Hospital's Sexual Assault Clinic, the Washington Coalition of Sexual Assault Programs, and the Office of Crime Victim Advocates for your wonderful ideas, help, or grants, which assisted us in providing the therapy. For their great editing abilities, we wish to thank Jon Conte (for sticking with us through so many years!), Georgene Marshman, Wayne Kritzberg, Lisa Brodoff, Jolie Sandoz, Katy Lusson, and Lucy Bayer. And John Konovsky and Don Martin, thank you for opening up your home and computer to us.

A joyous thank you and appreciation to our cover illustrators, 6-year-old Jesse and 9-year-old Micha Brodoff. Micha drew the loving hands with stamped hearts while Jesse drew children attending group. Jesse, as your mother says, "you are a blessing to her and now a blessing to others who have been hurt like you. You are so strong!" Thank you, Jesse and Micha.

Most of all, we would like to thank one another for writing this book together. It is said that what doesn't kill you makes you stronger. Melding three different writing and clinical styles (not to mention egos) is a major challenge and accomplishment. This book is an absolute combination of all three of our voices, beliefs, and styles. Over the years we have worked, taught, learned, laughed, and cried together. The book is much stronger because of this, and so are we.

Lynn Grotsky, Carel Camerer, and Lynn Damiano

I am forever indebted to and in constant awe of Lisa Brodoff, my life partner and soul mate, whose unflinching support, humor, and dedication to me and our children has allowed me to have the courage, confidence, and time to complete this book. In addition, I thank all my friends, my family, my children, Evan and Micha, and the Righteous Mothers, who have always been and continue to be there for me. After two decades of working with sexually abused children and their families, your friendship and support continue to humor, cajole, and cradle me, supplying me with the energy, vision, and compassion to continue with this work.

L.G.

I am ever so grateful to Lynn Damiano, my life partner and twin flame, whose light and commitment is an encouragement each day of this journey. Thank you for sharing your kind, gentle spirit and the brilliance of your wisdom. Songs, laughter, and love flow through you like water, soothing me and all the souls you touch. Thank you to my family for believing in me and encouraging me to complete this book, which at times was a daunting task. Old friends and new have offered such gracious support and thoughtful consideration throughout this project. Thank you to my dearest friends for five-element acupuncture and big feelings.

C.C.

It isn't everyday that the opportunity arises to profess private gratitudes publicly. I am thankful for the chance. To Carel Camerer, my life partner, best friend, and coauthor of all meaningful things, thank you for being you and loving me. No words are deep enough to express how your presence, love, and courage encourage me and everyone in your path. To my family, thank you for loving me through the hard and silent times and sharing in the good that came from them. To my friends, especially Shannon Osborne, Peggy Zorn, and Cathay Webb, thank you for your loving support, wisdom, and patience, and for listening even when your ears were threatening suicide.

L.D.

chapter 1

INTRODUCTION

Sexual assault is a trauma that affects the entire family as well as the community of the person assaulted. It is a social disease that affects human development and the ability to relate to others. It is treatable. The abused child is the primary victim and other family members are secondary victims. Without treatment, the effects of abuse can progressively undermine and overwhelm all areas of both the abused individual's and the family's functioning (Deblinger & Heflin, 1996; Everson, Hunter, Runyon, Edelson, & Coulter, 1989).

The courage to face the reality of childhood sexual assault as a society has led to increased awareness of the problem and skill in identifying its presence. Over the past two decades, the demand for therapy for sexually abused children has increased exponentially. To meet the growing needs and sheer numbers of often underresourced children and families, clinicians have looked toward the group therapy model for its therapeutic effectiveness and economy. Group therapy not only offers the advantage of serving greater numbers of children at lower cost, it also is believed to be an effective form of treatment for the broad range of cognitive, affective, and behavioral symptoms associated with childhood sexual abuse (Celano, 1990; Friedrich, Berliner, Urquiza, & Beilke, 1988; Mandell & Damon, 1989; Zaidi & Gutierrez-Kovner, 1995).

Group work with sexually abused children is not only effective, it is highly rewarding and creative. We believe that the sooner a child is treated, the easier it is to lessen the early effects of sexual abuse: shame, self-blame, low self-esteem, poor social functioning, fear, and isolation (Browne & Finkelhor, 1986; Gomes-Schwartz, Horowitz, & Cardarelli, 1990). By minimizing these destructive feelings and processing through the abuse, children regain a sense of safety and trust, and learn to relate genuinely and spontaneously again.

In 1989, Jon Conte, John Briere, and Dan Sexton presented research that identified more than 700 variables thought to have impacts on the sequelae of sexual abuse. Their

1

findings indicate that *family* and/or *other major adult support* and *peer support* can significantly reduce the long-term effects of sexual assault. When family members believe and support the victimized child, long-term symptoms are significantly reduced. Unfortunately, it is common that many nonoffending parents are untreated victims themselves, suffering from their own distress triggered by their children's disclosures (Deblinger, Hathaway, Lippman, & Steer, 1993; Kelley, 1990). These parents are often too wounded and unresolved to support their children's recovery. Even when parents were not abused as children, their children's abuse will inevitably cause them feelings of grief, anger, and victimization (Kelley, 1990; Sgroi & Dana, 1982). These feelings can temporarily overwhelm their capacity to take care of their children's needs.

A family's support is as vital to a child's safety as peer support is to a child's sense of belonging. Often, sexually abused children feel isolated from other children their age, believing that they are the only ones who have been sexually abused and that they brought the abuse on themselves (Carozza & Heirsteiner, 1982; Celano, 1990). They worry that no one would like them if the truth were known, and they fear they will be treated as outcasts by schoolmates. Imagine a child feeling alone and ashamed, coming into a room of six to eight peers and finding out that all these other children have also been sexually abused. For many, such an experience is the first time in their lives that they feel connected with and accepted by others. The impacts we see on abused children from this experience alone are significant.

Pamela Alexander (1993) discusses the importance of attachment in ameliorating the long-term effects of child sexual abuse. She states that the attachment the child develops with the therapist plays an important role in treatment outcomes. We believe that an abused child's ability to attach to family members, peers, significant adults, and therapists alike greatly decreases the child's symptoms.

Research also suggests that untreated childhood sexual abuse victims may grow up to have a myriad of other problems, such as depression, anxiety, sexual dysfunction, self-destructive behaviors, relationship problems, chemical dependency, and increased likelihood of revictimization (Browne & Finkelhor, 1986). A survey conducted by Benjamin Saunders and his colleagues found that children who were victims of physical sexual assault were more likely than nonvictims to meet the *DSM-III* diagnostic criteria for a major depressive episode, agoraphobia, obsessive-compulsive disorder, social phobia, and/or sexual disorders (see Saunders, Villeponteaux, Lipovsky, Kilpatrick, & Veronen, 1992). Also, a high percentage of women diagnosed with borderline personality disorder have been found to have been sexually abused as children (Linehan, 1993). These coping patterns are difficult to unlearn. When abused children are treated early, disorders such as these can be minimized or eradicated before they become enduring personality traits and treatment becomes a long and arduous process. Children do not have to maintain defensive coping once they learn that the abuse was not their fault, that other children have also been abused, and that they deserve and will receive love and protection.

To ensure positive treatment outcomes for children, we recommend that family and individual therapy occur in conjunction with group work. We also require that parents attend a parent/caregiver group while their children are attending the children's group. All parents of abused children need and deserve treatment, and those who receive it greatly enhance and accelerate their children's recovery (Deblinger & Heflin, 1996; Furniss, 1987; McCarthy, 1990; Ribordy, 1989; Sgroi & Dana, 1982).

WHO SHOULD USE THIS BOOK

This book was written for anyone trained to facilitate support or therapy groups for sexually abused children. This includes mental health therapists, advocates, school counselors, and clergy. For individuals to be effective facilitators, we recommend that they have specialized training in the following areas:

- The dynamics of sexual abuse
- The effects of victimization
- Grief and coping skills
- The roots of violence/oppression
- The state's mandated reporting laws
- Ethics rules and confidentiality requirements

To receive information about or to access training in the above areas, individuals can contact their local rape relief organizations or statewide sexual assault coalitions.

Although this book is intended to be used for group work, with a few modifications, most of the exercises included here can be used by therapists working with children in individual therapy.

HOW TO USE THIS BOOK

This volume is designed as a resource for facilitators of both therapy groups and support groups. Each exercise can be used on its own or in conjunction with others. The exercises come from a variety of sources. Unfortunately, some can no longer be traced back to their origins. Many have been passed along from one sexual assault program to another through the years. Others are derived from well-known children's games, stories, and therapeutic exercises that have been adapted to meet group goals. Many of the exercises were originated by our staff. Their creativity and enthusiasm constantly lead to new ideas as well as ways to adapt old ideas to each new group.

Following some of the exercises, we include sample materials written by members of our groups. In these materials, the names of the children and their family members have been changed out of respect for their privacy.

The appendix at the end of the book contains some sample outlines of groups for preschoolers, girls, boys, and adolescents. It includes outlines for therapy groups and support groups. We recommend the use of these outlines as jumping-off points for your groups. We always outline the plan for any group in advance. This helps to ensure that we will meet our goals and objectives for the particular group. We should note that these outlines are almost always later revised. For instance, there may be a particular child who could clearly benefit from a specific exercise, but on the day the exercise is planned, she is absent. Do you still go ahead and do the exercise? Is there enough flexibility in the plan that you can substitute another one that still focuses on your goals? Maybe next week, when the child has returned, you can do the originally planned exercise. Sometimes an exercise is so effective that the discussion leads in a direction that is totally different from the one you had planned. Go with that. Do not let your own agenda get in the way of the natural group process. On the other hand, do not let the group process force you to lose sight of the group's goals and objectives.

Some of the exercises presented here carry the notation "Therapy Group Only" in parentheses next to their titles. If you are leading a support group, *do not* do these exercises. Although they may sound exciting, they are exercises that may easily trigger memories or feelings to such a degree that children in the group deserve to have a trained clinician help them process their emotions.

The exercises, which are presented beginning in Chapter 6, are divided into seven topics: safety and trust, self-esteem, internal and external boundaries, dynamics of abuse, triggers, healthy body image and self-protection, and closure. Each of these represents a treatment goal. Because many exercises are suitable to more than one goal, we list all the goals for which each exercise is appropriate below the exercise title.

In each exercise chapter, we explain in an introduction why a particular goal is an important focus in work with sexually abused children. We explain normal development, the interruptions in development that may occur due to abuse, and the focus of the exercises in that particular chapter.

For the sake of ease, and to lessen confusion, for the most part we use only a single gender for the pronouns in each exercise. Using *he or she* and *her or his* can be quite cumbersome, so we have chosen to use male and female pronouns on a roughly alternating basis from exercise to exercise. All of the exercises can be done with either boys or girls.

At the end of each exercise is a section headed "Hints," which includes information about what to do if participants are not responding as expected or if there may be other ways to do the exercise. Facilitators should review all of the exercises thoroughly in advance of doing them in group.

chapter **2**

THERAPY GROUPS AND SUPPORT GROUPS

Differences, Goals, and Group Flow

There are salient differences between therapy and support groups. The purposes of a support group are to bring children and families with similar abuse issues together so that they will no longer feel alone, to promote awareness and understanding about the impacts and dynamics of sexual abuse, to connect abused children and their families with needed resources, to strengthen self-esteem, and to foster a sense of belonging and hope during a time of crisis. The intentions of a therapy group are not only to bring individuals together for support, encouragement, and education, but also to assess, challenge, and intervene in the psychological, emotional, and behavioral symptoms associated with child sexual abuse. In therapy groups, feelings are delved into, distorted thought processes are examined, and inappropriate behaviors are questioned at the same time new behaviors are modeled and taught. The lists below offer further clarification of the purposes of the two types of groups.

Therapy groups have the following objectives:

- Help children identify, understand, and ameliorate the effects of sexual abuse.
- Promote healing by helping children integrate the sexual abuse experience into their lives.
- Help children gain perspective on the role the sexual abuse plays in their lives.
- Assist children in reaching their own therapeutic goals.
- Confront distorted belief systems.

- Teach accountability for present behavior.
- Work actively to break down denial and defenses and rebuild a healthy ego.

The objectives of support groups are as follows:

- Provide emotional stability and avoid deep intensity.
- Build social skills.
- Decrease a sense of isolation and build a sense of belonging.
- Work actively to break down denial and defenses and to increase ego strength.
- Decrease self-blame.
- Support rather than confront.
- Help children make their own connections between feelings and actions.
- Help children reframe how they interpret situations.
- Support children in taking action when appropriate.
- Assist children and parents in obtaining therapy, when needed, by supplying them with information and referrals.

Many support groups remain permanently open to new members (open-ended groups), but we have found that trust among members is more easily established when groups are closed to new members. An open-ended group cannot be limited in size, but a closed support group is usually limited to 12 to 14 people. Naturally, the smaller the group, the more time each person will have to share. We believe that therapy groups should be small and intimate. They are most effective with only 5 to 7 children. Our therapy groups are always cofacilitated, closed, and time limited.

For many abused children, the sexual assault group provides an opportunity for them to no longer to feel alone or different, and friendships sometimes develop. When this happens, we advise the children's parents to supervise them closely, and not to allow them to play together behind closed doors. Parents of children who have histories of sexual reactivity are encouraged to disclose this information to the parents of any children in the group with whom their children become friends, in order to ensure the childrens' safety.

It is important to maintain the distinction between support groups and therapy groups. It is crucial that only trained clinicians facilitate therapy groups. Many children who have been sexually abused can be easily retraumatized. A well-meaning but untrained facilitator can cause great harm to a child by delving too deeply into the child's psyche before the child is able to handle such exploration.

We list below some examples of the kinds of goals and objectives we typically use when facilitating sexual abuse support and therapy groups. These lists may be used as they are or may be tailored to fit particular groups' needs. The amount of group time spent working on each goal is determined by the collective needs and progress of the members in the group.

- Goals and Objectives for Support Groups
   1. Trust and safety
      Reduce levels of fear, shame, and isolation.

2. Self-esteem

    Increase capacity to value self and others.

    Increase capacity to desire, believe in, and hold hope for a positive future.

    Increase ability to act appropriately in social situations.

    Increase friendships and a sense of belonging.

3. Dynamics of sexual abuse

    Understand the concept of grooming.

    Understand the basics of the sexual abuse.

    Understand societal influences of violence and oppression.

    Increase capacity for appropriate placement of responsibility and accountability.

4. Self-protection/healthy body image

    Introduce the concept of the rights and responsibilities of having a body to protect and nurture.

    Practice and increase self-protection skills.

    Learn what is age-appropriate sexual behavior.

5. Closure

    Bring conscious closure to the end of group.

    Summarize and reiterate the learning.

    Identify self-growth and put the abuse in perspective.

- Goals and Objectives for Therapy Groups

    1. Trust and safety

        Reduce levels of fear, shame, and isolation.

        Increase capacity to be vulnerable and to interact authentically.

        Increase ability to put the abuse experience in proper perspective without minimizing or maximizing it.

    2. Self-esteem

        Increase capacity to value self and others.

        Increase capacity to exert will and desire effectively and appropriately.

        Increase capacity to desire, believe in, and hold hope for a positive future.

    3. Internal and external boundaries

        Introduce the concept that thoughts and feelings create an internal interpretation of reality that affects behavior.

        Increase the ability to identify, comprehend, manage, and express thoughts and feelings appropriately.

        Increase the ability to make conscious behavioral choices.

    4. Dynamics of sexual abuse

        Understand and articulate the particular grooming dynamics used by the offender.

        Increase capacity to separate the self from the abuse/abuser.

        Increase capacity to place responsibility and accountability appropriately.

        Increase ability to define and express personal safety needs.

    5. Triggers

        Understand and articulate what trigger reactions are.

Identify and express the internal and external triggers that result in reactive coping behaviors.

Begin to decrease and desensitize trigger reactivity.

Begin to increase the ability to manage trigger responses.

6. Self-protection/healthy body image

Introduce the concept of the rights and responsibilities of having a body to protect and nurture.

Define age-appropriate sexual behavior.

Begin to decrease compulsive or sexually reactive behavior.

Begin to establish a subjective relationship with the body image that is consistent with objective reality.

Practice and learn self-protection skills.

Define own values in regard to sexuality.

7. Closure

Bring conscious closure to the end of group.

Summarize and reiterate the learning.

Identify self-growth and put the abuse in perspective.

THE OVERALL FLOW OF GROUPS

The flow of groups is vitally important. The pursuit of goals and the sharing of psychoeducational information follow a natural progression, with one concept leading to and integrating with the next. For instance, an initial goal of group is to establish trust and safety, which will continue to be a theme throughout all the sessions that follow. As new concepts are introduced, previous goals are revisited and related to the new concepts. For example, when teaching about triggers, the facilitator reiterates facts previously given about boundaries.

Of course, members will progress at different rates based upon their individual histories, symptoms, needs, and family and life circumstances. Learning how to pace the dissemination of information is a useful and necessary skill for the group facilitator. When concepts are introduced before children are ready, they will not be able to process the information or may even be retraumatized by it. Group facilitators need to rely on their best clinical judgment when determining what to do with the one or two children who require more assistance. Individual therapy can be a way of helping children keep pace with the group. An individual session can afford a child the time he or she needs to integrate and process feelings about the information received in group. Some children may simply need more individual attention in group. This may be possible when the adult-to-child ratio is small enough that a cofacilitator can easily manage the remaining group members. Ordinarily, within the first three sessions it is possible to determine by children's behavior whether or not they are truly ready to participate in group. Children who are highly distracting or very dissociative throughout these initial sessions are not recommended for group.

Below, we provide overviews of the different ways support and therapy groups ideally flow from one goal to another. We furnish more detailed information concerning the importance of each goal in the introductions to the exercise chapters.

Overall Flow of a Support Group

Support group facilitators want first of all to establish safety and trust. The use of exercises such as "Check-In," "Safety Rules," and "Group Mascot" can build a sense of safety in group. When children feel comfortable in group they begin to take risks with each other and with the facilitators. They may start sharing more of their feelings and thoughts. As facilitators begin to notice the children's increased levels of comfort, they can move on to self-esteem exercises.

Self-esteem exercises are designed to enhance the children's sense of worth and value by encouraging them to interact with one another in meaningful and healthy ways. These exercises motivate children to notice and affirm the positive qualities in themselves and others. During this process, children will naturally begin to demonstrate their abilities to be cooperative with and supportive of one another. When group members begin to display this level of cooperation, they are ready to progress to the next goal.

The exercises concerning the dynamics of sexual abuse focus on decreasing children's sense of shame and self-blame while increasing their ability to place responsibility for the abuse on the offenders. Therefore, it is helpful for facilitators to have the children define what sexual abuse is. The facilitators should also explain to the children the concept of grooming (see Chapter 9). Children need to understand that their abusers knew what they were doing and knew that it was wrong.

To convey adequately the concepts involved in the dynamics of abuse, it is imperative that facilitators recognize and understand the influence of societal violence and oppression. This understanding will help facilitators to address such issues as (a) male victims' fears of homosexuality when they have been abused by males; (b) the importance of empowering females to be assertive and self-protective; (c) the need for young males to express their feelings verbally instead of physically; (d) all persons' rights to be treated with respect and equality no matter their gender, race, sexuality, and so on; and (e) the responsibility of those in roles of authority and power to observe and protect the rights of others. Understanding these dynamics can help children to move away from self-blame and shame, because they can then put the responsibility where it lies, with the abusers.

Once they understand the dynamics of abuse, children gain perspective and separation from the abuse and become psychologically available and ready to learn self-protection skills. Through the self-protection exercises, children are taught to be assertive and to seek help from adults who will protect them. They come to understand that the best way to stay safe is to talk about their feelings and not to keep secrets. They also realize that their bodies are their own, and that they have the right to choose who can and cannot touch them. When children reclaim their bodies and integrate their rights and responsibilities, it is time for them to practice these new skills and to live their lives with less focus on sexual abuse.

As the group approaches closure, a process of review begins. Closure in group is a time to celebrate the children's accomplishments and to summarize all that they have learned. Children are given the projects they have worked on in group and certificates of accomplishment or medals to commemorate their success.

Overall Flow of a Therapy Group

When a child has been sexually abused or has grown up in a highly dysfunctional family, normal developmental tasks, emotional growth, and often physical growth are interrupted. A therapy group may serve as a surrogate family for such children. Facilitators assume a role similar to that of parent as they model positive nurturing, boundary setting, consistency, and predictability. Throughout the group process, children are essentially reparented and are given the opportunity to gain the skills they need for emotional and psychological development. Children will not necessarily completely achieve a particular developmental task before moving on from one goal to the next, but they will have at least experienced it. When a therapy group is working at its optimum level, the group will progress as described below.

All group work begins with the establishment of trust and safety among the members (see Chapter 6). The collective creation of clear rules and guidelines, along with the facilitators' reminders to follow them in a consistent manner, defines the environment and helps children know what to trust. When children perceive themselves as safe, they will risk being vulnerable and begin to interact playfully with one another. Children sometimes test their environment for safety, and the group facilitators' responses need to be consistent. We have found a perfect definition of what it means to be consistent with children on a parenting tape presented by Barbara Colorosso: "You say what you mean, you mean what you say, and you do what you said you were going to do." When these elements are present, children will learn to trust in themselves, in others, and in the group as a whole. As children connect and develop a sense of belonging, they gain the support they need to grow stronger and more fully into themselves. This is a favorable time to introduce children to situations in which they can develop their self-esteem.

A child's sense of self-esteem develops over time and in the context of that child's relationship to the world and others. The self-esteem exercises presented here are designed to create circumstances in which children can explore and improve their social skills and increase their level of self-confidence. When children receive positive peer and adult attention, they experience a level of acceptance that allows them to relate to others openheartedly.

When children are cared for, they begin to believe that they are important enough to be seen and listened to. When this occurs, it is time for the group to move on to boundaries work (see Chapter 8). This begins with children's learning about their external boundaries—that is, their own personal space and comfort levels with other people. When children learn how to express their needs in respectful ways and are responded to appropriately, they learn that they can positively affect their world, which helps them to feel their worth and value.

Internal boundary work is concerned with the mechanics of reality making. It teaches children how their thoughts, feelings, and bodily sensations relate to their actions and behaviors. In group work, we teach children about their internal boundaries by introducing a version of Bennett Brauns's (1993) BASK (behavior, affect, sensation, knowledge) model:

- *Behavior:* What am I doing?/How am I acting?
- *Affect:* How am I feeling emotionally?
- *Sensation:* What am I feeling in my body?/Where am I feeling it?
- *Knowledge:* What do I know/believe about myself and my situation?

Initially, we teach the children to identify their feelings. Once they attain some proficiency with their emotions, we teach them how to relate their feelings with their thoughts and bodily sensations. The "Life Vest" exercise and "My Own BASK Book" are extremely effective tools for teaching children these concepts. When children can separate their inner reality from external events, they learn that they have choices about how they want to act or react in any given situation. A healthy boundary system restores a child's will, choice, and power. When children feel safe enough to know their thoughts, identify their feelings, and express their needs directly, they have less need to defend or act out.

Once they have acquired healthy boundary systems, children can learn to separate themselves from the abuse. As children begin to view abuse as an event instead of an identity, they are able to confront the dynamics involved in their own abuse, such as how they were groomed, who was responsible, and what really happened (see Chapter 9). Children need help to understand how they were manipulated into believing the abuse was their fault. "The Butterfly and the Spider" and "The Alligator River Story" exercises are especially helpful ways to communicate this information. When children are able to transfer responsibility to their abusers, their shame is lessened and their egos are strengthened.

As children achieve a measure of distance, they gain perspective and are able to explore their unconscious reactions to the abuse (see Chapter 10). The facilitators help the children to identify the sensations, feelings, and thoughts they associate with their abuse and/or their abusers. The exercises "101 Dalmatians" and "Elizabeth's Triggers" are useful metaphors for teaching children how to identify triggers and gain perspective on their abuse. Perspective brings the ability to differentiate the past from the present. Once they learn this concept, children begin to understand that their reactions (triggers) have origins (the past) and sources (the abusers). This teaches them that it is safe to be present, and that when they are being triggered by something that happened to them in the past, they can become safe by centering themselves in the here and now.

When the children are fairly well able to understand that the hurt was in the past and that they have some control over their trigger reactions, their level of internal threat is greatly reduced. Their anxiety decreases and their self-confidence grows stronger.

With this awareness, children learn how to make decisions from a place of understanding, presence, and clear choice. These skills enable children to feel safe, take risks, assume responsibility, and take control over those things within their ability to control.

By this point, the children feel very connected with other group members, have a sense of belonging, and feel confident and accepted. They acknowledge their abusers' responsibility for the abuse and have skills to manage their trigger responses.

The children's final task is to reclaim their bodies. Healthy body image and self-protection exercises are designed to help children accept and establish body images that are based in objective reality (see Chapter 11). This is not always easy, as many abused children separate from their bodies as a way of coping with the abuse. Helping these children to develop realistic views of their size, weight, and appearance gives them clearer pictures of themselves. The more reality based children are, the safer they become.

Once children recover their bodies from the abuse, they need help in learning how to nurture and protect their bodies. Certain rights and responsibilities are inherent in body ownership. To help children understand this concept, we present each one with a "Body Bill of Rights" charter. The charter describes what their rights are, and the exercises show them how to demonstrate those rights within their lives. Practicing self-protection means learning how to control their actions and take responsibility for their attitudes. By learning to become mindful and aware of their own thoughts, feelings, and actions, children learn how to protect themselves as well as how to relate to others with respect.

By this time in group, children are feeling connected to one another and are strong and proud of themselves. Sexual abuse is becoming an event of the past and the children are ready to resume their lives. It is time for closure (see Chapter 12). The closure process allows the children time to make the transition from group back into their everyday lives. During this stage of group children are encouraged to reflect on what they have learned over the many weeks. The "Debriefing and Evaluating Group" exercise helps children map their progress by asking them to describe how different they are now from when they entered group. Closure is also a time to instill hope for the future. The facilitators' summarizing of the children's efforts, achievements, and resources helps to remind them of both their skills and their ability to be safe in the world. To celebrate their success, the children all receive certificates, awards, and/or folders containing all the exercises they did in group as a reminder of the extraordinary personal work they have accomplished.

chapter 3

SPECIAL CONSIDERATIONS IN SETTING UP GROUPS

Many factors must be taken into consideration in the setting up of therapy and support groups. For instance, how many children should be in a group? How many facilitators? What should be the age range of each group? Where will the group sessions be held? Should groups include a mix of genders? Should a group be open or closed? The following are some of our thoughts on these issues as well as some tips based on what we have discovered in our own group work through the years.

FACILITATORS

The success of a particular children's group will depend largely on the facilitators' skills and personalities. Their confidence level in supporting sexually abused children, comfort level with children in general, understanding of child development, ability to have and use outside support, and unique personalities all play roles in how the children will respond.

It is essential that facilitators with a history of sexual abuse be in successful recovery from its effects. Being in a group surrounded by sexually abused children is an extremely triggering situation. All facilitators must have reliable support systems and the ability to contain and manage their own emotions.

A group for sexually abused children is not a place for adults who need to rescue or save children. Many abused children are caught in the dynamics of a legal system that is not protective of them or in home situations that are not safe or supportive. As such children act out against or withdraw from these circumstances, their behaviors may keep them isolated from peers. Facilitators must establish boundaries and limits that are both clear and firm. Otherwise, they may be overwhelmed by the neediness of the children, and as a result the group could become too chaotic, exhausting, or ineffective.

Effective Facilitators

To be effective, facilitators need to develop particular skills. We recommend the following:

- *Be enthusiastic and express your excitement about the group.* Greet children by their first names as they arrive and help them feel noticed by acknowledging something unique about their attitudes, behavior, or social skills. For example: "Sarah, you have the most wonderful laugh. I feel warm inside every time I hear it."

- *Treat each child with respect.* We often use talking sticks or talking stones in our groups. The person with the talking object is the only one allowed to speak. The object is passed around so that everyone has a turn to talk uninterrupted. When a child is disruptive, be firm and ask for quiet in a kind manner. For example: "Trish, I am having trouble hearing what Mary is saying. Remember, you will get a chance to speak."

- *Act childlike at times, but remember, you are the adult!* Join in with the children during the exercises. Your involvement as a role model will give the children permission to be themselves. Be silly and active, yet remain aware of how the group members are responding and participating.

- *Share real feelings with the children.* Let group members know why you do this work; share your personal feelings. For example: "When I was a child, someone touched me and I was too frightened to tell anyone"; or "I am feeling very sad today because my cat just died." This will encourage the children to express their feelings openly. Be careful, however, not to dominate the group with your own feelings. The group is for the children, and your input is appropriate *only* when it facilitates *their* healing process or is pertinent to the group topic or goal.

- *Physically stand or sit at the children's level.* Looking up at a looming adult is both intimidating and a physical strain for children. When you are physically on the children's level it is easier to develop rapport and a sense of trust with them.

- *Be clear about your own boundaries.* Do you feel comfortable having a child sit on your lap, and is it therapeutically appropriate given the child's history? How much distraction are you able to tolerate? Act as a role model by clearly stating your own needs in the group. For example: "The noise is too loud for me in here. Let's all whisper for a few minutes"; or "For this game we need to hold hands. I like people to ask permission to touch me so I always try to ask others for permission before I touch them. Do you mind if I hold your hand?"

- *Be flexible with your planned activities.* Although it is very important to plan for each group in advance, you must also be willing to change those plans. During check-in, children might reveal information that should be dealt with quickly, or a conflict may arise between group members that demands immediate attention. Be prepared to deal with these issues right away rather than your planned activity. Your own goals and plans are important, but they can often be reached by following the group process.

- *Respond sensitively to group members' disclosures of abuse.* Sexually abused children will rely on your responses to them in determining how much information they will disclose. Therefore, it is very important that you monitor your responses. Do not show shock, disgust, extreme anger, or fear while a child is sharing her story. She needs to know that you can handle anything she says, and that her story is not so different from others you have heard. It is fine to show empathy while a child is sharing her story. For example, you might say, "How did you feel when he did that?" or "From the look on your face, it looks like you felt frightened." Children need to know that you are listening and that you care. Do not put them in the position of having to take care of your feelings as well as their own.

- *Seek outside support and consultation.* This work is very demanding. Often, facilitators can be triggered by the stories they hear in group. Consult with other skilled clinicians regularly, and allow time after each group session for facilitators' debriefing.

COFACILITATING GROUPS

It is difficult to run a group with just one facilitator. Our groups are always facilitated by at least two therapists. We recommend this for a variety of reasons, including the following:

- *Bonding/attachment:* The opportunity for each child to find at least one adult with whom he or she will be able to bond increases when a group is led by two or more facilitators. Each child will also be more likely to receive nurturing from one of the group leaders during the group process.

- *Role models and boundary setting:* Many sexually abused children are extremely needy and starved for appropriate affection. They may ask for a lot of attention in such forms as being held, being listened to, and other kinds of close contact. With at least two facilitators in a group, one facilitator can be free to teach about appropriate boundaries (e.g., "You need to ask me if I want to be hugged" or "You can sit next to me, but not on my lap right now") while the other continues to focus on the group as a whole.

- *Competition for attention:* Many abused children are extremely needy; others have learned to be antidependent. The presence of two or more facilitators allows each adult to give additional special attention to each child. However, cofacilitators should be aware that some children may try to create a split between them. It is important for cofacilitators to stay aware of their own issues and not take it personally if some children gravitate toward the other facilitator.

- *Opportunity to confront or challenge:* With two facilitators in a group, one can play a more nurturing role while the other can be more confrontational. The cofacilitators can then alternate these roles. (This technique is used more often in therapy groups than in support groups.)

- *Better observation and response:* When a group is cofacilitated, while one facilitator is leading an activity, the other has more freedom to manage behavior(s) through observation, response, and intervention.

- *Dividing the group:* When a group has two facilitators, the group can be divided in two for specific activities that work more effectively with fewer children. This allows each smaller group to have its own facilitator.

- *Dividing case management:* With two facilitators, the responsibilities of the children's case management needs are cut in half. It is extremely time-consuming, but essential, for facilitators to keep in touch with every child's individual therapist as well as teachers, parents, and so on. Good case management results in a stronger support network for the child and helps to establish a more cohesive and unified treatment plan and intervention strategy on the child's behalf.

- *Focus on note taking:* At times, facilitators want to take notes in group. A child may say something significant that a facilitator wants to be sure to remember, or the group may be brainstorming thoughts or feelings that should be recorded. When a group has two facilitators, one can take notes while the other directs the session. This is especially useful when a child makes a spontaneous disclosure during group.

- *Management of discipline and dissociation:* If a child is being triggered, his or her response may require individual attention, regardless of whether the child's behavior is dissociative or disruptive. In a cofacilitated group, one facilitator can work with the triggered child's behaviors while the other continues activities with the remainder of the group.

GENDER OF FACILITATORS

There is no single absolute right or best way to establish the gender makeup of group facilitators. Although many argue for same-sex facilitators, others, with equally sound clinical reasons, argue for mixed-gender facilitators, and a few argue that gender is or should be irrelevant. The resolution to this controversy is far beyond our scope.

Gender alone can negatively trigger some children's abuse histories and defenses, interfering with their ability to participate in group. Facilitators need to be mindful of children's potential to generalize and transfer their abuse issues to gender or to the facilitators themselves. The more aware facilitators are of each child's history, the more effective they can be and the more precise they can be with interventions.

We are most comfortable staffing our girls' groups with two female facilitators and our boys' groups with one male and one female facilitator. Children need and deserve to have both males and females introduced as healthy role models at different times in their recovery process or whenever possible.

GROUP SET-UP

We discuss below some of the issues that are important considerations in the setting up of groups.

Open Versus Closed Groups

When a group is open, new members can join at any time. There may not be a designated ending date, in which case group members leave when they feel ready to do so. Closed groups consist of the same members, who usually meet for a designated number of weeks.

We strongly believe that all therapy groups should be closed, and we encourage the same for child sexual abuse support groups. Closed groups have clear beginning and ending dates. The establishment of these dates provides perspective for the children on the work they will do and an understanding that it is for a limited period of time. Closed groups help to create a sense of trust and safety at a faster rate, as new people are not entering the group week after week. Closed groups allow for predictability and consistency, which make deeper therapeutic work possible. They also keep the group rules consistent and understood by everyone.

In a closed group, a sense of family can be created. Children learn how to relate to one another in new and healthy ways. As in any family, conflicts and other problems will inevitably arise between group members. With trust established between members, each can be taught how to express and resolve these conflicts in constructive ways that build, strengthen, and deepen their relationships with each other. Group members form much stronger friendships in closed groups than in open ones and take more risks regarding what they share about their sexual abuse and themselves. Because of this, closed groups are able to cover more ground, and participants feel they are moving forward rather than repeating the same old material every time new people join.

The benefits of closed groups became clear to us through our work with teens who lived in a small town. There was a lack of support services available to the community, so we set up an open group to accommodate more teenagers. The first week began with 5 girls; the next week they brought their friends, and by the third week we had 15 with absentees and newcomers. This made it difficult to establish trust among group members. Some of the teens had a basic understanding of the dynamics of sexual assault and others had just disclosed sexual abuse the day before. With group members at such different levels of awareness, it was difficult to do many of the planned exercises. A lot of time was spent with the newcomers explaining the dynamics of their abuse and having everyone share basic information about themselves over again. We also learned why group members were less apt to come on a weekly basis: When the duration of a group is open-ended, it suggests a feeling of "we can always work on this another time." It also seems to imply that healing from sexual assault trauma will take forever.

This is not to say that open support groups cannot work. Open groups need to be less structured than closed groups. It may be enough for an open support group to focus on a different emotion each week. The wonderful part about an open group is that those who have been attending for a while can take leadership and support roles with new members. This can increase their sense of self-worth, and it may even free them up to share more feelings than they would have otherwise because they want to be good role models. In a school setting, an open group can work well to lessen isolation, because it offers immediate support for a child who has just disclosed: Not only are there others this has happened to, the "others" are even students in the child's own school.

An emphasis on confidentiality is especially vital in a school setting and must be strictly adhered to, or group members may be teased or ostracized by their peers. If children attend a group during school hours, it should have an innocuous name, such as "friendship group." The facilitators should go over the rules of confidentiality individually with each child before he or she even enters the group. An explanation of confidentiality needs to include simple examples of how a child can answer other children's questions about the group. Further, the issue of confidentiality should be revisited with the group as a whole every few weeks.

Age Categories

Groups operate most effectively when the group members are close in age. Children within a 2-year age range will usually be at close developmental levels, making them similar in their abilities to verbalize, read, and draw. They will have comparable understanding of sexuality and the abuse. Also, they will be at similar levels in their intellectual capacity to assimilate and comprehend what is being taught in group. In addition, age often affects a child's ability to pay attention. Whereas a 5-year-old may have trouble sitting for more than 5 minutes, an 8-year-old can usually sit for 10 to 15 minutes. Thus the exercises chosen for groups should vary accordingly.

What 5-year-olds may reveal about their abuse is often very different from what 9-year-olds might say. Older children might describe their experiences in more detail than younger children are capable of hearing or understanding, and as a result, the younger ones might be disruptive in group. We have found that the age span can be a little more spread out with older children, so we offer one group for 11- to 13-year-olds and another for 14- to 18-year-olds.

The placement of a child with a group is determined during the initial screening process. A developmentally delayed child who acts much younger than his or her chronological age should be put in a group with children at a comparable developmental level. When deciding which group is right for a given child, facilitators should consider the child's abilities to read, write, and so on as well as the child's capacity to understand the information presented. If a child is exceptionally mature, it is best to keep him or her with others of the same age unless it is clear the child will not fit in. This helps to discontinue the pattern of forcing the child to grow up too fast or to act in a parentified manner. Every child deserves to be a child and to act childlike while receiving protection from supportive adults.

Sometimes there are not enough children of the same age to form an effective group. In such cases, we recommend making a comfortable-sized group covering a broader age span and adding at least one facilitator for every 2 years of age difference. For example, if a group has six children ranging in age from 6 to 10, it should have three facilitators. This allows the facilitators to split the group up into smaller groups for specific exercises. Extra facilitators can also give age-appropriate prompting to children and provide more individual attention.

Size of Group

A group needs to have enough children that it feels like a group yet not so many that each child cannot get some individualized attention. When considering size, facilitators should make sure that there are enough members to absorb the inevitable absences without disrupting the feeling of being in a group. Our ideal size for a therapy group is six children. If there are two facilitators to a group, each child gets some focused attention and the group can easily be divided in half for role-plays, letter writing, and other exercises when even smaller groups are desired. A support group can tolerate a higher ratio of children to facilitators.

Same-Gender Versus Mixed-Gender Groups

Many facilitators run mixed-gender groups. Sometimes such groups are formed because it is difficult to have enough children to form a group if only a boys' group or a girls' group is offered. The issues raised by the inclusion of both boys and girls within groups are similar to those raised regarding whether groups should be led by facilitators of the opposite sex.

We have found same-gender groups to be more effective than mixed-gender groups. This is true both because of the developmental differences between boys and girls and because girls seem much more willing to disclose facts about abuse when boys are not in the room. The only mixed-gender groups we offer are for preschoolers.

Preschool Groups

Naturally, there are limits to how much preschool children can understand and should be told about sexual abuse. We facilitate groups for children 4 to 5 years old. Our preschool groups are gender mixed, but we always try to have more girls than boys in a group to maintain a calmer level of energy. At least two boys are needed in group, so that a lone boy does not feel isolated or singled out. The focus of a preschool group is to help the children learn to identify and express their feelings appropriately. This includes feelings in general and feelings specifically about the abuse. They learn about safe and unsafe touch and how to assert themselves if someone is trying to touch them. Young children are also taught about being tricked and about what secrets should be told. Finally, they are helped to identify who the safe adults are in their lives and how to go to them for protection.

Puppets are wonderful teaching tools for showing preschoolers the dynamics of abuse and other prevention skills. Preschool children also love stories that work on a metaphorical level. Many popular fairy tales and their Disney adaptations contain messages about grief, survival, and the importance of hope and resilience. We use an exercise based on *101 Dalmatians* to explain about both trickery and trigger reactivity. Songs are also highly effective with preschoolers. Facilitators can pick a goal or subject and make up a ditty to be sung to one of the children's favorite tunes. The parents will report the children's singing the new words everywhere.

Our preschool groups are usually just 8 weeks long and last for only an hour each week. When the children arrive, we ask their parents to encourage them to use the bathroom before the group starts. This is essential—otherwise we would have a sudden mass exodus in the middle of the group session. We always do a very quick, fun check-in, and then we play a game that is tied in with our goal for the week. This is followed by the group's singing a song that pertains to the goal and a drawing exercise. We do another game, often one such as Duck, Duck, Goose, and end with story time and a snack (pretzels or popcorn and juice) to eat while everyone listens to the story. The story is always one that ties in with the objective of the week. Preschoolers also love being videotaped. We often videotape them doing an exercise and then replay the tape for them (review childrens' abuse history before videotaping them). This repetition serves the further purpose of reinforcing the goal for the week.

It can be especially difficult to contain preschool children when the group is dealing with an uncomfortable topic. Their anxiety level is often so high that they will do anything to avoid their feelings. To help with containment, we put everything away—toys, drawing materials, paper, and snacks—so the children cannot see them until they are ready to be used. We also hang posters on the wall of children expressing different feelings.

Also to help with containment, we have small chairs for preschoolers to sit in, so they are not stretching out and kicking one another or rolling into each other. As we begin doing exercises, we move the chairs back and sit closely together on the carpet. At that point the children are more focused, and each is better able to stay in his or her own space.

Often in preschool groups there will be someone who is too anxious to stay seated. We allow that child to walk around as long as he or she is not disturbing others. Many times children will want to sit on the facilitators' laps. We leave that up to each facilitator, depending on both the facilitator's individual comfort level and the child's individual issues. A sexualized child may be stimulated by sitting on a facilitator's lap.

It is common in a preschool group to have at least one child who wants to leave the room or be with a parent (or other caregiver) during the group session. In this case we do one of two things. If the child's parent is someone who will not disrupt group, but will sit quietly and unobtrusively in the room, we will allow the parent in for the first 15 minutes or so of the session, until the child is comfortable. A second option, which we use to avoid distracting the other children, so they all don't want their parents in the room too, is to allow the child to go and sit with the parent in the waiting room. We instruct the parent not to entertain the child or make the time in the waiting room fun. We ask the parent just to sit quietly with the child. The child is told that he or she is welcome back to the group whenever he or she wants to rejoin it. Usually, after leaving two or three times, a child will choose to join the group on a regular basis and not try to leave the room again. Because facilitators are trying to establish safety and trust, they should never try to force a child to stay in the room.

Girls' Groups

Girls' groups are usually the easiest to facilitate. Ideally, we have a 5- to 6-year-old group (which would include the more mature 5-year-olds), a 7- to 8-year-old group, and a 9- to 10-year-old group. Groups work best when they include from five to seven girls. In general, girls are more adept at articulating their feelings than are boys. They often enjoy discussions and can stay focused on exercises for fairly long periods. They are excited to connect with the other girls in group and want to build friendships with them.

Overall, if members of girls' groups rebel, it is more often by withdrawing than by acting out. Early on (see the rule-setting exercise in Chapter 6), the facilitators can help them express what they need from the group when they do start to withdraw or act out. Generally, we start the group with a snack as everyone is coming in. We run our girls' groups for 15 weeks, and each session is $1\frac{1}{2}$ hours long.

Boys' Group

Boys' groups can be quite challenging and invigorating to facilitate. Boys need more active exercises than do girls, and the exercises need to be shorter. In general, sexually abused boys have a harder time discussing issues regarding sexual abuse, and they are unable to sit still and focus long enough to do thorough processing. Many of them feel anxious just walking into the room and will express this anxiety through physical aggression or loud, raucous play. Boys, however, often become enthusiastic when they recognize the common ground they share with others in group, and want to develop friendships.

The boys' groups that we have run most effectively have been led by two to three facilitators, including at least one male and one female. Our boys' groups run for 8 weeks. In our experience, by the fifth or sixth week of group, boys seem to develop a "pack mentality" such that they join together against the facilitators and against the idea of wanting to work on the issues of abuse. By that point they've formed a "boys' club" and are ready to play. Therefore, 8 weeks is more effective for boys to make connections, break down their sense of isolation, and work on the abuse issues. Any remaining concerns can be effectively dealt with in individual and family counseling. Our younger boys' groups meet for 1 hour each week, and the older boys' groups (10+ years) meet for $1\frac{1}{2}$ hours.

We usually pass out snacks in boys' groups when we want to have a discussion or want to process an exercise. This settles them down for a little while. Boys like to be videotaped, so we line them up one behind the other and have each answer a question in turn while looking at the camera, and then have them go to the end of the line again to wait for another turn. If there is time at the end of the session, we watch the video together. This is great to do using exercises such as "Talking to the Offender Psychodrama," "Triggered Memories," and "My Safety and Comforts." To safely use video cameras in group, ensure that no member of the group was videotaped while being abused. Using a video camera may be a volatile trigger for such children.

Because boys tend to be physically active, boundaries need to be clearly defined so that they do not hurt each other in their play. We have our boys all sit in chairs in the beginning of group so that they do not accidentally bump into one another (we recommend the use of sturdy chairs, as they always try to tilt them backward).

The goals of boys' groups are to create trust and safety and to teach them gentle ways to show affection, nonhurtful ways to express anger, and how to protect themselves in the future. In therapy groups, boys are also helped to understand when they are being triggered and how to manage their triggers (see Chapter 10). They are given the opportunity to express their anger about their offenders (see "Letter/Video to the Offender" and "Talking to the Offender Psychodrama").

Adolescent Groups

Working with teenagers can be fun and enlightening as long as the groups are led by facilitators experienced with teens. Many teens love to participate in long discussions. One of the roles of the facilitator in an adolescent group is to keep the teens on track, talking about themselves and the abuse, as opposed to talking about their friends (including the ever-popular topic of who has a crush on whom).

Many teens in sexual abuse groups are sexually active. They often make poor choices when they are hanging out with friends—for example, they may be pregnant and still smoking cigarettes or drinking alcohol. It takes a skillful facilitator to join with the teens and concurrently guide them without being judgmental. Some exercises that work especially well with teenagers are "How We Sabotage Ourselves," "The Alligator River Story," and the "Date Rape" role-plays.

In our adolescent groups, we spend one session with a guest speaker from Planned Parenthood who discusses sexuality and answers any questions group members may have. (Group facilitators who elect to do something similar must make sure that they receive written permission for teens to attend this session from the group members' caregivers.) We also have a question-and-answer box in a discreet place outside of the group room, where teens can anonymously deposit any questions they have. We periodically go through the questions in group and answer them to the best of our abilities.

Teens, for the most part, gravitate toward and love coming to group. Often they want to socialize with other group members outside of group, too. If they do, facilitators must talk to the teens' parents about the importance of setting strict guidelines relating to safety, responsibility, and curfew. We have heard about more than one incident in which teens from a group have gotten together and gone out on the streets after midnight or shown up at parties that put them all at risk. To prevent such situations, facilitators should spend group time doing role-plays about peer pressure and how to resist it.

Teens usually get a snack halfway through the session in our groups. They often also beg for cigarette breaks, which we do not allow. Our teen groups run for 15 weeks, and each session is $1\frac{1}{2}$ hours long. We give the teens the choice of whether they want to sit on the floor or in chairs.

Group Setting

Children in a group need to feel safe before healing can begin. Facilitators should choose a meeting place that is both private and kept secret from offenders. Children in the room should not be visible from the street, and no one but group members should be able to walk into the room during the group session.

It is important for the children to feel they have privacy from their parents (or other caregivers), as this enables them to share their thoughts and feelings relating to their abuse. They often will censor themselves if they think their parents may hear what they are saying. The best way to ensure privacy is for the group room to be situated away from the waiting area. Otherwise, the group room should be well soundproofed, and the facilitators should demonstrate to the children that it is.

It is important that the group room feel comfortable and inviting for the children. A kids' space can be created with brightly colored posters. We have learned through the years to be very selective about how many things are within children's reach in the group room or they will be too easily distracted. Teenagers feel more comfortable in a setting that is used for adults, something like a living room. We also have tape recorders, drawing materials, old magazines, and other craft materials on hand but out of sight for the various exercises. Usually, we put projects that kids have completed on display in the group room for a few weeks before they take them home. This gives them a sense of ownership and belonging, which boosts their self-esteem and offers comfort in the group setting. Writing a group list of safety rules to post in an easily visible spot helps begin this process, as does displaying the group's "mascot" if one has been made.

Accessibility

Accessibility of both the waiting room and the group room is another issue to consider. We have worked with a number of children who are differently abled, some in wheelchairs as well as some visually impaired and hearing impaired. Accessibility for such children is not a problem as long as the facilitators are prepared and the space is properly equipped. Some advance planning is necessary for these children, and any special help they need should be set up ahead of time. This may involve securing the services of an interpreter for hearing-impaired children or special transportation for those with physical disabilities. Facilitators should think about what the group members need help with and be sure they can do the exercises that are planned for the group. Differently abled children should also be given a chance to lead activities at times in group so that they will feel equal in ability with the other group members.

Confidentiality

Confidentiality in work with sexually abused children is extremely complicated. What group facilitators can and cannot keep confidential often depends on individual state laws. All facilitators must know their states' reporting laws and should inform the children of their reporting responsibilities. We usually tell children at their screening sessions that we will not report anything to their parents without their permission. We then go on to say that sometimes the law requires us to report to a social worker or a detective any suspected circumstances in which children may be harmed or may cause harm to others. We also tell them that we must report if a child is actively suicidal. We tell children that if we feel we need to report something (and it will not be detrimental to them), we will let them know first, before we report. We also review this information during the first session of group with all the children.

Caseworkers, parents, attorneys, and school personnel often ask facilitators how particular children are doing in group. Facilitators can respond in general terms, explaining the types of exercises used and how well a child is participating. Before a facilitator can give out more specific information, a release form must be signed. The facilitator should let the child know in such a case that he or she will be speaking with others about the matter in question. The facilitator should ask the child if there are things that he or she wants or does not want the facilitator to talk about with the questioner. The facilitator should try to gain an understanding as to why the child might have these needs and determine what conversation with the questioner might be most effective. Again, as we have mentioned, in certain legal situations facilitators do not have a choice—they must report what children have disclosed.

Record Keeping

Whether or not facilitators should keep detailed records of group sessions is quite controversial. Some state laws require that notes be taken in group. In many states, all records can be subpoenaed. Because of this, many group facilitators are tempted not to take any notes. On the other hand, writing down what happened in group and how children responded to various exercises can be very helpful for facilitators in their planning for group goals week after week. It is all too easy to forget who said what in group a week or two later. Unless a facilitator is required by insurance or a managed care company to keep notes on individuals in group, it generally comes down to a personal choice as to how many notes to take. It is especially important, however, for a facilitator to take detailed notes if a child is disclosing any new information regarding the abuse that by law needs to be reported to the proper authorities.

Absences

It is essential for children to attend every group session. Inconsistently attending therapy group can be very harmful to the child as well as detrimental to the group. The child's issues may be triggered, and without the support of therapy, he or she may not have the skills to manage or contain the triggered feelings. In group, children learn to care for each other, develop concern for one another, and rely on one another. If a child misses too many sessions, he or she may not be able to continue in group. Aside from the disruption this causes for the other children, the frequently absent child may be unable to experience the same level of connection that other group members share, or may miss out on vital information and processing.

To make a final determination about a frequently absent child's group status, facilitators must judge, based on the dynamics of the group, whether the goals for the child can be met given the absences and whether the child's parents are able to follow through. If the facilitators determine that the child could benefit from continuing in group but the parents are unable or unwilling to follow through, finding an adult sponsor for the child may be a viable option.

chapter **4**

GROUP FORMAT

Our group sessions consist of directed play through planned exercises and discussions. We use a variety of methods derived from many theory bases, including cognitive and behavioral theory, grief work, attachment theory, child development, learning theory, and object relations and other psychodynamic theories. In our experience, groups need to be directed and focused, with set goals, and yet flexible enough to allow for processing of spontaneous incidents and statements that arise during group sessions.

For both support and therapy groups to be successful, they must, on a weekly basis, provide children with (a) trust and safety, (b) predictability and consistency, and (c) skills for containing emotions. Trust and safety are created through the setting of specific guidelines or rules regarding confidentiality, how each person will be treated in group, and the types of behaviors allowed and not allowed in group. Group needs to be a fun and warm place where each child is cared for, respected, and has worth. It is critical that participation in any of the exercises and discussions be voluntary.

Predictability and consistency increase the potential for trust and safety. Because many sexually abused children come from homes where they have experienced violence or the unpredictable nature of a chemically dependent parent, it is vital that facilitators remain supportive and in consistent good humor each week. Facilitators provide further predictability by following through with appropriate interventions when any rules are disregarded. Predictability also is reinforced when the group starts and ends in similar ways each week. We usually start our groups with check-in and end with a fun, upbeat exercise or a story. In addition, children ages 8 and older often appreciate being told what is on the agenda for the following week. They then know what to expect each week when they walk in the door. Children also feel more secure if the group is held in the same room each week.

The middle part of each week's session usually includes an exercise that reinforces the goals of the week before and one or two new exercises that pertain to the current week's goals. For example, if the previous week's goal concerned boundaries, the group does one boundary exercise and then moves on to one or two other exercises related to the next goal, understanding the dynamics of abuse.

At the close of group each week, children need to leave feeling that they can handle their emotions and not fall apart. Exercises are done that help bring a sense of centering, balance, and closure to the group's work that day. The children know that the group room is a place to think and feel about the abuse. They learn how to release feelings and thoughts so they do not leave the session overwhelmed by emotion.

When trust and safety, predictability and consistency, and containment needs are all met, the group gains the feeling of a healthy family. The children now have a relatively secure place where they know what to expect, feel validated, are given guidance, and are nurtured.

chapter 5

SCREENING GROUP MEMBERS

The screening process is the backbone of any good group. A solid screening procedure increases the likelihood of the formation of a cohesive group made up of children with similar issues and ages who are ready and excited to participate. Screening also allows the group facilitator to explain the group's goals and objectives to both parents and children. In this chapter, we provide general information on screening for both support and therapy groups. We include information on the purposes of screening, hints on the screening process, and, at the end of the chapter, a screening tool that helps determine readiness for group (Table 5.1).

PURPOSES OF SCREENING

In screening sessions, information is gathered from parents and children to determine whether the children's issues can be addressed by the goals and objectives of the group and, conversely, whether the group is relevant or suitable for the children's issues. The fact that a child has been sexually abused does not necessarily mean that he or she is an appropriate candidate for group therapy, or that he or she is ready for group. For those children who need only additional parental protection, the screening process can also serve as a tool to educate parents on safety and protection issues so that their children can become ready for group. In deciding whether or not a given child is ready to participate in group, a facilitator must consider and compare many factors. Whether screening for therapy groups or support groups, facilitators should address the following issues.

Has the abuse been reported to the appropriate authorities? The facilitator must find out whether the abuse has been reported to a child protective services agency or to law enforcement. If not, by law, the facilitator is required to report the abuse. If the parent has not reported the abuse, the facilitator should find out why—the answer may help to determine how protective of the child this parent is. If the parent has not reported in order to protect the perpetrator, then the parent is putting the needs of the abuser above the needs of the child and may not be adequately protecting the child. In this case, the child may not be in a safe enough situation to allow the vulnerability needed to recover from the abuse, and group might add to the child's sense of isolation and confusion. If the parent has not reported the abuse because of a lack of understanding of the legal system or because she is minimizing the abuse, the screening session can be used to educate the parent about the system and about the dynamics of sexual abuse. With additional information, the parent may then be in a better position to protect the child. As the child feels safer, he or she will find it easier to work through the feelings of the abuse in a group setting.

Has there been any legal activity regarding the abuse? Is there any past, present, or potential legal activity relating to the abuse, such as a criminal case against the abuser or a child custody case involving the abuser? If so, the facilitator and/or his or her records may be subpoenaed. The parent should be informed of this possibility. We tell parents that we will not release the records without their permission. If they do not give their permission, we require a judge's order before we will release them. In a custody battle, the facilitator should try to ascertain whether the parent's motivation for therapy is related to the child's recovery or to the belief that therapy will help her win custody. If the latter is the case, it may be in the child's best interest to put off entering group therapy until after custody is determined, so that the facilitator and/or the child does not end up a victim of the battle. If criminal prosecution is pending, some prosecutors may consider the child's participation in group harmful to the case. This is often true when the children are young, as the defense can raise issues around their suggestibility. Defense attorneys may argue that a child has been influenced by the group process and made to believe that the abuse happened after hearing the stories of other children. Therefore, it may be prudent for the facilitator to talk to the prosecutor on a child's case before accepting that child into the group.

What has the child disclosed? The facilitator needs to determine what information the child has given the parent (or other caregiver) about the abuse. Has the child been able to tell the parent details of the abuse? Is the parent able or willing to hear details about the abuse? Children who deny the abuse, become anxious or frightened at the mention of abuse, or cannot talk about the abuse at all may be better served in individual therapy, as their anxiety may prove to be too disruptive to the group process. Parents who do not want to know any details of the abuse may need to be in individual therapy to help them better support their children through the group process. Gaining specific information from the parent about the abuse can also help the facilitator to understand the symptoms the child is displaying and to get a clearer sense of what the child may be exhibiting in his or her play. Sometimes children are willing to talk more openly to facilitators about the abuse when they know the facilitators already have the information and they can see that the facilitators manage and contain it effectively. Knowing a child's abuse history prior to screening may offer the facilitator the opportunity to tell the child about others in group (without revealing names) who have similar abuse stories. This can help the child feel less isolated and may lessen his or her anxiety about attending group. Any information about the child's abuse will be useful in proceeding with an effective treatment plan for a therapy or support group.

How was the abuse disclosed? The facilitator should discuss with the parents (or other caregivers) how they discovered their child was being abused and what their reactions have been to this information. This communication provides a valuable education about parent-child relationships and how able the parents are to support their child's recovery. This information is crucial for the facilitator in deciding whether the family is capable of the effort needed to support the child's return to health and safety. Often, a child's disclosure of abuse will activate a parent's childhood feelings and issues, which may include abuse. These feelings can interfere with the parent's capacity to provide support for the child, and some may sabotage the child's efforts to heal. In such a situation, the child should not be in group without the parent also being in individual or group therapy to work through his or her own issues.

Is there still contact with the abuser? This information is relevant because the child may not be safe, or may not feel safe enough to disclose information about the abuse. When contact with the abuser continues, it is difficult for the child to process thoughts and feelings. The recovery process is slowed or halted when the child is in a threatening or potentially dangerous situation. The needs of a child in this position would be better met through individual and family therapy, and/or legal intervention. Children who have supervised visitation with their abusers may do well in group as long as they are well protected during the visits.

Will the parents be able to follow through with treatment? The facilitator should explain to the parents (or other caregivers) their responsibilities if their child participates in group. These include transportation, scheduling, finances, and the ability to protect the child from contact with the offender or allies of the abuser who might try to undermine the child's recovery process. The parents must have a reliable car, or access to public transit and a willingness to use it, and/or a reliable person who is willing to provide transportation weekly for the family. They must have the ability to arrange their schedules and meet at the appointed times for groups. They must have the necessary finances or know how to access financial resources to cover the cost of group. (Families who are involved with state social health service systems often have case managers who can be of assistance with these issues.) A parent who still allows the child to have contact with the offender (even by phone or mail) or contact with the offender's allies who disbelieve or minimize the abuse is unlikely to have the capacity or desire necessary to support a child's emotional needs throughout the duration of the group. A parent in this situation most likely needs her own individual therapist to direct and educate her in protective parenting skills. If, however, another protective adult— whether family member or friend—is willing to take responsibility for the child's support and participation in group, the child may still be considered appropriate. (When this alternative is not available, we have successful graduates from previous groups who volunteer to sponsor families in these situations.) If the parents cannot meet all of these requirements, the child is not appropriate for group.

Has there been any assessment for chemical dependency? Older children and all parents and other caregivers need to be assessed for chemical dependency, and the screening process should address their use of drugs and alcohol. The facilitator should develop an abstinence contract for them to sign in which they agree to abstain from using all mood-altering substances for the duration of group. Participants need to agree that, in the event that they find they are unable to meet the terms of the abstinence contract, they will receive a professional drug/alcohol evaluation if the facilitator deems it necessary. We insist that parents abide by the abstinence contract, too, as they often must drive their children to and from group and need to be clean and sober to help their children through the recovery process. Failure of child or parent to agree to these conditions makes the child inappropriate for group.

Has the child been sexually acting out? Although it is common for all children to have some sexual curiosity, abuse can stimulate sexual acting out. We sometimes allow sexually reactive children to participate in group when we have determined that they are not exhibiting extremely coercive, obsessive, or offending behavior. Children who are very aggressive or controlling of others need to be in a group that focuses specifically on the abusive behavior.

Was the abuse exceptionally violent or ritualistic in nature? Children with histories of extremely sadistic abuse may not be appropriate for group. When their abuse has been very severe, they need more individual attention than a group setting can provide. Survivors of ongoing violent or sadistic abuse are often highly dissociative. Individual therapy is a more effective modality of treatment for children to process these traumas. Trauma reenactment in a group setting is not therapeutic for anyone. A facilitator who is considering for group a child who has been violently abused should meet first with the child's therapist to be certain that the child has worked through enough of the trauma to make the group experience a success for all participants.

Does the child also have a diagnosis of attention deficit disorder? Abused children diagnosed with attention deficit disorder (ADD) have difficulty concentrating and are more easily distracted than other children, making them more reactive and less able to process their thoughts and feelings about the abuse. Children with ADD do better in group settings after they have learned how to manage, tolerate, and contain their feelings through their work in individual therapy.

SCREENING THE PARENTS OF
CHILDREN BEING CONSIDERED FOR GROUP

We highly recommend for both support and therapy groups that the parent always be screened before the child. This will give the facilitator a much clearer picture of the family dynamics, the child's history, and the child's readiness for group. We also suggest that the screening session be administered by the child's group facilitator. This allows one of the group's cofacilitators to be acquainted with both the parent's and the child's issues before the group actually starts.

While screening the parent, the facilitator should establish the level of the parent's ability to follow through with therapy and to support and protect the child. Regardless of whether the screening is for a support group or a therapy group, the facilitator should look for a parent who (a) supports the child emotionally, (b) allows the child to clarify his or her own needs and to be assertive, and (c) permits the child to get well (without sabotaging the child's efforts).

Information to Give Parents During Screening

Educating adults is a vital part of the screening process. It is helpful during screening for the facilitator to give parents a sense of how their children are likely to respond to sexual abuse. The facilitator can discuss the child's symptoms with the parent and determine whether or not the parent noticed the child acting differently after disclosure. The facilitator can also explain how research shows that children who have parents who believe, support, and protect them have increased capacity to heal from the abuse.

During screening, the facilitator can discuss with parents the more common behavioral changes that are displayed by sexually abused children. For instance, children frequently regress to behaviors that are normal for younger children, such as thumb sucking, baby talk, clinginess, bed-wetting, throwing tantrums, and being fearful of the dark or of abandonment. The facilitator can reassure parents that, although it can be difficult, they will be able to help their children through such behavioral changes. We often hear comments from parents such as "We thought she had outgrown this a long time ago." Caregivers need to understand that, although their children have outgrown certain behaviors, the trauma of abuse can cause regression. The facilitator can explain to parents that the regression helps free the child from any feelings of responsibility for the abuse. After all, how could a helpless baby possibly be responsible for what happened? Or perhaps the regression is the child's subconscious attempt to return to a time of safety.

It is beneficial for parents (and other caregivers) to understand that their children will likely have feelings surface during group. These feelings, especially feelings of anger, may be misdirected toward the adults they feel closest to, usually nonoffending parents. Children can have difficulty accepting that their nonoffending parents were unable to protect them from the abuse. Some children focus anger inward, blaming themselves for the abuse. Throughout the duration of the children's group, parents will need support in learning how to cope with their children's anger and other emotions affecting their behavior. Screening sessions are a good time to get parents started in a positive direction to help their children.

If it appears from the parent interview that the child may be appropriate for group involvement, the facilitator should set up an appointment to screen the child. If the facilitator finds that the parents are unable to protect the child or to commit to the child's safety or recovery and there are no other responsible adults to take on this role, he or she should refer the child and family to other appropriate resources.

Screening the Parents of Children
Considered for Therapy Groups

The screening session for a parent (or other caregiver) whose child is being considered for therapy group is used to gain a history of the child's abuse and to assess the child's compatibility with group goals. It is also a time for the facilitator to judge the parent's capacity to protect and support the child in recovery. By gaining a better understanding of the parent's coping style, the facilitator gathers a more complete view of the child. A glimpse into a child's family environment allows the facilitator to determine how safe and protected the child actually is.

Screening for a therapy group is a considerably longer process than screening for a support group. The type of information to be assembled is multifaceted. Often, we screen the parents in two separate sessions. The initial session is scheduled for 90 minutes and is concerned with establishing the history of the abuse, the parent's ability to provide transportation, the legal aspects of the case, and an understanding of the child's symptoms. If at that point the parent is still interested in group for the child and, from the information gathered, it appears that the child is a likely candidate for group, we make an additional 1-hour appointment to assess the child.

A side benefit to screening and assessing the parent to determine the child's appropriateness for group is that it allows us to assess appropriate treatment for the parent. We require parents to attend our nonoffending caregivers' therapy group. While interviewing parents, we evaluate them for traits associated with personality and/or character disorders such as narcissism, borderline personality disorder, and dependent personality disorder. By doing a thorough assessment, we can clarify the goals for each child and family member. Depending on the severity of any detected disorders, some parents may need to be in individual therapy rather than group therapy. However, if a parent's symptoms are relatively stable, a combination of individual and group therapy may be beneficial to both parent and child. This evaluation helps us to determine what to focus on in individual, group, and family therapy. It may also play a part in the establishment of group makeup. We have found it especially helpful to have parents with similar issues in our parent groups.

Screening the Parents of Children
Considered for Support Groups

The main reasons for screening the parents of a child who is being considered for a support group are to gain a general history regarding the child's abuse, to find out if the child is currently safe, and to assess how the child feels about the abuse and about participation in a group.

Screening for support groups generally requires less time than does screening for therapy groups, because of the type of information being gathered and its relatively lower level of complexity. A parent screening for a support group can usually be completed in one 60-minute session.

We recommend that the parents of children in support groups attend a "parents' support group" while their children are in group. Because many support groups are open attendance, a commitment to have the child attend each week is not vital, but it is preferable. However, assessing the child's current safety is of critical importance.

SCREENING A CHILD FOR GROUP

When screening a child for either a support group or a therapy group, the facilitator should meet with the child alone. Children who are unable to meet with a facilitator without a parent in the room are probably not ready for group. They may first need to establish a level of comfort through family or individual therapy.

Facilitators should attempt to build rapport with children during screening. They might let the children know that they like children and ask open-ended questions about their schools and their families. To elicit more than simple yes or no responses, they should word questions in such a way that they require full answers. Some good ways to start the conversation include asking the child to "tell me about your school" or "tell me about your family," or the facilitator might ask, "What kind of games do you like to play?"

We keep some drawing materials, a sand tray, and toys available during screening sessions for the children to play with. Having an activity to do, such as coloring or playing with clay, helps children relax. When children appear nervous at screening, facilitators should ask them if they are feeling nervous and what they think might help them to feel more comfortable.

The facilitator should let children know the boundaries right away, explaining limits and expectations. This helps them feel safe. For example: "This is our play therapy room for kids. You can do anything here as long as you don't hurt yourself or anyone else. We'll talk and play for about an hour today and then we will clean up when it is time to go."

Early in the session, the facilitator should ask the child being screened if he or she knows the reason for the meeting. The sooner this is addressed, the better for the child, who will then no longer need to anticipate or avoid the topic. If the child does not know, the facilitator should ask if the child was ever touched in a way that made him or her feel uncomfortable or confused. If the answer is no, the facilitator should state the information he or she has in a general way; for instance, "Your mother had some concerns about unwanted touch." If the child denies being touched again, the facilitator can profess confusion and ask the child if he or she knows what the child's mom might be talking about. If the child still says no, he or she should be referred to individual therapy to become more comfortable discussing the abuse before being placed in a group situation.

Facilitators should not push children at screening to tell about their abuse. Children need to be able to decide who they will tell. The more comfortable a child feels with an individual, the more likely he or she is to tell that person what happened. The facilitator should try to normalize the child's feelings; for example, "There are other children in group who experienced being touched, or touching others in their private parts." If a child fears that no one in the group will like him or her, the facilitator can tell the child that most of the other kids feel that way too. The facilitator might tell the child that he or she reminds the facilitator of someone else who will be in group and how much fun they might have together. We always tell the children that group is an exciting place because they can be completely themselves and not have any secrets. All the other children have been touched, too, and share many of the same feelings.

Sometimes a child will ask whether the interviewer has been abused. Each facilitator must use his or her own judgment when answering such questions, taking into account how impressionable children are and what the particular child's motivation might be in asking. If a facilitator who has been abused decides to disclose that fact, he or she should give very few details. The facilitator may decide to share some of the feelings he or she had then as a point of connection with the child. The focus needs to stay on the child, however; it should not shift to the facilitator.

Young children who have already disclosed often later recant. While screening a child who has recanted, a facilitator should use the history obtained from the parent as well as any corroborative background received from individual therapists, teachers, school counselors, extended family members, and others. Facilitators must rely on their own experience and intuition in trying to determine whether particular recantations are made out of fear or the child really was not abused. We reassure children in these situations that if they want to tell what happened, it will be kept private unless there is a chance of their still being hurt. We also let the children know that many children "wish the disclosure away." Because disclosure often results in many changes in the lives of children and their families, children often hope that by saying the abuse didn't happen everything will return to normal. If at this point a child is still uncertain and nondisclosing, we explain to the child that we understand and that we would like him or her to participate in individual therapy now, and possibly in group later.

Facilitators should tell the children who are accepted into group what they can expect from group, including specifics about games and other activities. The facilitator's enthusiastic descriptions can make group sound like fun. The facilitator should also take the time to explain that groups help sexually abused kids become friends with one another, so they will no longer feel alone.

Children should be given a choice about being in group. If they don't want to be there, they may be disruptive, and the other participants may suffer. When the facilitator has a strong sense that a child would both like and benefit from group but the child is unsure, the facilitator might suggest that the child try it for 3 weeks and reevaluate after that time.

In the event that parent and child information gathered at screening is markedly incongruent, or the child discloses unreported abuse, the facilitator should reevaluate any decision and take appropriate steps to meet the emergent needs of the situation. If, however, after assimilating all the facts, the facilitator feels the child and family are ready for group, he or she should take the following steps: (a) Inform them of their acceptance into group; (b) provide them with a group itinerary that includes dates, times, and places; and (c) review the commitments and responsibilities of participation.

Screening Children for a Therapy Group

The primary reason for screening children for therapy groups is to determine their readiness to disclose and process their thoughts, feelings, and behaviors about the abuse. A child is ready for a therapy group when all of the previously mentioned criteria have been sufficiently met and when the child can say who abused him or her, has some memory of it, can be in group without being too disruptive or dissociative, and can interact with other children safely and appropriately.

Screening Children for a Support Group

The main reasons for screening a child who has adequately met the previous criteria for support groups are to determine whether the child is safe, able to talk in general terms about the abuse, able to do well with other children in a group setting, and able to contain his or her feelings well enough in a group; and to determine which age group best fits the child's needs.

In a child's support group it is not absolutely necessary to group children according to their ages. However, it is most effective to do so, and we recommend it whenever possible. The exception to this is when a child's development is delayed or advanced beyond his or her age group.

Once screening is completed, it is time to start the groups. In the following chapters we provide exercises for both support groups and therapy groups. Remember that all of the exercises can be used for both, except those exercises marked "Therapy Group Only." You will also notice that *within* some exercises certain portions are labeled "Therapy Group Only." Do not use these parts of the exercises in work with support groups. To help you further with group organization, we provide in the appendix some sample outlines for preschool groups, boys' groups, girls' groups, and teen groups.

TABLE 5.1 Screening Children for Support Groups

Child Support Screening	Child Readiness Questions	Ready for Group	Not Ready for Group
Psychological/emotional: ability of the child to acknowledge and share thoughts and feelings about the abuse	Do you know why you are here today? How do you feel about being in a group for children who have been touched? Would you tell me a little about the touch?	Child acknowledges abuse and shares thoughts and feelings about it. Child expresses interest in group participation.	Child is unable to talk or cooperate, denies abuse, and is frightened and anxious.
Behavioral: the child's capacity to interact safely with others in a group setting	Do you want to play a game or draw while we talk? What kind of games do you like to play? Are their behavior problems that might interfere with group?	Child is cooperative and interacts safely and appropriately.	Child's behavior is disruptive and dangerous to self and others.
Intellectual: ability of the child to understand and integrate the concepts introduced in group	Do you go to school or day care? Tell me about your school. Who do you go to when you need help?	Child perceives environment realistically, is able to understand questions, and responds appropriately.	Child is unable to perceive reality accurately and is unable to concentrate, comprehend, or respond coherently.
Developmental: ability of the child to participate in group based on emotional maturity	Do you have friends you play with? What do you like to play? What age group does the child seem appropriate for?	Development is average and compatible with other children in the same age group.	Child is not developmentally compatible with same age group, but may be compatible with younger or older age group.
Resources and systems: ability of the child to receive the necessary emotional and practical support	Who do you trust or feel safe with? If something really bothered you, or you needed something, who would you talk to?	Child has adequate support or knows who to go to and where to go for help.	Child's support system is impoverished or is too unstable to support recovery needs.

NOTE: In a child's support group, it is not absolutely necessary to group children according to their age. However, it is more effective and we highly recommend it whenever possible. The exception to this is when a child's development is delayed or advanced beyond their age.

TABLE 5.2 Screening Children for Therapy Groups

Child Therapy Screening	Child Readiness Questions	Ready for Group	Not Ready for Group
Psychological/emotional: ability of the child to identify, articulate, and process issues	How comfortable is the child with you? How does child respond at mention of sexual abuse? How does child feel about being in group? Can you tell me about the touch? What happened? Tell me more about the abuser. What parts of the abuse do you remember a lot?	Child is able to talk about the abuse, share feelings, and interact appropriately.	Child is unable to talk, unable to cooperate, denies being abused, and is frightened and anxious.
Behavioral: the child's capacity to interact safely with others in a group setting	Are there behavior problems that might interfere with group? Is child sexually aggressive or reactive? Is child on any medication that may affect behavior in group?	Child's behavior is containable and manageable, not harmful to self or others. Medication has no negative influence on behavior.	Child's behavior is disruptive and dangerous to self and others. Medication side effects interfere with concentration and performance.
Intellectual: ability of the child to understand and integrate the concepts introduced in group	Now that everyone knows about the abuse, what is it like at your house? Have you ever been in a therapy group before?	Child is able to perceive environment realistically, is able to understand questions and respond rationally, and is intellectually functional.	Child is unable to perceive reality realistically. Child is unable to concentrate, comprehend, or respond effectively. Child has developmental delays.
Developmental: ability of the child to participate in group based on psychosocial, psychosexual, and emotional maturity	What age group does child seem to be appropriate for? Is child sexually active? How extensive was the abuse? Would disclosure in the group stigmatize the child?	Developmentally, child is compatible with other children in the same age group. Child's psychosexual experience and level of maturity are compatible. Severity and extent of abuse is in accordance with others.	Child is not developmentally compatible with same age group, but may be appropriate for younger or older age group. Extent and severity of child's abuse experience is potentially traumatizing to others, or child's abuse experience is subtle, thus the child may be traumatized by the severity of others' abuse.

(continued)

TABLE 5.2 *Continued*

Child Therapy Screening	Child Readiness Questions	Ready for Group	Not Ready for Group
Resources and systems: ability of the child to receive the necessary emotional and practical support to assist in recovery	What adults in your life do you trust or feel safe with? If your friend talked you into taking candy from the store, and you felt bad about it, would you tell anyone? Who? What do you think they would do?	Child has adequate emotional, psychological, and physical resources to support recovery obligations and commitments.	Child's support system is impoverished or is too unstable to support recovery needs.

TABLE 5.3 Screening Parents of Children in Support Groups

Parent Support Screening	Parent/Child Readiness Questions	Ready for Group	Not Ready for Group
Psychological/emotional: the ability of parent(s)/caregiver(s) to protect and support the child's recovery process as well as their own	What happened when abuse was disclosed? Was it reported? How did you respond to child? History of your child's abuse? If not disclosed, why not? Does child have contact with offender? If yes, do you believe child is safe? Do you use alcohol/ drugs or take any medication? Does the child?	Parent believes the child and is able or willing to learn how to use social and legal systems to prevent further contact with the abuser.	Parent blames the child for family and legal problems. Parent is unable or unwilling to utilize social and legal systems to protect the child. Parents are unwilling to acknowledge how their own issues and reactions are interfering with their child's ability to recover.
Financial: the ability of parent(s)/caregiver(s) to meet financial obligations and commitments or ability to access financial resources	Do you have adequate financial resources to care for your family's needs (food, clothing, shelter, medical, therapy, legal, and transportation)?	Parents are able to meet the family's basic needs on their own or are willing to learn how to access resources.	Parents are unable to meet the family's basic needs and are unwilling to accept assistance.
Community: the ability of parent(s)/ caregiver(s) to access and utilize emotional and practical support to assist in the child's recovery	Do you have any family support or other outside support? Do you have reliable transportation, or access to public transportation?	Parent has adequate emotional support or is willing to develop it with family, friends, or outside community organizations. Parent is willing to prioritize scheduling and transportation needs for support group.	Parent is unwilling or unable to develop or maintain emotional support within the family, among peers, or within the community. Parent has no reliable transportation and/or is unwilling to access other resources.
Child and family issues and concerns: the ability of parent(s)/ caregiver(s) to assess, attend to, and report on issues relevant to the child's safety and the abuse, the effects of the abuse on the child, and/or any other circumstances affecting the family's coping	How does your child cope with the abuse? Are you aware of sexual acting out? If yes, how do you deal with that? How does child relate to peers? How does child feel about coming to a support group? What does child need most from group? Any legal actions expected?	Parent is willing to learn about the impact of the abuse on the child's emotions and behaviors. Parent is willing to learn how to supervise, protect, maintain, and report on child's behavior, health, emotional, and safety needs.	Parent is severely overwhelmed, unwilling or unable to supervise, protect, maintain, or report on child's behavior, health, emotional, and safety needs.

TABLE 5.4 Screening Parents of Children in Therapy Groups

Parent Therapy Screening	Parent/Child Readiness Questions	Ready for Group	Not Ready for Group
Psychological/emotional: ability of parent(s)/caregiver(s) to believe in, protect, and support the child's recovery process and their own	What happened when the abuse was disclosed? If it was not disclosed, why not? Who abused the child? Is the suspected abuser still in contact with the child? What steps have been taken to ensure the child's safety? How did you respond to your child? What are your feelings about the offender? Do you have contact with the offender? How often? Where is your child during that time? Describe the details of your child's abuse. Has your child ever been sexually abused before? If the offender is a spouse or boyfriend, ask about physical, sexual, or verbal abuse. How are you handling the fact of the abuse now? Do you use alcohol or drugs, or take any medications? Is this typical? Were you ever sexually abused? Are you or your child in individual therapy?	Parent believes the child and is able to protect child from abuse by either enforcing no-contact orders or supervised visitations when court ordered. Parent is willing or able to meet child's recovery needs by separating their own feelings from child's feeling about the abuse and the abuser. Parent is able to empathize with and emotionally support child appropriately. Parent is willing or able to participate in own recovery.	Parent blames and punishes child for family and legal problems resulting from the abuse. Parent is unwilling or unable to provide safety and protection for child. Parent is incapable of placing child's needs above own and actively sabotages child's safety and recovery. Parent is dysfunctionally self-absorbed and incapable of providing or unwilling to provide emotional and physical support necessary for the child's recovery.

chapter **6**

SAFETY AND TRUST EXERCISES

The initial goal of group is to establish a safe and trustworthy environment for the children. Safety is a basic human need and a necessary condition of survival. Children rely without reservation or choice upon adults for protection. Those who are secured from danger are free to thrive. Over time, a thriving child comes to believe in, trust in, and even hope for a continuous future. A child's dependence upon others for physical, psychological, emotional, and spiritual well-being is an interactive process. It requires the participation of both the caregiver and the child. If the parent is a healthy or adequate caregiver, the interactions of parent and child will be experienced as mutually successful and satisfying. The experience of the world as a benevolent place prepares the child to negotiate his needs with others effectively and confidently. This simple act of relationship helps to develop a sense of belonging, of being a part of a family, a community, and a society.

Trust and safety are often primary issues for children who have been sexually abused. Many of them have been violated, manipulated, and betrayed by family members or trusted family friends. Power and control have been substituted for relationship, and the children are left without resources to manage confused and overwhelming feelings.

One of the roles of a group facilitator is to be a resource for the children. Facilitators provide a consistent and predictable environment with clear and appropriate boundaries while they model effective communication skills. Responding to children's fears or confusion with empathic acknowledgment helps them to feel that they are being connected with and understood by someone who cares. This helps to reduce feelings of anxiety. Encouraging children to express their thoughts and feelings verbally greatly reduces the potential for destructive acting-out behavior. Reassuring them of their present safety and offering them suggestions for future self-protection help them with emotional management and containment.

41

Trust-building exercises are initially used to help children feel comfortable in the group setting and with one another. Nonconfrontational activities help to create safe connections among group members (see "Imaginary Object," "Check-In," and "Group Mascot"). Subsequent trust and safety exercises are designed to shape and influence behaviors and beliefs distorted by abuse and to strengthen healthy attitudes and the children's ideas about themselves, others, and the world around them (see "Ball Toss," "Going Camping," and "Group Collage About the Abuse").

Safety- and trust-building techniques are good opening and closing activities and are a consistent thread woven throughout the entire group experience. In addition to the exercises described below, thematic variations on common children's games—such as Duck, Duck, Goose; Musical Chairs; Operator; Telephone; and Mother, May I?— work wonderfully with the children. To create bonds and to reduce feelings of anxiety in the initial session, facilitators can have each child make a collage of him- or herself and share it with the group. For other activities, *The New Games Book* (Fluegelman, 1976) is a resource filled with many fun, group-focused games. The children often have many great ideas, too. Facilitators can use games that they know and suggest. Even quick, simple techniques such as a group hug, group cheer, or applause for a session well done can go a long way toward building a sense of safety and belonging.

Imaginary Object

GOAL

To build feelings of trust and safety

AGES

4 through 8

TIME

10-15 minutes

PURPOSE

This exercise provides a creative way for children to introduce themselves in group, using their imaginations.

DO THIS EXERCISE TO

- Reduce levels of fear.
- Set a fun and creative tone for group.
- Build connections among group members.
- Validate group members for who they are and what they have to say.
- Increase group members' ability to relate authentically.

DO NOT USE THIS EXERCISE WHEN

There is no reason not to do this exercise.

WHAT YOU NEED

No special materials needed

INSTRUCTIONS

Direct group members to stand or sit in a circle facing one another. Begin this exercise by pretending to hold something in your hand. Describe the imaginary object and state what it is. It may be a cat, roller skates, a rowboat—anything. Describe the object by using your voice and hands, and by making body movements to illustrate clearly what the object is. For example, if your object is a mouse, hold your hands really close together and make a petting motion. Explain that you are holding a mouse and what you like about mice. Then answer the questions you want the children to answer while you are still holding and petting your imaginary object. When you are done, pass your object gently on to someone else in the group. The following are examples of some questions you may want group members to answer. Ask no more than three questions at a time:

- What is your name?
- What school do you go to?
- How old are you?
- What is your favorite thing to do?
- If you could have any pet in the world, what would you have?
- How do you feel about being in this group?
- What do you like about yourself?
- What is your favorite story?

As the imaginary object is passed, each person changes it into whatever she wants it to be. Ask each child about why she changed it into what she did. Have the child answer the questions you are asking for the day and then pass the imaginary object on to the next person. The next person can change the object into anything of his choosing.

HINTS

Children generally love this exercise. We give group members time to ask their own questions about the object, too. We had a boy who turned an object into a cat. We asked him what he liked about cats and whether he had a cat. It turned out that he had a cat that he cuddled with when he felt sad.

As the facilitator, consider making your object something active, like a ball. Then you can pretend to bounce it, throw it up in the air, jump around with it, and toss it to someone else. This stimulates everyone's imagination and sets a tone that encourages the children to be relaxed and enthusiastic.

Check-In

GOAL

To build feelings of trust and safety

AGES

4 through 18

TIME

5-20 minutes

PURPOSE

This exercise helps group members become present in their thoughts, which enables them to focus on group while providing them with ways to both express and contain their feelings. This exercise encourages a sense of trust in members and offers them an opportunity to develop their social skills.

DO THIS EXERCISE TO

- Discuss current concerns the facilitators or group members may have.
- Bring focus and direction to that day's session.
- Teach basic communication skills, including listening, empathic response, and appropriate disclosure of thoughts and feelings.
- Give children a sense of safety by providing a predictable beginning to each week's session.

DO NOT DO USE THIS EXERCISE WHEN

There is no reason not to do this exercise; however, you need to put clear time limits on it.

WHAT YOU NEED

No special materials needed

INSTRUCTIONS

Have everyone sit in a circle facing one another. Decide whether you want to go around the circle, pick people randomly, or have individual members respond to your initial query.

This exercise helps direct the children's attention and awareness to their present emotional state or most recent concern. It places them in context with one another and the issues they are dealing with. The questions asked can be either general or specific, open-ended or directive. Typical general check-in questions are open-ended and invite voluntary responses from members. Questions such as "How are you today?" and "How has your week been?" allow current or new information to arise and be processed. We prefer to let children respond on a voluntary basis so that we can witness their interactive styles. Although long silences between responses can be somewhat uncomfortable, they yield useful information. Noticing who responds first or last, who waits to be called upon, who dominates, and who distracts or dissociates increases our capacity to assess and treat each child's specific needs.

Time limits are helpful for group management and may vary depending upon age group and daily group agendas. You may want to set a time limit for responses, such as 2 minutes. To encourage responses that have emotional content and informational relevance, we ask the children to explain their opinions and feelings. For example, when a child responds that she is feeling "fine," the facilitator or another group member will ask for more information or clarification by asking why, or what is helping her to feel fine.

The specific check-in is a more focused and directive technique. It is typically used to tie activities from one week to the next or as a lead-in to the current session's topic or activity. Following are some suggestions for directive check-ins:

- What was the most outrageous thing you did this week?
- What thoughts or feelings did you have this week regarding the sexual abuse?

- Finish this sentence: The worst thing about being sexually abused was . . .
- Share a dream you had this week.
- Share one great thing and one rotten thing that happened this week.
- Share one way you were tricked or manipulated this week.
- Was anyone triggered this week? Talk about one thing that happened.
- How has the sexual abuse affected your feelings about dating?
- What's your favorite thing about group?
- If you could change one thing about yourself, what would it be?
- Has being sexually abused changed you in any way? If so, how has it changed you?
- Is there anyone you trust? If so, what about them helps you to trust them?
- Do you think you could have stopped the sexual assault? If so, how?
- Do you have a secret that doesn't feel good? What stops you from telling it?
- Name three things you like about yourself.

HINTS

Teenagers can really get off track during check-in, spending a lot of time talking about anything but sexual abuse issues. You should definitely place a time limit on a "general" check-in so that you don't spend an hour of your session discussing boyfriends, school, or who dropped whom as a friend this week.

Be sure to keep group members on track. Let them know in a kind way when they are getting sidetracked or if they are taking up too much time. Gentle confrontation helps them learn appropriate communication skills. Make sure that group members are answering the questions you asked and that they are talking about themselves and not their friends down the street.

When doing check-in as an exercise, be flexible with your agenda. Important information is often disclosed and can need immediate attention. For example, during check-in we have had children mention plans to visit their offenders for the first time that evening. Another time a child had just learned she had to go to court the following week to testify. One of the hardest surprises we experienced during check-in was when a girl was told, while walking into our office to attend the group session, that her grandfather (her offender) had just committed suicide. Naturally, these issues took precedence over our previously planned activities and became the focus of group that day.

Helping children deal with their immediate issues and situations in a group setting helps everyone and generates a great deal of strength, support, and confidence.

Safety Rules

GOAL

To build feelings of trust and safety (Always do this in the first group session.)

AGES

4 through 18

TIME

10-15 minutes

PURPOSE

Creating clear group rules establishes a safe, consistent, and predictable environment. The involvement of group members in developing the rules builds cohesion, a sense that their input is important, and a feeling of ownership of the group and its process. Most of all, it encourages them to express their needs and to be empowered to speak up when the rules aren't being followed.

DO THIS EXERCISE TO

- Create/establish group cohesion and a sense of control and predictability in the group.
- Increase the capacity of group members to risk being vulnerable and to express their needs safely.
- Stress the importance of confidentiality among group members.
- Increase group members' understanding that a sense of safety is both internal and external.

DO NOT USE THIS EXERCISE WHEN

Always do this exercise.

WHAT YOU NEED

- Large sheets of paper, and a place to hang up the rules
- Markers

INSTRUCTIONS

Instruct group members to think about what they need to feel safe in the group. Give some examples, asking:

- Would you feel safe if anybody could walk through the door?
- Would you feel safe if people could get really wild in here and jump on all the furniture?
- Would you feel safe if anything you said in here could be told to other people?

When they respond negatively to such questions, ask them what would help them to feel safe in the room.

THERAPY GROUP ONLY: Continue by asking the group members how their insides tell them they are not feeling safe. Give examples:

- Some people get a stomachache when they do not feel safe.
- Others think thoughts like "I don't like you" or "She hates me."
- Others want to go in a corner and hide.
- Some people get angry and start hitting objects or people.

Continue by saying, "For example, if someone said something that hurt your feelings, how would your body tell you that you did not feel safe? What would you do?" If a child says, "I'd hide," or "I'd yell," ask the child how the group could help her feel safe and connected again if that happened. Offer ideas to be considered by asking questions such as the following:

- Would you like the group to ignore you?
- Would you like someone to gently put a hand on your knee or shoulder?
- Would you like us to joke with you?
- Would you like us to check in with you and ask you how you are feeling?

Examples of internal safety rules children have chosen in the past include these:

- *Jenny:* If not feeling safe she will withdraw and we leave her alone.
- *Sally:* If not feeling safe she will cry or get teary. The facilitator can sit near her and hold her.
- *Diane:* If not feeling safe she will say mean things to others. Group members can let her know they notice she is not feeling safe and tell her why they like her.

For both therapy and support groups, as kids make suggestions, write them on a piece of paper marked "Rules for Safety in Group." (For **therapy groups,** make sure you include the above internal safety rules on your list.) Children will need some prodding and some help with ideas. Typically our groups include many of the following rules:

- No hitting, kicking, spitting, or slapping.
- No touching another person without his or her permission.
- Whatever is said in this room stays in this room.
- Hugs are great if a person asks for one.
- Always listen to the person talking.
- Show you are listening by being quiet and looking at the person who is talking.
- Respect all group members by being nice to them and treating them as you want to be treated.
- Use your words to describe how you are feeling.
- All feelings are okay.

Make sure all of the children understand each of the written rules. The rule that will need the most discussion will probably be one about confidentiality. The children need to agree that they will not reveal the names of other children in the group. Each group member has a choice about who he wants to tell about his own abuse. It is not permissible to disclose details of any other group member's abuse. If that is done, the group's sense of safety will be destroyed.

Confidentiality can be a difficult concept to explain. We tell group members not to share anything private that another group member has said. They also should not tell others the last names of anyone in group. We tell group members it is okay to talk to a parent about group and share what they are learning and how they are feeling. They may want to say, "Johnnie shared something that happened to him and it happened to me too. I want to talk about it."

Be sure to review the group rules during the second session and allow group members to add any new rules they have thought of during the week.

HINTS

Display the rules on the wall each week, so that members have a visual reminder of them. Don't drag this exercise out too long, or you'll lose their attention.

Group Mascot

GOAL

To build feelings of trust and safety

AGES

3 through 18

TIME

45-60 minutes (Aside from check-in and a quick closing exercise, this exercise easily takes an entire group session for children ages 7-18. For 4- to 6-year-olds, the exercise takes about 20 minutes.)

PURPOSE

Building a mascot together gives group members a sense of cohesiveness and ownership of the group. It is a fun way to express their individuality while simultaneously learning to work cooperatively together. This exercise works best if it is done the second week of group. Patricia Godleman brought this exercise to us. The children love it.

DO THIS EXERCISE TO

- Reduce levels of shame.
- Build group cohesion and a sense of belonging.
- Increase group members' capacity to be vulnerable and to interact with other group members authentically.
- Teach cooperation.

DO NOT USE THIS EXERCISE WHEN

There is no reason not to do this exercise.

WHAT YOU NEED

- One large piece of poster board
- A selection of large pieces of colored paper and white paper
- Colored markers
- Glue sticks

(Glitter, buttons, ribbons, and so on are also great to have on hand for added decoration)

INSTRUCTIONS

Part I: Begin with a guided imagery for ages 7 and older. Have younger children simply close their eyes and imagine an animal, real or pretend, that they would feel safe with. Then ask them some of the questions listed below. Instruct older group members to lie down or remain in a sitting position, whichever they are most comfortable with. Have them close their eyes and take three relaxing/cleansing breaths. Instruct them to feel themselves becoming more and more relaxed and to allow their bodies to rest comfortably on the floor. Then instruct them to picture a place in their minds that feels safe and wonderful. This can be a real place or a made-up one. Ask them to imagine what the place looks like. Lead them through an exploration of the place: How do you feel inside your body when you are there? Notice if it's dark or light there. What is the temperature there? Look around and notice what about this safe place fills your heart with warmth. While in that safe place, you notice an animal. It can be a real one or a made-up one. This animal will protect you. Notice how good and safe you feel when you are near it. Look at the animal closely. What do you notice about it? Notice the animal's colors and its expression. Look at its face, ears, tail, feet, and body.

- Does the animal have fur, scales, hair?
- Is it big or small?
- Where does it live? Under your bed? In the closet?

- Does it have wings, eyes, teeth, horns?
- Does it have special powers to protect you?

While the group members' eyes are still closed, assign a different section of the animal for each person to study closely. For example: "Jan, you notice your animal's eyes, ears, and the top of the head. Sally, you notice your animal's nose, mouth, chin, and neck. Rosie, you focus on the animal's legs. Jean, notice what your animal's body, the torso, looks like."

Tell them that they will be leaving their safe places, but their animals will be able to see them, be with them, and protect them wherever they go. Tell them to begin to feel the floor beneath them and to notice sounds they're hearing around them. Tell them to return to the room by slowly opening their eyes.

Part II: Instruct the group members to draw the sections of their animals they were assigned. Have them draw their sections on pieces of paper large enough to fit on the poster board in proportion to the rest of the pieces of the animal. Remind them to draw only the parts of their animals that you assigned to them. For example, if a person pictured a lion and you assigned him the tail, he is only to draw the lion's tail.

Part III: Have each member cut out the body part she just drew and have the group together arrange and glue the body parts onto the poster board to create a protector animal. This mascot may have a lion's legs, a snake's tail, and a shark's teeth.

Part IV: Together, decorate the animal. Ask the children questions about the animal as it is being formed. For instance, "Does it have any extra qualities, such as poison sacs, eyes that see everything, lightning bolts to electrocute offenders, or scales all over that emit slime?" As time permits, while decorating, ask each member about the individual animal he visualized.

Part V: Ask group members what the group mascot will say to protect them. Write up these words on a piece of paper and place them so that they are coming out of the animal's mouth, as if the animal is saying them.

Part VI: Ask the group to come up with an agreed-upon name for the mascot (this process alone can be quite fascinating). Then have the group decide if the name will be accepted by majority rule or consensus. Should there be silent voting? Notice the dynamics in the group while a name is being chosen. Does one member take charge? Do others follow her? Is one upset if the name he suggests isn't chosen?

DISCUSSION (THERAPY GROUP ONLY)

Following the exercise, discuss the process. Is everyone happy with the mascot? Describe the ways they cooperated and the times when cooperation broke down. Ask them how they felt when or if it broke down. Ask if everyone felt heard and recognized during this process. If not, why not? If you notice a child had shut down, ask her what that felt like for her. Ask her what she would like the group to do if this happens again. Does she want to be recognized or ignored? Would she like a hug or someone to sit near her? Would she like people to joke with her or be serious? This is the same process that is done in setting up the rules for the group. This gives you a chance to expand on the importance of group members' learning to identify and express their needs.

If there is time, ask the same question of every group member: If you are feeling not included, or sad, scared, or angry, how can you let the group know and what would you like from the group?

HINTS

Some group members may be resistant to drawing only parts of their animals. Encourage them to do so anyway. Once they join in on the group animal they'll enjoy it and be proud of their particular contributions.

The mascot is now an important member of the group. Therefore, always be sure to display it in the room for every subsequent group session.

Often, the facilitators will go to a copier store and photocopy reduced colored copies of the mascot for each member to take home.

Going Camping

GOALS

To learn about internal boundaries; to build feelings of trust and safety

AGES

4 through 6

TIME

30 minutes

PURPOSE

This exercise, developed by one of our therapists, Karen Farber, helps group members increase their ability to self-soothe and control their anxiety. It helps them to identify and express their needs and thus get their needs met.

DO THIS EXERCISE TO

- Build a personal sense of safety.
- Teach the children to express their feelings and articulate ways they feel safe.
- Give the children a sense of control over their environment.
- Increase group cohesiveness.
- Increase the children's capacity to be vulnerable and to interact authentically.

DO NOT USE THIS EXERCISE WHEN

- Any child in the group was abused on a camping trip (in such a case, you could turn this into a day hike in the forest or a day at the beach)

WHAT YOU NEED

- Items used on camping trips, such as a children's tent big enough for all group members (or a card table and a large bed sheet), stones for a campfire, one flashlight for each child, a couple of pieces of firewood
- Enough chairs for each child
- Paper
- Colored markers
- A stuffed animal that each child brings from home (have a few extras available in case some children forget to bring them)

INSTRUCTIONS

Part I: Tell the group that you are all going on an imaginary camping trip. Arrange the chairs as if they were the seats in a car, and have everyone get in the car and buckle their seat belts. Drive to the beach, describing some of the sights you see on the way.

Part II: When you arrive at the beach, have the children help set up the tent and gather firewood and rocks for the fire circle. (If you have no tent, make one by putting the bed sheet over the card table.) Then make a campfire by putting the rocks in a circle and placing the wood in the center. Cook up and eat an imaginary dinner, and then have everyone brush their teeth and get into bed in the tent. Pass out the flashlights so that each group member has one.

Part III: When everyone is in the tent, explain that it is nighttime and it is getting dark. Ask everyone if it is okay to turn out the lights to remind them it is nighttime. Turn off the lights only if everyone agrees. Now ask, "Are you scared of the dark? What are you afraid of in the dark?" If they're afraid of monsters and animals, ask them why they are not afraid of these things during the day. They'll probably mention that they can see them during the day. Let them know that people can see at night, too. When you first turn out the lights it is dark and hard to see, but then your eyes adjust and you can see a lot of things, even in the dark. Ask them, when they are feeling scared, how they can feel safe? Have them try everyone's ideas; for example:

- Let's turn on the flashlights.
- Let's sit on someone's lap.
- Let's sing a song.
- Let's hold hands.

Part III: When everyone lies down to go to sleep, ask, "Did anyone hear that noise? I think it's a bear. How can we scare the bear? Let's figure out ways to feel safe from the bear together." Some suggestions might be:

- Turn the flashlights on.
- Make lots of noise.
- Call on the cellular phone for help.
- Hold each other.
- Remind ourselves that bears are really scared of people and don't want to be around us so we just have to be loud enough to let the bear know we're here.

Part IV: Have everyone lie down for a peaceful sleep, then wake them up and tell them it is morning. Have everyone help pack up, and then drive home in the car together.

Part V: Back in group, talk about how members can feel safe at home. Ask questions such as the following:

- Does anyone get scared when there is a storm and lightning?
- Is anyone scared of spiders? The dark?
- What can you do at home to feel safe?
- Who can you tell that you are scared? Will they help you?
- What can you do to help yourself feel less scared? What can you think in your head? What can you feel in your body? What can you hold or draw?

Part VI: Have each group member draw a picture that shows something he is afraid of and what he can do to feel safer.

HINTS

Put away the flashlights when you pack up the car, or you will have major distractions.

When children have difficulty thinking of ways to be safe for their drawings, make suggestions, such as getting help checking that all the doors and windows are locked at home at night or asking someone to check under their beds and in the closets before they go to sleep.

Group Collage
About the Abuse

GOALS

To learn about internal boundaries; to build feelings of trust and safety

AGES

5 through 18

TIME

60-90 minutes

PURPOSE

Doing a collage together builds a group bond and provides a safe outlet for expressing feelings about the abuse.

DO THIS EXERCISE TO

- Build group cohesiveness.
- Introduce a safe way to begin identifying and expressing feelings about the abuse.

DO NOT USE THIS EXERCISE WHEN

- The group room is too large for everyone to work side by side comfortably.

WHAT YOU NEED

- One large piece of butcher paper
- Crayons and markers
- Old magazines
- Yarn and glitter
- Photographs
- Construction paper, tissue paper
- Scissors
- Glue and tape

INSTRUCTIONS

Part I: This exercise can be done as an introduction for group members to tell their personal abuse stories. Roll out the butcher paper so that everyone is sitting side by side with the paper in front of them. Then instruct the group members to use the materials at hand to describe all their feelings and thoughts about the abuse, even though some may be contradictory or confusing.

Part II: When the collage is finished, have the group members share what they have created. Encourage them to ask questions about others' creations. Point out the feelings that the children have in common with one another. Hang the collage up to use during future sessions as a reminder of the multitude of emotions children feel when they are abused.

HINTS

Do not give too many directions on this exercise. If kids want to work on a section together, fine. You'll find that they are taking notice of what others are doing and will be talking and commenting throughout the exercise. This exercise also gives you a glimpse into their social skills as you observe how they interact and how willing or unwilling they are to share their materials. (Because the finished collage may be displayed in a room with some public viewing, ask the children not to use swear words or their names.)

Consider having many precut pictures available for younger children. Otherwise, finding the pictures and then cutting them out can take the entire group time.

This can be a calming exercise. We had a group of wild 7- and 8-year-olds, some of whom were so full of rage they had difficulty sitting for more than 2 minutes at a time. Others in the group were so ashamed of the abuse that they had only revealed who touched them and nothing more. They were completely engaged during this exercise, which had a more cathartic and cohesive effect on the group than did any other. Group members took great care in the pictures they drew and cut out. They began helping each other write comments next to their pictures. The following week, when we discussed each person's section, we found out that one member was still having contact with the offender and was overwhelmed with fear that the abuse might happen again. Another felt "dead" during the abuse and began to describe how she completely dissociates whenever she remembers it. A third finally admitted that she was abused by an additional offender recently, and others graphically described their own feelings of anger and fear toward their offenders.

Let It All Out/Sound Train

GOAL

To build feelings of trust and safety

AGES

4 through 18

TIME

2-5 minutes

PURPOSE

This is a wonderful exercise that helps to release pent-up emotions in the group in a safe way. It provides support and permission to acknowledge and express big feelings instead of acting them out or avoiding them altogether. (This is a quick, fun warm-up or closing exercise.)

DO THIS EXERCISE TO

- Release feelings of fear, shame, and isolation.
- Release feelings after the group has done some hard emotional work.
- Teach stress management and containment skills.
- Relieve feelings of anger, disgust, or hurt before group members leave the room.

DO NOT USE THIS EXERCISE WHEN

There is no reason not to do this exercise.

WHAT YOU NEED

No special materials needed

INSTRUCTIONS

There are two versions of this exercise. For both, group members stand next to one another in a circle, about half an arm's length apart. In the first version, "Let It All Out," the facilitator starts by making a sound and motion that expresses how she is feeling, such as a karate yell with a karate chop. The rest of the group then copies that same motion and noise. Then another group member who chooses to do so makes a noise and sound, and again the entire group follows by simultaneously making the same sound and movement. Continue doing this until everyone who wishes to has initiated an emotional release.

The second version, "Sound Train," is very similar. The only difference is that after the first person demonstrates a sound and movement, this action and sound are slowly built upon. The person to the initiator's right does the same sound and motion while the initiator keeps doing it. Then the following person joins in, so now three people are doing it all at once. This continues until finally the entire group is imitating the initial person. Once that sound train is completed, someone else initiates a sound and movement and the process is repeated.

End both versions with one or two quiet and calming motions to help group members settle down before they leave the room.

HINTS

You can use this exercise often, whenever you believe feelings need to be released or the group is growing restless. Once the children are familiar with this exercise, they will often recognize their need for it and request it themselves.

My Own Safe Place

GOALS

To learn about internal boundaries; to build feelings of trust and safety; to learn to manage triggers

AGES

3 through 18

TIME

15-20 minutes

PURPOSE

This exercise helps each child find and define his own safe place in the world. This place may be real or imagined. It is a place where a child can momentarily escape when feeling threatened; where he can bolster his strength and confront his fears.

DO THIS EXERCISE TO

- Increase the children's understanding that a sense of safety is both internal and external.
- Increase the children's capacity to risk being vulnerable and to express their needs safely.
- Increase the children's ability to identify, comprehend, manage, and express thoughts and feelings appropriately.

- Decrease dissociative behavior when abuse is mentioned.
- Increase the children's ability to manage trigger responses.

DO NOT USE THIS EXERCISE WHEN

There is no reason not to do this exercise. In fact, we believe it should be done in all groups.

WHAT YOU NEED

- Drawing paper
- Markers or crayons

INSTRUCTIONS

Part I: Instruct everyone to close their eyes for a few minutes and to imagine the safest place possible. This can be a real or imagined place. Ask them:

- How does this place help you to feel safe?
- Are there other people there? If so, who?
- Are there animals there?
- What does this place look like?
- Is it indoors or outdoors?
- What is the temperature like?
- Are there colors, sounds, or sights you especially notice?

End the image by stating, "Know that this is a place where no one can harm you. You will always be safe here. In your mind's eye, add in everything you need to be safe in this place."

Part II: Instruct everyone to open their eyes and to draw their safe places. Encourage them to include as much detail as possible.

Part III: Have everyone share their drawings with one another by describing their safe places and what about their places helps them to feel safe.

HINTS

You will be able to use the image of a safe place over and over again. When doing other guided imagery exercises, you can have each child first imagine her safe place as a way to hasten the relaxation process. We often mention the children's safe places on the personalized certificates they receive at the close of group (see "Completion of Group Ceremony").

Some sexually abused children have never had a sense of safety and so have a difficult time imagining a safe place. Work with these children individually to help them begin to visualize the possibility of such a place existing. Ask each child if she can remember one time when she felt happy. Have her describe that time to you. Ask her if she can remember a place where she felt she might have some protection. Have her describe that place to you. Use the child's answers to help her develop an image of a safe place. Sometimes using the word *soothing* in place of *safe* can help a child to develop an image.

chapter 7

SELF-ESTEEM EXERCISES

The development of a child's self-esteem is not an event, but a process. Self-esteem evolves over time and within the context of relationships. Developing healthy self-esteem is an inside job that requires outside help. To develop a strong sense of self, a child must learn that she is a valuable person who is loved, enjoyed, and respected. She must be afforded opportunities to feel and demonstrate that she is an integral part of her family and community. How well she develops this positive sense of self is strongly influenced by the main caregivers in her life.

We believe that there are five stages in the development of a healthy self-esteem: safety, attachment, affection, achievement, and socialization. All of these five stages are intricately woven between the child and the relationships she has with those around her.

Let's begin with safety, which has both physical and emotional components. *Physical safety* protects the integrity of the body. It provides the child with an environment that will ensure her ability to thrive. Parents with healthy self-esteem are able to be present and focused on their children's needs. When the child is very young, the healthy parent makes sure the child is safe. She protects the child physically from a dangerous environment filled with cars, hot burners, and myriad other potential harms.

Emotional safety requires conditions that allow and contribute to a child's emotional safety and development. Children need guidance to navigate successfully the uncharted world of sensations, emotions, and events. They need help learning to put words to their feelings. They need to be encouraged, comforted, and corrected so that they can learn to nurture themselves and relate empathically with others. A parent who is sufficiently attuned to her child's needs will positively influence the child's ability to learn how to identify, interpret, tolerate, and regulate emotions. When the child gets hurt, the parent soothes her with comforting words and gentle embraces. The words also teach the child about emotions and thoughts. A 4-year-old who bursts into tears when the family dog runs by and knocks her over would be swept into the arms of an emotionally healthy parent and held. That parent may comfort her by saying, "Oh, honey, are you all right? That must have scared you. You were standing there as happy as could be and then boom, you're on the floor. I don't think you're hurt. I'm glad you're not. It's okay to cry, sweetheart." In such an interaction the child's feelings are validated and mirrored, and she is taught words for her emotions. She is also told that it is okay to express those emotions and to receive comfort when she needs it. A parent with the capacity, energy, and desire to recognize and respond to her child's physical, psychological, and spiritual needs adds greatly to her child's feelings of emotional safety and esteem.

Attachment is a way of describing feelings of connection and belonging. The experience of feeling connected or belonging to something or someone benevolent and greater than oneself is at the heart of human relationships. A person's first experience of attachment begins during infancy. You have probably noticed how babies often try to maintain eye contact with their parents as the parents are moving away. Very young children can follow only with their eyes, but as a child becomes mobile he will physically follow the parent. You may have watched a baby happily respond when he hears his mother's voice. Although the infant is unable to articulate feelings, his movements demonstrate the attachment he has already developed with the parent.

It is through this relationship with the parent that a child learns about the world and himself. How he feels and relates to others will be largely determined by the quality of this primary relationship. In the example above, of the little girl accidentally knocked down by the family dog, the mother compassionately intercedes and provides the child with comfort, understanding, and perspective about the event. The mother's empathic response teaches the child how to relate to life's experiences with shared understanding and compassion.

When attachment fails to develop adequately between a parent and child, the child is at risk. A parent too wounded or self-absorbed to respond to a child's needs may not provide a sufficient experience of bonding (Horney, 1991). At worst, this could result in the child's failure to thrive, disorders of attachment, or sociopathy. At best, it could lead to the child's impaired ability to relate to the world, other than in an antagonistic or objectifying way.

Affection may be pictured as the emotional energy that allows attachment to occur. It is an emotion that conveys warmth, positive regard, and love. Over time, this feeling of affection flows toward a child, creating a core belief and a felt sense that she is, at center, someone who is both lovable and worthwhile. Children who feel loved and valued are more secure and confident. They are able to handle new situations, changes, and difficulties with some measure of hope and composure. When Mom sweeps her capsized little girl into her arms and says, "Oh, honey, are you all right?" she is conveying concern about her daughter's physical condition and emotional experience. She is affectionately letting her child know that what happens to her matters and that she deserves time, attention, and comforting.

When children are neglected or abused, their self-esteem is greatly impaired. If a parent ignores or punishes a child for expressing needs for affection, attention, or help, the child will learn to adapt—at a grave cost to himself. The absence of affection in combination with other negative treatment may cause feelings of abject worthlessness. Children who feel bad about themselves treat themselves and others in ways that demonstrate their lack of self-esteem.

Achievement is the ability to transform ideas into actions. When children have an underlying sense of emotional security and confidence, they have the courage to assert themselves effectively in the world. Children need more than encouragement, however, to be successful. They need skills. They need to learn how to direct and sustain effort in order to achieve desired results. A child who is learning to walk first crawls and most often falls. Parents who teach their children how to tolerate the frustrations that come with learning, by modeling patience and commitment transfer skills, and greatly increase their children's potential for success. When the little girl in our example learns how to dodge her overly enthusiastic dog effectively, she feels a sense of accomplishment. When her parents teach her how to communicate with the four-legged family member through commands such as "sit" and "stay," she is deeply impressed with both herself and the dog. Her burst of pride comes from acquiring skill as well as from establishing a means of communication and relationship with her dog. Children who are guided, corrected, and praised become adults who know their limitations and realize much of their potential.

We have observed that when children are made to feel incompetent, they have difficulty with performance. Parents who shame, humiliate, or inappropriately punish their children for exercising their will damage their child's self-will and self-esteem. These children often feel defeated before they even start. They frustrate easily when things don't go just right and they sometimes fear that there will be retaliation for mistakes made.

Socialization is learning gained from a system of collective values, practices, and habits. Children initially are socialized through their interactions with their parents and other family members. Ideally, children are guided by their parents. They are taught *how* to think and behave, instead of *what* to think and do. A child's ability to grow into responsibility and become a positive member of society depends on his capacity to understand the values or consequences of his actions and their effects on the whole. If our little girl's impulse to kick her dog because he made her fall were to go uncorrected, she might never learn how to manage her problems or hurt feelings in ways that lead to self-respect and consideration of others. She might similarly mishandle other life situations as well, and her relationships would suffer.

Children who learn at the hands of parents who themselves are irresponsible, immature, or mentally unbalanced usually have difficulty relating effectively to others. In situations where children are sexually abused by parents or other family members, lessons of responsibility and accountability are confused and distorted.

When a child has been sexually abused on an ongoing basis, her self-esteem is greatly impaired. Instead of learning about mutual relationships through the love and respect of an adult, the child learns about power and control (power over someone or something substitutes for connection with others). Instead of learning how to express herself and negotiate her needs, she learns about manipulation and control. Instead of learning about attachment, she learns to feel guilty and responsible for others' feelings and behaviors. Instead of learning about loving affection and to trust the support of others, sexually abused children learn that people are dangerous and can hurt you.

The group is a perfect venue for sexually abused children to develop healthy self-esteem. Through facilitated social interaction, children learn what to value and trust inside themselves, in the environment, and in others. Self-esteem exercises promote cooperation as well as competence, which enables children to gain confidence as well as a sense of belonging.

The role of the group facilitator is to model and teach the concepts of safety, attachment, affection, achievement, and socialization through self-esteem exercises. Self-esteem is the heart and soul of a child's life. Every exercise contained within this book offers an opportunity to address one or all of the components of self-esteem. Children want to be liked, want to belong, want to get along and have friends—reminding them of this and helping them to learn these skills is both a necessary and a gratifying responsibility.

The following exercises emphasize the creation of a positive self-image (see "Ball Toss"), a sense of belonging with other group members (see "Friendship Medals" and "Yes/No/Maybe Continuum"), rebuilding children's views of themselves based on reality ("Me, Through the Years"), thus helping children develop a sense of hope for a positive future.

Yes/No/Maybe Continuum

GOAL

To build self-esteem

AGES

6 through 18

TIME

10-20 minutes

PURPOSE

This exercise is used to help reduce levels of fear, shame, and isolation that children often feel when disclosing the details of their abuse. The ways in which the children respond to questions can generate new information about their circumstances, attitudes, and behaviors. This exercise also allows the children to witness other children's experiences of abuse, which increases a sense of belonging and decreases a sense of feeling different from everybody else. This exercise is adapted from a psychodrama workshop we attended in the 1980s led by psychodramatist Ann Taylor.

DO THIS EXERCISE TO

- Reduce levels of fear, shame, and isolation.
- Increase group members' capacity to be vulnerable and to interact authentically.
- Create a strong feeling of group cohesiveness and identity.

DO NOT USE THIS EXERCISE WHEN

There is no reason not to do this exercise.

WHAT YOU NEED

- Three signs: one that says "Yes," one that says "No," and one that says "Maybe"

INSTRUCTIONS

Prior to beginning the group, post the three signs along a straight line in the room, with the "Maybe" sign in the middle.

Begin expressing yourself with excitement and enthusiasm about this exercise to get and keep everyone's attention while you explain the instructions. Explain how group members will stand under the signs, using their bodies instead of their voices to answer the questions being asked in this exercise. For example, if the question is "Do you like frogs?" you will stand under the "No" sign if you really don't like them or under the "Yes" sign if you do like them. You will stand under the "Maybe" sign if you sort of like them or sometimes do and sometimes don't.

When everyone understands how the "game" is played, begin by asking some fun and nonthreatening questions. This will encourage everyone's involvement, even those who might otherwise be reluctant to participate in group activities. For example, you might ask, Who likes chocolate? pizza? dogs? cats? snow? to swim? music? and other "get to know you" questions. After everyone gets the idea, begin asking questions that are more specific and therapeutically oriented.

The questions used in this exercise include two different types: (a) the "fun joining" or the "get to know you" questions, such as "Who likes to walk in puddles on rainy days?" and (b) the therapeutic questions. The first kind of questions can be ad-libbed and are asked mainly by facilitators, though we often invite children to ask these or any other kinds of questions they have. When the game is well under way, we begin asking therapeutic questions, using the sequence shown below.

The first time a group does this exercise, use these therapeutic questions. (Remember to begin with fun joining questions.) The following 10 questions work well for a new group:

- Did you feel scared about coming to group?
- Are you still feeling scared?
- Are you still feeling nervous?
- Has anyone been touched in a way that made them feel confused, uncomfortable, or yucky?
- Were you touched by someone you knew?
- Did you think it was your fault?
- Do you think the person who touched you should not have?
- Do you want to help everyone feel safe in this group?
- Do you want to have fun in this group?
- Are you ready to go home now?!

For the second session of group in which this exercise is used, ask these questions after some initial "get to know you" questions:

- Was anyone here touched by their brother/uncle/stepdad/grandfather/father/neighbor?
- Did you tell your mother/friend/teacher/etc.?
- Were you believed?
- Did anyone here have to talk to law enforcement?
- Did anyone have to go to the doctor because of the touch?
- Do you or did you go to court?
- Does anyone worry about their body?
- Does anyone think people know about the abuse by looking at you?
- Does anyone have bad dreams about the stuff that happened?
- Do you feel safe in your room at night?
- Do you think a family member/friend is mad at you for telling?
- Did you think you were the only one who was touched?
- Were you told you would be hurt or thought something awful would happen to you if you told?
- Did you think, or were you told, that someone else would get hurt if you told about the touch?
- Are you glad you told about the abuse?

- Do you think it was [start here with the facilitators' names, then the least shy person in group, until everyone's names have been used] fault they were abused?

THERAPY GROUP ONLY: Later on, this game can be used to teach children the BASK (Behavior, Affect, Sensation, Knowledge) model when the focus is on internal boundaries and the expression of thoughts, feelings, and actions. Some items for yes/no/maybe responses would then include the following:

1. When I was touched, I thought I was bad.
2. When I was touched, I thought Mom would get mad.
3. When I was touched, I thought, "I wish this would stop!"
4. When I was touched, I thought I would get in trouble.
5. When I was touched, I thought, "This is fun."
6. When I was touched, I felt frightened.
7. When I was touched, I felt angry.
8. When I was touched, I felt alone.
9. When I was touched, I felt confused.
10. When I was touched, I felt embarrassed.
11. When I think about the abuse, I feel shivers in my body.
12. When I think about the abuse, I feel like someone's still touching me.
13. When I think about the abuse, I feel pain.
14. When I think about the abuse, I feel excited.
15. When I was touched, I pretended I was asleep.
16. When I was touched, I pretended to fly away.
17. When I was touched, I touched back.
18. When I was touched, I closed my eyes and waited for it to stop.
19. When I was touched, I froze and couldn't move.
20. When I was touched, I kicked and hit.
21. When I was touched, I did what I was told to.
22. When I was touched, I said no.

HINTS

Be sure to word questions in this exercise in such a way that they can be answered with *yes*, *no*, or *maybe*, on the continuum. After the children respond to a question it is useful to ask other variations of the initial query. For example, if you ask, "Who was sexually abused by your dad?" then add "stepdad?" or "mom/stepmom?" or "brother/stepbrother?" there may be a few children who answer no to all the questions being asked about the offender. Therefore it is important to ask specifically, "Who was the person who touched you?" (As the facilitator, you should already know the answer to this question for each group member. If anyone comes up with a different person, note it for the individual therapist.) When a child is hesitant to answer, give him room and wait until he is ready to talk later.

Often, more information is volunteered without any prompting. Pay particular attention to these cues as they often reveal details of the abuse that may not have been initially reported. It is especially important to take careful notes when there are court cases pending.

Children may not have the vocabulary to describe their feelings. However, when feelings are named through questions such as "Who felt angry, or sad?" group members can more easily identify and recognize emotions. Children can also better understand feelings when they are allowed to express their personal experiences of feelings. In one group a little girl asked, "Who had a hurt heart?" This gave her permission to share her knowledge of sadness, which in turn encouraged others to talk about their feelings.

While you are asking questions, be sure to keep track of the answers that kids have in common with each other. Note the similarities for the children; for example, "Wow, everyone here was touched by a male" or "Everyone felt confused." Children will then begin to notice the things they share with others, which will help to build bonds and a sense of belonging to the group.

One question we always ask is, "Who has a friend?" In one group, we had a child who responded with a no to this question. The other group members spontaneously responded by offering their friendship, with each child saying, "You can be my friend." As the group progressed, we often checked in with this little girl who hadn't felt that she had any friends, to remind her she had made friends with all of us. After 10 weeks of group, she was confidently boasting to her family about how many friends she now had.

If you do allow the children to come up with some of their own questions, limit them! You may decide that each child can ask one question only, or that each question must be about the touch. Without limits, this exercise will turn into the only one you do that session.

This exercise is a real hit in groups. It has repeatedly been the favorite of many children. Often when we have a little extra time at the end of a group, someone will request that we play the "Yes/No/Maybe Game."

Grotsky, Camerer, and Damiano, *Group Work With Sexually Abused Children*. Copyright 2000, Sage Publications, Inc.

Ball Toss

GOAL

To build self-esteem

AGES

3 through 18

TIME

10-15 minutes

PURPOSE

This activity promotes social interactive skills among group members while increasing their capacity to value themselves and others. It also assists children in learning the names of others in group.

DO THIS EXERCISE TO

- Increase the children's capacity to value self and others.
- Gather information related to the children's feelings and beliefs about themselves and others.
- Help group members get to know each other.

DO NOT USE THIS EXERCISE WHEN

There is no reason not to do this exercise.

WHAT YOU NEED

- A soft ball or small stuffed animal

INSTRUCTIONS

Have the group form a circle, either standing or sitting. Explain that one person will start by tossing the ball (or stuffed animal) to someone else in the circle while saying something he likes about that person. The person who receives the ball will then gently throw it to another person and compliment her. The ball can be tossed to anyone—it doesn't have to go in a circle or in any specific direction. Play continues until everyone in the group has received at least three or four compliments.

This exercise is very versatile and can be used as a fun way to elicit a variety of information. There are many kinds of statements you can have the children make as they toss and catch the ball. Some examples:

- Something about myself that I am proud of is . . .
- The best part of being in this group is . . .
- I feel most scared when . . .
- I'd like to be friends with you because . . .
- I am a good friend when I . . .

HINTS

As the facilitator you'll need to fill in the gaps during this exercise. There may be one or more group members who are not so popular. You can help them feel included by directing your compliments toward them and by asking other group members to choose someone they have not chosen before for each toss.

If you have concerns about someone being left out by others, prior to starting you can add more structure. For example, in some groups we have asked each person to say something he likes about each individual in the group.

Group members will often need help to recognize the difference between behaviors and appearances. Because sexually abused children are often quite or overly focused on their appearance, we suggest that compliments be made about behaviors only. We have found it is necessary to exaggerate a bit to model this clearly for younger group members. For example, you might start by saying something like,

---

"Let's see, what do I like that Sara does in group? Oh, I know, I like how well Sara listens while other people are talking."

Young children will often copy the child who went before them. Therefore, with 3- to 6-year-olds, you may want to set a rule that each person must say something different from what the person who went before them said.

The younger the group, the faster paced the exercise needs to be, otherwise children will lose interest. You may want to tell them that the ball is a "hot potato," so they need to pass it fairly quickly.

You may also use this exercise as a name game. If it is being played this way, have the child with the ball say her name first, then the name of the child she is passing the ball or stuffed animal to.

Me, Through the Years
(Therapy Group Only)

GOAL

To build self-esteem

AGES

7 through 18

TIME

45-60 minutes (This can be done over two sessions: In the first session, draw the lifelines; in the second, share them.)

PURPOSE

This exercise helps to put the sexual abuse in perspective. Being sexually abused is not the only identity group members have. They also are students, children, artists, writers, and more. Like anybody, they have had both good and bad experiences in their lives. Rather than having the sexual abuse be their entire focus, this exercise helps build their self-esteem by encouraging them to remember some of the other experiences in their lives.

DO THIS EXERCISE TO

- Increase the children's capacity to separate the self from the abuse/abuser.
- Increase the children's capacity to desire, believe in, and hold hope for a positive future.

DO NOT USE THIS EXERCISE WHEN

- Any group member has suffered a great deal of misery and at present is probably not safe. It may reinforce to him that his life truly is horrible and may decrease his sense of hope for a positive future.
- Any group member is easily triggered and gets overwhelmed and out of control when this happens.

WHAT YOU NEED

- Pieces of newsprint from 3 to 5 feet long (the older the group, the longer the newsprint)
- Markers, pens, and/or crayons

INSTRUCTIONS

Part I: Instruct group members to draw timelines of their lives. These can be straight lines or lines with many twists and turns. Ask them to start their lifelines with the age of 0 and go through the ages they are now. Have them leave room at the end to include the future. Tell them to include the following on their timelines:

- *Positive memories in their lives:* These may be events they remember or that others have told them. They may include being born, special birthdays, starting school, learning to ride a bicycle, and the like.
- *Memories that are not happy:* These include the abuse. If the abuse happened more than once, they should include the number of times they remember and a little about what happened. These memories may also include deaths of loved ones, times they were hurt, and so on.
- *Anything else that stands out in their minds:* These memories may include different places they have lived or schools they have attended.

At the very ends of their timelines, have them draw their wishes for the future. What will their futures look like? Who will be there with them? What will they be doing?

Let group members know that they can use more paper if they need it. For each age on the timeline, beginning with 0, they need to include everything, good and bad memories, before moving on to age 1 and then age 2, and so on. They can write or draw pictures to explain their memories.

Part II: Display all the lifelines on the wall. One at a time, have each person share his lifeline. As each person shares, ask him to talk about each memory one at a time, telling about it and expanding on what is on the paper. Group members may ask clarifying questions.

Part III: As each person finishes sharing his timeline, have the rest of the members tell him about a wish or a hope they have for him for the future. Have him write these wishes and hopes down in the space for "future" on his timeline.

HINTS

Group members who want to avoid feelings regarding the abuse will rush through this exercise and try to do it very superficially. Slow them down and ask them about each year. Prompt them to come up with more examples, both positive and negative. Remind them that the abuse was then, and this is now. They are safe now. Remind them that once they learn how to process through the painful memories, those memories will no longer carry such a powerful emotional charge in their lives. They are just memories. Remembering will eventually help them to have more control over their feelings and over their lives.

If a child does not want to share his timeline with the entire group, then try to encourage him to share it one-on-one with a facilitator. If he will not agree to that, then tell him you will give the lifeline to his individual therapist and he can share it there.

During sharing, be aware of any children who are fidgety or withdrawing. Check in with them about how they are doing and determine if they are being triggered. Ask them what they need from the group to help them stay present. They may need to be held or to sit close to a person they feel safe with in the room.

This exercise may bring up previously undisclosed incidents of abuse. Therefore, it is helpful to ask permission of the group members to share the lifelines with their individual therapists. Those therapists will know if any further reporting needs to be done or if further therapeutic interventions are needed.

The other place group members get lost in this exercise is when considering the future. Some of them may assume they will not live to be adults. Help them to imagine what their lives could be like as adults. Will they want children? Is there any type of work or job they might like? Where might they want to live? Guide them in imagining realistic futures. Many may want to imagine themselves as unicorns or fairies. Ask

---

them what they like about those things and try to take those qualities and form them into something that could really be. For instance, a child may respond, "I like unicorns because they can fly, and they are kind, people are nice to them, and they are magical." You might respond with, "Well, you can't really grow up to be a unicorn, but you could learn to fly. Maybe you could be a pilot and fly a big airplane. I think that it is very magical how in a short time you could fly thousands of miles and make your passengers so happy. People are usually really nice to pilots and have a lot of respect for them. Would you be interested in something like that?"

Friendship Medals

GOAL

To build self-esteem

AGES

7 through 18

TIME

20-30 minutes

PURPOSE

This exercise helps group members learn to give and receive positive feedback. It also builds a sense of identity by showing them how others perceive them. This exercise also gives group members concrete reminders of their connections with other children who have experienced abuse, which in turn reduces their sense of isolation.

DO THIS EXERCISE TO

- Build a sense of identity and worth.
- Increase group members' ability to recognize and verbalize their own personal qualities.
- Increase group members' social skills.
- Decrease isolation among group members.

DO NOT USE THIS EXERCISE WHEN

- There is someone in the group who is disliked by all or most of the others in group and there is a likelihood others will have nothing positive to say about her.

WHAT YOU NEED

- Small strips of paper with a group member's name on each one
- Enough 8- to 12-inch brightly colored circles of paper for each member
- Paper doilies or ribbons to be used for borders on the circles
- Markers, glitter, and stickers
- Glue

INSTRUCTIONS

Part I: Have each group member choose a colored paper circle to make into a friendship medal for another group member. Have each person pick, with eyes closed, a slip of paper from the pile of slips with group members' names. (If someone draws her own name, have her return it to the pile and pick again.) Ask the group members not to tell whose names they have drawn. Each member then decorates her medal for the person whose name she drew, leaving room for others to add positive comments. (An element of surprise makes this exercise fun and exciting.)

Tell group members that they should decorate their medals in ways that express their appreciation for the persons who will receive them. Encourage them to personalize the medals by drawing or writing what they like about the persons as friends. For example, a child who has a nice smile might have a big smile drawn on his medal. Another child's medal might have written on it an expression that the receiver likes and uses in group. Other children might put nicknames on their medals as a way of expressing affection.

Part II: When everyone has finished making their medals, have them come together in a circle and take turns passing them out. Then ask each person to express to the recipient why she is a friend or what qualities she has that make her a friend.

Part IV: After each child has given her medal to the person it was made for, circulate the medals around the group so that each person can write a positive quality on everyone's medal.

HINTS

We treat these medals as awards for friendship. They are very important. Be sure group members understand the concept of awards, their significance, and the reasons they are given to others. Usually, from our enthusiasm and the fun of receiving the medals, group members do not need any reminders to be proud–they just are.

A variation on this exercise is to have group members decorate their own medals and to write down 10 things they like about themselves. We ask them first to write down as many things as they can come up with on their own and then ask other group members for further ideas.

Sharing Our Stories (Minimal Disclosure)

GOALS

To build self-esteem; to build feelings of safety and trust; to learn about the dynamics of abuse

AGES

5 through 18

TIME

15-30 minutes (depending on the size of the group)

PURPOSE

For people who have been sexually abused, the healing process begins when they learn that it is safe to talk about what happened with others they trust. Usually, as survivors talk more about the abuse with other survivors, they feel less shame, fear, and isolation. They recognize similarities they share and learn that they are liked, even with their "terrible secrets." This exercise helps build tremendous bonds among group members.

DO THIS EXERCISE TO

- Reduce levels of fear, shame, and isolation.
- Increase the children's capacity to be vulnerable and to interact authentically.

- Increase the children's ability to put experiences or events into proper perspective, without minimizing or maximizing them.
- Increase the children's ability to identify and express feelings.

DO NOT USE THIS EXERCISE WHEN

There is no reason not to do this exercise.

WHAT YOU NEED

- Big pillows to sit on, or chairs for each member (to provide a sense of personal space)

INSTRUCTIONS

Have everyone sit in a circle. Explain to the group that sharing their stories of abuse helps survivors to feel better and rids them of the "awful secrets" that they have kept inside. Also, children may realize that others have had similar experiences and that they are no longer alone.

Ask each person in the group the same questions, starting with the facilitators as models:

- What is your name and what was your age at the time of the abuse?
- Who was the abuser?
- Are you safe now?

Keep disclosure at this level. It provides boundaries and safety so that there is predictability about the limited amount of information to be disclosed. Although these questions may seem basic, they are difficult to answer, and for a child to answer them he must feel trust and safety. Some children may want to disclose more. We ask younger children to wait to disclose additional information with their individual therapists or privately with a group facilitator.

THERAPY GROUP ONLY: With children 8 years old or older, in the following week of group we go through this exercise again, using the same group of questions and adding other questions. Again the leaders answer the questions first, acting as models for group members to follow:

Grotsky, Camerer, and Damiano, *Group Work With Sexually Abused Children.* Copyright 2000, Sage Publications, Inc.

- What is your name and what was your age at the time of the abuse?
- Who was the abuser?
- Name one feeling you had at the time of the abuse.
- Name a thought you had at the time of the abuse.
- How did the abuse stop?
- How do you feel now?
- Do you ever see the person who touched you? If yes, how do you feel when you see that person?

The following week, in **therapy group** for children 8 to 18, ask the following additional questions:

- What is the worst part about the abuse to you?
- Do you think you are a different person than you would have been if you hadn't been abused? If yes, how are you different?

These questions are harder than they seem, even the second time around. Your positive encouragement really helps the group members to feel capable and confident.

HINTS

It is helpful to set a relaxed yet serious tone for sharing sexual abuse stories. What you decide to do will vary depending upon the makeup and size of the group. Here are some ideas to try. We have turned the storytelling into a ritual by lighting a candle as each person tells his story. The candle represents taking the dark secret that's inside and bringing it out into the light of day. In another group we gave each person a shell that represented her own beauty and strength. We told each group member that she was like a shell that had been tossed and turned in turbulent waters, then washed ashore and bathed in the sunlight, becoming stronger, brighter, and more beautiful than before.

Sometimes we give group members lumps of clay to work with to help them release their tension as they tell their stories. The transformation of the clay during a child's telling of his story consistently matches the relief the child feels after sharing his story with the group. We encourage group members to make positive comments about the changes they see in the clay. We ask the children who have told their stories to leave their clay visible to help other group members as they tell theirs.

Younger children may be frightened by other children's stories. We have found that children who have been molested by relatives are sometimes frightened to hear that other children were abused by friends, relatives, or strangers. Take the time to talk about these fears and explain what group members can do to protect themselves. Remind them that if someone attempts to make them do anything they do not want to do, they can tell someone they trust. Assure them also that most people do not behave in this way.

We have had some therapy groups where minimal disclosure has not been enough for the children. In some cases, the children wanted to disclose more and not allowing them to do so created the impression that the abuse was too shameful to talk about in detail. In those cases, we divided the intitial group into two smaller groups, and each child told more detailed accounts of the abuse to the smaller group. In doing so, we could determine which member was appropriate for which group. Those that were abused once, or were fondled as opposed to violently raped were put into separate disclosure groups.

At the end of storytelling, you may want to give each person the choice of asking for something she wants or needs from the group. This may be a hug, a cheer, or positive feedback from everyone in the group. Ending activities for the whole group are equally important.

London Bridge
(The Escape Version)

GOALS

To build self-protection skills and a healthy body image; to build self-esteem

AGES

4 through 8

TIME

5-10 minutes

PURPOSE

This exercise encourages children to work cooperatively and teaches them how to negotiate and make choices. As they learn to ask for help, their self-esteem is enhanced and they discover how much stronger they are working together than alone.

DO THIS EXERCISE TO

- Increase the children's ability to make conscious behavioral choices.
- Increase the children's ability to define and express personal safety needs.
- Increase the children's capacity to exert their will and desire appropriately and effectively.
- Increase the children's capacity to value self and others.

- Introduce the rights and responsibilities of having a body to protect and nurture.

DO NOT USE THIS EXERCISE WHEN

- Any child in the group is too afraid, or too uncomfortable, to have the level of physical contact that this exercise requires.

WHAT YOU NEED

No special materials needed

INSTRUCTIONS

Find out if the children in group know the game London Bridge. Explain to them that you will be playing a different version of London Bridge. Introduce the song first, to make certain everyone knows the words:

London Bridge is falling down,
Falling down, falling down.
London Bridge is falling down,
My fair lady.

Take the keys and lock her up,
Lock her up, lock her up.
Take the keys and lock her up,
My fair lady.

Usually, the two facilitators should start out by being the bridge. Later on, children sometimes want to try being the bridge with one of the facilitators.

Begin singing and have the children walk in a circle under the bridge until, on the words "My fair lady," the person under the bridge is captured.

While the second verse of the song is being sung, encourage the child who has been captured to get free if he doesn't want to be locked up. Have everyone else in the group try to help the captured one escape. The captured child can go under or over the bridge, or the others can just pull him free. The people forming the bridge should break their hold when the captured child tries to escape.

With a little encouragement, the children really get into singing and helping each other escape. They have a lot of fun with this one.

HINTS

Sometimes children like the feeling of being held gently by the bridge because it feels like safe and soothing touch. When a child is captured and she chooses to be held by the bridge, we gently rock her while singing.

After this exercise, be sure to spend a little time talking with the group about how it felt to be helped by others. Encourage them to ask for help when they need it and ask them who they can go to for help in their lives (away from group). One little girl in our 4- to 5-year-old group kept choosing another little girl in group when we asked her who was a safe person she could go to for help. After a few times it was clear that she felt very safe with her group friend, but that still didn't answer the question of who was safe at home. Finally we asked, "Before you were in group, who were the safe people in your life?" She came up with several family members, but still wanted her new friend on the list.

The Parent Within
(Therapy Group Only)

GOAL

To build self-esteem

AGES

9 through 18

TIME

60-90 minutes

PURPOSE

Learning about the parent within helps group members learn techniques for self-soothing and self-love. It lends perspective and understanding to the victim's inability to stop the abuse when it was happening. This exercise also helps reduce shame and increases the children's confidence and ability to empathize and support themselves and others.

DO THIS EXERCISE TO

- Reduce self-blame for the abuse.
- Reduce the negative effects of adults who responded nonsupportively to disclosures of abuse.
- Increase the children's capacity to desire, believe in, and hold hope for a positive future.

- Lessen the children's sense of isolation.
- Increase the children's capacity to value self and others.

DO NOT USE THIS EXERCISE WHEN

- Any group member lacks the maturity needed to be attentive enough to follow the stages of the exercise.

WHAT YOU NEED

- Pencils or pens
- Writing paper

INSTRUCTIONS

Part I: Divide the group into smaller groups of three. Assign the letter A, B, or C to each group member. A is the child, B is the parent, and C is the scribe.

Part II: The facilitators first demonstrate a role-play of an abbreviated version of a disclosure. In this role-play, the child tells the parent that he has been touched on his private parts. For the group members' role-plays, assign ages to those playing the child's role that are younger than their present ages. For example, have a 9-year-old role-play a child at age 7. If many children in the group were abused by relatives, use a family member as the abuser in your scenario. Have the parent respond exactly as she would if a 7-year-old child actually disclosed to her. Remind the children role-playing parents to be emotionally supportive rather than jumping to immediate solutions such as "I'll call the police right now." During the role-play, the scribe quickly writes down everything the parent says.

Following is an example of what a facilitator role-playing the parent hearing the disclosure might say:

Oh, honey, I am so glad you told me this. That was very brave of you. I love you and I'm so sorry this happened to you. I will do everything I can to protect you and keep you safe from him. Everything is going to be okay. You are going to be okay. Now that I know, I can get help for you. Others can make sure that he gets help so he doesn't do this to other children. I am so proud of you for telling me. Is there anything else that he said or did that is frightening you? Is there anything more you want to tell me now? I want you to know that I'll always be here for you so if you want to talk about this again, we can. You are so wonderful. I LOVE YOU!

Part III: Have the groups of three do similar role-plays of a child disclosing to an adult. Have each member spend at least 5 minutes being in each role.

Part IV: Guided imagery is a method that directly communicates to the subconscious the supportive messages of the "parents." Darken the room slightly and have everyone sit or lie in a comfortable position. Begin with a progressive relaxation routine: Have the children flex and then relax their feet, legs, pelvis, back, chest, shoulders, and so on. Tell them to take deep breaths and feel their bodies resting closer and closer to the chair or the floor. Help them remember themselves at 7 years old. Ask questions such as these:

- What did you look like at 7 years old?
- How did you feel at 7?
- What clothes did you wear?
- What adult did you trust the most?
- What made you feel happy when you were 7?

Tell group members to imagine themselves playing or doing something that makes them feel good all over. Remind them that they are safe and cannot be hurt. Then have them imagine walking up to the person they trust the most. Tell them to see and hear themselves telling this person that they have been touched.

While the children are still relaxed and quiet, have them imagine their trusted person comforting them while you read aloud all the papers from the scribes. When you are done, tell the children that they are safe and very brave. Reiterate that the abuse was not their fault. Remind them that they can protect themselves. Whenever they feel sad, lonely, guilty, angry, or the like, they can say their scripts to the little children inside themselves. They know just what to do to take care of themselves. They will never be alone again.

HINTS

The kids may balk at first about doing the imagery and start to giggle. Remind them that they need to give it a fair try and should be as quiet as possible. Their cooperation makes this a very powerful exercise.

During the role-plays, make sure that the children who are hearing the disclosures understand that they are playing adults, not themselves. After the role-plays are completed, you may wish to collect the scripts and type up copies to be given to each child at the next session.

Four examples of scripts from our groups follow:

That sounds pretty scary. Can you tell me what happened? Have you told anybody like your Mom? I'm glad you told me. It's important that we make you safe so it won't happen anymore. Well, I think that you and I can go talk to your Mom together and tell her. I know it is scary but it is brave of you to tell me so we can tell your Mom and make it stop. (Barbara, age 12)

Hey! I'm really glad you decided to talk to me about this. I know how radically scared, confused, and overall freaked you must feel. My dad did just about the same thing to me when I was about your age. Everyone you've ever trusted has turned their backs on you, and overall there isn't a lot of things I can tell you. Please, if not for yourself, for me, tell somebody who has the power to help you out, don't turn yourself inside out, don't be a massively violent person, don't hide what you feel, because once you start, you can't stop. I guess I've begun to drone, so I will sum this up, I can't make you help yourself, but, PLEASE don't turn away from what you feel, make him PAY! Don't let him kill you inside, don't feel bad. Believe in yourself, I do. (Sarah, age 15)

1. Have you told anyone else?
2. He's a pervert.
3. It's not your fault.
4. Get him help.
5. I'll help you.
6. Who cares what people think as long as your privacy is protected.
7. Tell someone you trust.
8. It's not your fault.
9. He's sick.
10. Don't blame you, blame him.
11. Put it out in the open. (Tricia, age 11)

Well, I'm really glad you came and talked to ME about this, 'cause something similar happened to me when I was your age. I want you to know that it was not your fault 'cause the only way this can happen is if the person who did this to you is SICK—I don't mean like a cold. I mean there is something wrong with them down where you keep their guts. You are probably really mad about this and I can relate to that, but don't let what happened and your feelings about it tear you up inside. 'Cause if you let it get to you it'll turn your heart black—not literally—but that is how you will feel. And when that happens to you, you let that happen and it'll take a lot of time and energy to make you feel right with the world again. (Jill, age 14)

chapter **8**

INTERNAL AND EXTERNAL BOUNDARIES EXERCISES

A child's capacity to organize and interpret reality effectively is strongly influenced by the development of a healthy boundary system. The boundaries we develop affect how we process and respond to information and experiences about ourselves, others, and the surrounding world. Like gatekeepers, boundaries allow us to select with discernment what can safely be shared between the inside and outside worlds. Until children learn to negotiate their own boundary systems, their parents act as their external regulators. Like guardians at the door, they monitor and protect children from physical and psychological harm.

Boundaries also delineate where one person ends and another begins. Boundaries act as thresholds that both separate us from and connect us to the world. Children's ability to conceptualize the difference between themselves and others is a fundamental predictor of their future success in relating to the world in realistic and effective ways.

People with poor boundaries perceive little or no separation between themselves and others. Like sponges, they soak up others' beliefs and emotions, unable to separate out their own values, thoughts, sensations, and feelings. Other people wear their boundaries like armor, to shield themselves from the harmful words and intentions of others.

The exercises in this chapter are designed to help children learn their rights and responsibilities in relationship to others by teaching them to identify and express their own thoughts, feelings, and behaviors in safe and respectful ways. The exercises focus on showing that boundary systems play a fundamental role in helping children to understand that they

> exist,
> have bodies,
> live in relationship to other people and things,
> have both inner and outer experiences of reality, and
> have rights and responsibilities regarding all of the above.

Exercises concerning external boundaries are the first to be introduced in group. These exercises bring up issues of personal space, physical touch, and psychological distance and intimacy. Children who have been guided by emotionally healthy parents learn how to protect themselves in the world. They learn that their bodies are important and need the proper food and care to keep them healthy. They learn that they have the right to say no to touch that feels uncomfortable or invasive and that they have the right and responsibility to assert themselves in situations that feel disrespectful or dangerous to them. They know they are separate individuals with their own thoughts, feelings, and preferences.

We have observed that children who have suffered ongoing sexual abuse often display behaviors associated with boundary impairment. The invasive, insidious nature of sexual abuse can distort a child's developing perception of self. Abused children's ideas about who they are, who others are, and what the world around them is like are often corrupted. Abused children can experience the world as dangerous. Their trust, innocence, and sense of safety and connection are diminished. Their ability to trust in their own internal experience is confused by the bewildering and sometimes violent words and actions of their abusers. The projections and actions of their abusers divert these children from developing healthy relationships with themselves and others. Instead, abused children must direct their energy toward the development of adaptive behaviors in order to survive.

Children with external boundary issues have difficulty knowing where they begin and end as individuals. Consequently, these children experience confusion about physical distance, touch, personal rights, and responsibilities. They are often detached from their bodies, unaware of simple sensations such as cold or hot, pain or comfort. They sometimes feel they deserve to be hurt physically or used sexually, having adopted the distorted thinking of their abusers, believing these are expressions of love. Other sexually abused children display confused external boundaries by being extremely clingy and overly demonstrative or physically or sexually aggressive. One exercise that helps to heighten children's awareness of their external boundaries is "Boundary Line."

Once the children in group have demonstrated an ability to understand and practice appropriate external boundaries, they are introduced to the concepts of internal boundaries. Internal boundaries involve identifying and processing feelings, thoughts, beliefs, and sensations about reality in order to make appropriate behavioral choices and decisions. Children brought up in healthy environments learn how to identify, express, and manage themselves and their circumstances successfully. When they are scared, they can tell others who will help them feel safe. When they feel hurt by what someone says to them, they can respond rather than react. When they lash out in anger, they are allowed to express it, but are taught how to do so without harming themselves or others. These children have a sense that they are valued, understood, and heard. With guidance and practice they learn how to identify and express their own needs while respecting the needs of others.

Children who have been sexually abused often have a difficult time knowing and expressing directly what they need or want in any given situation. They have often been told that their feelings are invalid. To cope, they minimize, deny, avoid, act out, project, or dissociate. Unexpressed emotions in children also surface as somatic symptoms, such as stomachaches, headaches, panic attacks, and bed-wetting. When they have expressed anger about spending time with their abusers, they have sometimes been admonished, misunderstood, threatened, or punished, which creates overwhelming feelings of shame and self-doubt.

Some sexually abused children learned to *disassociate*. Disassociation is a way to numb and separate from emotions. This is a survival technique used by some children enduring abuse. The feelings of fear, pain, panic, and anger are too overwhelming to experience, so these children "numb out." They escape from the unmanageable reality of abuse by retreating into the world of imagination. Some children imagine themselves crawling into the wall, flying out the window, or floating above their bodies. The end result is a separation of body and mind and a learned technique of cutting themselves off from any feelings. Often these children "daydream" in school or are yelled at for not paying attention.

Abused children can be so detached from their inner lives that they are unaware of their own thoughts or feelings. Because they are so removed from themselves, and have been taught to fear retaliation if they are direct about their needs, their attempts to meet their needs are often manipulative, indirect, and unsuccessful. They can be passive or aggressive depending on their experiences and coping styles.

To avoid revictimization, abused children need to separate *from the abuse,* not from themselves. They need to learn to distinguish between what happened to them, who they truly are, and how the abuse affected their beliefs about who they are. This enables them to take the information that their feelings provide and protect themselves. For instance, if a child is not allowed to feel fear, he will not know when to fight or flee from a dangerous situation. This is why it is critical for abused children to understand their feelings and to rely on them.

In our group work with children, we teach internal boundaries by interweaving versions of Bennett Brauns's (1993) BASK model into the exercises. The model consists of four parts:

- *Behavior:* What am I doing?/How am I acting?
- *Affect:* How am I feeling emotionally?

- *Sensation:* What am I feeling in my body?/Where am I feeling it?
- *Knowledge:* What do I know/believe about myself and my situation?

Children learn that their thoughts and feelings create an internal interpretation of reality that affects behavior. Our use of the BASK model is more fully explained in the exercise "My Own BASK Book." Other exercises that are useful to help children with internal boundaries include "Life Vest," "Internal/External Self," and "Boundary Line."

We teach the BASK model by first teaching children to identify their feelings. Once they begin to be able to do this, we teach them to associate their feelings with their thoughts and also with any bodily sensations they may have. Finally, we teach them that by being aware of their feelings, and the thoughts that go with those feelings, they can give themselves choices about how they want to act or react in any given situation.

Boundary Line

GOAL

To learn about internal boundaries

AGES

4 through 18

TIME

15-20 minutes

PURPOSE

This common self-defense exercise, which has been passed down through the years, teaches group members to pay attention to their inner feelings and their intuition. As a result they are able to make educated choices based upon their own inner messages.

DO THIS EXERCISE TO

- Help facilitators assess group members' senses of personal safety with each other.
- Introduce the concept of the rights and responsibilities of having a body to protect and nurture.
- Increase the children's ability to make conscious behavioral choices.
- Increase the children's ability to define and express personal safety needs.

DO NOT USE THIS EXERCISE WHEN

There is no reason not to do this exercise.

WHAT YOU NEED

No special materials needed

INSTRUCTIONS

Part I: Begin by asking the group members to imagine that they do not know any of the other people in the room. Have them divide into two equal lines and have the lines stand on opposite sides of the room, facing each other. Each person in one line should be standing across from a person in the other line. Ask each person to stand across from someone she does not know well.

The cofacilitators then demonstrate the exercise to the group members by taking the following steps:

1. Face each other with about a 10-foot space between you.
2. One facilitator stays still while the other slowly walks toward her.
3. The facilitator who is standing still tells the other facilitator to stop walking toward her when she notices herself beginning to feel uncomfortable.
4. The facilitator who is standing still holds out her arm to gauge how much space she needs in order to feel safe. (For example, she may need one arm's length from most people, but maybe she needs the length of two arms in order to feel safe.)

Part II: Designate the two lines as line *A* and line *B*. Have those in line *A* (the *A*s) move toward those in line *B* (the *B*s) while those in line B remain stationary. Each *A* is to move toward the *B* across from him until *B* senses that being any closer would be too close and uncomfortable. B then says, "Stop!" Each individual decides when to stop *A* based upon his own feelings.

Part III: Take a few minutes to discuss the experience the group members just had. Select someone to start and find out how he decided when his partner was close enough to him to tell him to stop. After a person from line *B* responds, ask that person's partner from line *A* to share his experience. The children will often make statements such as "He couldn't look at me anymore," or "He started to smile." Ask, "Did anyone from line *A* want his partner to say stop sooner than he did?" If anyone answers yes, ask, "What did you do to let the person know you wanted him to say 'stop?'"

Part IV: Mix up the order of persons in both lines so that no one is with the same partner as before, but all are still in the same lines. Now have the *B*s follow the instructions you previously gave to the *A*s.

Part V: Repeat this exercise but *A* should stop when he believes that *B* really wants him to stop. This means that *B* must use a very serious and strong voice when saying "Stop!" and he must not smile.

HINTS

Try using different scenarios with the boundary line exercise to help participants be sensitive to their personal boundaries in a variety of situations. We use scenarios involving (a) a stranger, (b) an acquaintance, (c) someone you are angry with, (d) a good friend, (e) your mom or dad, and (f) a person who is drunk.

This exercise works best when each person takes it seriously and makes it real. If a child is having difficulty saying "Stop!" convincingly, have him say "No!" or "Go away!" If these don't work, have him imagine that he is a fierce animal, such as a lion, a tiger, or a gorilla. Then have him try saying "Stop!" while imagining the fierce animal inside of himself.

Many kids have a difficult time being assertive when saying "Stop!" One of the facilitators should do this exercise with any child who needs help being assertive. Have him stand while you walk toward him, and keep walking toward him if he doesn't say "Stop!" or if he says it so quietly you can hardly hear it. Repeat the steps until he blasts you away with "Stop!" Videotaping this exercise and playing the tapes back for the children can help them see how they look and sound to others. Many are able to react in a stronger manner after viewing themselves on tape.

Children really can be assertive and can trust their bodies if you give them the chance to practice and learn. Unfortunately, assertiveness is something that is not taught to a lot of children, so be patient and keep trying.

Internal/External Self
(Therapy Group Only)

GOALS

To learn about internal boundaries; to build self-esteem and feelings of safety and trust

AGES

8 through 18

TIME

30 minutes (This exercise can be done over two sessions: 10 minutes the first week and 20 minutes the second.)

PURPOSE

This exercise helps members understand that they have feelings and thoughts inside of them that they may or may not show to others. When a person has incongruent internal and external selves, often her personal needs are not met, and many of her actions may be misinterpreted. For example, a person who feels shy and uncomfortable in social situations but does not communicate this may be considered snobby and arrogant by others because she hardly ever talks to them. Understanding this can help children to realize that they have some power to create their own reality. The more they can feel confident in themselves and show their vulnerable sides to others, the better they will be understood and the more likely they will be treated in a manner congruent with their needs.

DO THIS EXERCISE TO

- Introduce the concept that thoughts and feelings create an internal interpretation of reality that affects behavior.
- Teach that when thoughts and feelings are not expressed, others will often misinterpret who you are based on your behavior.
- Increase the children's capacity to exert their will and desire effectively and appropriately by understanding the self and expressing thoughts and feelings.
- Increase the children's capacity to be vulnerable and to interact authentically.

DO NOT USE THIS EXERCISE WHEN

There is no reason not to do this exercise.

WHAT YOU NEED

- "Inside Thoughts and Feelings" and "Outside Thoughts and Feelings" worksheets
- Pens, pencils, or fine-tipped markers

INSTRUCTIONS

Part I: Pass out the "Inside Thoughts and Feelings" worksheet to all group members. Instruct them to write down, within the drawing of the body on the worksheet, how they view themselves on the inside. Ask the following questions to help guide them:

- What thoughts go through your head about yourself?
- Are these thoughts sometimes conflicting, such as "I'm a good friend" and "I'm a mean friend"? Write all conflicting thoughts down.
- Do you have any thoughts about the abuse such as "I could have stopped it" or "I liked the way the touch felt"? Write those thoughts down also.
- Do you have thoughts about what others think about you—thoughts such as "No one likes me" or "They think I'm smart but I don't think I am"?

- What feelings do you have about yourself? "I feel happy," "I feel like crying a lot," "I feel like hurting others"? Write all your feelings down.
- Do you have feelings about the abuse? Write those down too.

Pass out additional worksheets if members need more space to write down all of their thoughts and feelings.

Part II: Pass out the "Outside Thoughts and Feelings" worksheets. Ask the group members to write on the worksheets, around the figure of the body in the middle, their thoughts and feelings about how they think others see them. To help them get started, ask:

- When someone first meets you, what do you think they would say about you? "She is nice," "She is shy," "She seems friendly"?
- As they get to know you better, what would they say about you?
- How would they describe you as a friend?
- How would they describe how they think you feel on the inside?
- How do you think their view of you would change if they knew all about your inside feelings and thoughts?

Part III: When everyone has completed both worksheets, come together again as a group and have members take turns sharing what they have written. Note the congruencies and incongruencies that you notice for each child. If a child says she is a good friend but her outside worksheet states that people do not like her or think she is mean, ask her how that happens. If she thinks she can be a good friend, why don't others know that? Follow up these questions with an assignment for each person to choose one thing she can do in the coming week that will better match her inside feelings or thoughts to what she shows others on the outside.

HINTS

This exercise can give you a quick glimpse into how group members view the world and can help you to assess whether individual children's views of themselves are based on any reality. You will need to share much of what you learn from this exercise with group members' individual therapists, so they can focus more in depth on any distorted cognitions the children may have.

It is a good idea to separate group members somewhat during this exercise, so that they do not copy off of each others' papers.

If a child in the group shows that she has no concept of how she is viewed by others, or if her view is extremely distorted, then during the full group discussion ask other members to share their views of that child. Make sure that this is done sensitively and that you elicit a lot of positive comments.

**INSIDE THOUGHTS
AND FEELINGS**

OUTSIDE THOUGHTS AND FEELINGS

Feelings/Thoughts Mask

GOAL

To learn about internal boundaries

AGES

5 through 9

TIME

45-60 minutes

PURPOSE

This exercise allows facilitators to assess the adaptive responses or coping behaviors that group members use on a day-to-day basis, some of which may be harmful to them over time. The exercise allows group members to identify their feelings and thoughts and to recognize which ones are difficult for them to express; it then gives them permission to express them.

DO THIS EXERCISE TO

- Help group members identify their own adaptive responses to trauma.
- Help group members make more positive behavior choices.
- Increase group members' ability to understand that their thoughts and feelings affect their behavior and actions.
- Give group members something concrete to lessen feelings of isolation and give them visual images to remind them of what they are learning in group.

DO NOT USE THIS EXERCISE WHEN

- Any group member has been ritualistically abused or masks were used during the abuse.

WHAT YOU NEED

- Plain brown paper bags, one for each child, each large enough to fit over a child's head (or you may substitute, for each child, two large paper plates stapled together, with a Popsicle stick glued in between them)
- Markers, paints, and/or crayons
- Chalkboard and chalk or a large piece of paper
- Optional: glue, pipe cleaners, feathers, felt, fabric scraps

INSTRUCTIONS

Pass out one paper bag to each child and explain that they will be using the bags to make masks with two faces. Talk with the group members about the kinds of feelings and thoughts they are comfortable sharing with most people. Then ask them what feelings and thoughts are harder to share with others, and ask whether any of them have feelings or thoughts they haven't ever told to anyone. As part of this discussion, generate a list of the feelings they feel comfortable sharing and a list of those they don't. Do the same regarding thoughts. Write the lists up on the chalkboard or on a large piece of paper that everyone can see. Following are some examples of some very short lists:

Feelings Shared	Feelings Not Shared	Thoughts Shared	Thoughts Not Shared
Happy	Mad	I like you.	I'm ugly.
Sad	Hate	Nothing bothers me.	I'm stupid.
Funny	Embarrassed	You're mean.	No one likes me.
Goofy	Scared	I'm cool.	I'm bad.
Lonely	I want to hurt myself.		

Encourage the children to take their time and do their best at making their own two-sided masks. On one side, each child should depict the side of himself (the feelings and thoughts) that he shows to other people; the other side should represent the side of himself (the feelings and thoughts) that he keeps to himself and doesn't usually share with anyone.

Discussion: Once the masks are completed, take time for all group members to show and talk about both sides of their masks. Ask them to talk about why they made their masks the ways they did. Have other group members ask questions and point out similarities and differences between the masks. Also, talk about why no one wants to share all his feelings with everyone. Ask the children how they determine who is a safe person to share feelings with. Have them name the people they trust and can go to when they need to share their feelings with someone. Encourage each child to share his mask with one of these people during the next week and to share one feeling or thought he has not shared before.

HINTS

We have found the first part of this exercise to be the key in making it a success. Children need to identify their feelings before they do this exercise so that they can determine what feelings are okay to share with others. It is very useful to talk with group members about what they can do when they feel sad, or mad, or when they have any other feelings. When children do not know what to do with their feelings about the sexual abuse, or when they do not have someone to share their feelings with, it is helpful for them to hear other kids' suggestions. We also encourage each child to choose one person he would be willing to go to with his feelings.

In one of our groups, we worked with a girl who had really suppressed her anger. Making her mask helped her to recognize and begin expressing this anger once again. Having access to her anger allowed her to feel more powerful and less victimized.

Life Vest

GOAL

To learn about internal boundaries

AGES

6 through 18

TIME

30-45 minutes

PURPOSE

This exercise is a wonderful tool for teaching children how to choose what they will allow into their hearts. Each individual has the right to decide how she will take in and respond to others' comments about her and actions toward her. Group members learn to use their hearts (feelings), heads (thoughts), and hands (actions) to respond to others. This is all done with a powerful, imaginative, protective vest that they can take with them anywhere.

DO THIS EXERCISE TO

- Increase the children's ability to define and express personal safety needs.
- Teach the children how to distinguish between constructive comments from others and nonconstructive comments.
- Increase the children's ability to make conscious behavioral choices.
- Increase the children's ability to identify, comprehend, manage, and express thoughts and feelings appropriately.

DO NOT USE THIS EXERCISE WHEN

- There is not enough time for the children to process the feelings it raises.
- You do not have two facilitators.

WHAT YOU NEED

Imagination!

INSTRUCTIONS

Part I: Have group members sit in a circle. Tell them that each of them is going to put on the most beautiful, magical, wonderful vest there is. Take a moment for all the children to close their eyes and imagine what their vests look like. Ask questions such as the following:

- What color is your vest?
- Are there any designs or pictures on it?
- It is the most comfortable vest in the world. What is it made of?

Tell group members that their vests are also very strong, and that nothing can penetrate or push through them. But notice, there is something extra special on each vest. Why, it is a little zipped pocket right over the heart! Does everyone see it? Put your hand on that pocket. Yes, there it is!

Instruct the children to hold their vests out in front of them and admire them, and then have them put their vests on very carefully. Once they are on, make sure they are buttoned or zipped closed. Also, instruct everyone to check the pockets over their hearts and make sure those are zipped closed too. Now have everyone open their eyes.

Part II: Explain that you are going to do some role-plays with the vests on. These vests will protect everybody and help them decide if they want to take in what others say to them. Any comment a child does not want to take in will just bounce right off the vest and back to the person who made the comment. The facilitators then demonstrate how the life vest works:

First facilitator: You look funny in blue shoes with yellow polka dots.

Second facilitator: Hmmm . . . How does my heart feel? It hurts. It doesn't like that comment. . . . What does my head think? My head thinks, Is what she is saying true for me? No, I don't think I look funny in these shoes, I like them. . . . So, what will my hands do? They want to push this comment away. So I am going to keep the pocket zipped and let the comment bounce right back to the person who made it. And I'm going to say, "Well, maybe you think they look funny but I don't. . . . I like them!"

The second facilitator continues by explaining the process she just went through:

So my heart, which is my feelings, was hurt. With my head, or thought, I realized that I like these shoes. With my hands, or my actions, I had a choice about what I wanted to say or do about this. I could have gotten all sad and let the comment get inside me and feel terrible. Or I could have thought that maybe she is right and then given up my shoes. But in this case I realized that this is just her opinion. I have a different opinion. I like these shoes! Once I realized that, I knew I did not have to let her comments into my pocket. I didn't have to think like her. I also did not have to be mean to her. I could nicely, but firmly, tell her how I felt.

Now the two facilitators switch roles. One says something mean to the other, such as "You're mean." This time, while the second facilitator goes through the same process of heart, head, and hands, she should realize that there is some truth to this statement. She feels hurt and attacked at first, but then she thinks about the statement and realizes that there have been times when she has been mean. So what does she decide to do? She decides to say, "Gee, I guess I have done some mean things to you. I'm sorry, I would like to be your friend." She should mention that she has taken some of the comment into her pocket and then used it to help her be nicer.

Part III: Remind the children that they are wearing their vests. Now it is their turn. Start with a facilitator making a positive comment to each child, such as "You are really nice" or "I love how helpful you are in laying out the pillows when we come into the room." Go through the process with each child by asking these questions:

- How does it feel in your heart when I say this to you? (Happy? Good? Scary?)
- What do you think in your head? ("It's true" or "I'm not really very nice.")
- Now, how do your hands want to respond? (They want to hide, or they want to say thank you.)
- Okay, now, how would you respond back to me?

Grotsky, Camerer, and Damiano, *Group Work With Sexually Abused Children.* Copyright 2000, Sage Publications, Inc.

- Finally, is this a comment you want to open your pocket up for and let into your heart?

Part IV: Now have a facilitator make a negative comment to each child, but make sure that all comments are farfetched and clearly have nothing to do with the children they're directed toward; for example, "When you hiked to the top of Mount Everest you looked weird!" Make a different comment to each child and see how each responds. For every comment, go through the heart, head, and hand process with the child. Then ask the child to decide if she wants to let the comment into her pocket or have it bounce back to the person who said it.

Part V: As a homework assignment, tell the children to wear their vests all week and to practice using them. The following week, at check-in, have each give examples of how she used her vest and explain what she felt, thought, and did.

THERAPY GROUP ONLY: If there is time left in the session, before assigning homework, do the exercise again, this time making a mild negative statement to each child such as she might hear at school (e.g., "You act too silly" or "You eat too much sugar") Let the children practice with these kinds of comments. Pay close attention to whether any statements are hitting too close too home, causing withdrawal or acting out. If this happens, process with that child exactly how she is feeling and how she can use her vest to protect herself.

HINTS

The children love this exercise, but younger ones can be extremely sensitive and may take even the slightest negative statements to heart. When we were doing this in a group recently, 6-year-old Amy looked crestfallen when my comment to her was, "You are such a klutz, you always fall off your bike." She immediately went quiet. I responded, "Oh no, Amy. Do you have a bike and you've been falling off of it?" She nodded affirmatively. We immediately used that to say, "Use your vest. How do you feel in your heart?" and so on. She went through the process and then I said, "See, Amy? I had no idea you even had a bike. I totally made up that comment to sound jerky. Now you could have left here feeling miserable, but because of your vest you were able to realize, 'Hey, I'm not a klutz. I'm just learning how to ride my bike and everyone falls off their bike when they are first learning.'" She, more than anyone in the group, understood how life vests work after that. She started becoming much more assertive in group following this exercise.

Grotsky, Camerer, and Damiano, *Group Work With Sexually Abused Children.* Copyright 2000, Sage Publications, Inc.

Feeling Image

GOAL

To learn about internal boundaries

AGES

7 through 18

TIME

20-30 minutes

PURPOSE

This exercise helps group members to identify and develop visual images of the feelings they have related to the abuse. Understanding the magnitude of these feelings is a preliminary step to learning how to manage them.

DO THIS EXERCISE TO

- Help facilitators assess group members' adaptive coping styles.
- Reduce feelings of isolation and shame.
- Increase the children's ability to identify, comprehend, manage, and express thoughts and feelings appropriately.

DO NOT USE THIS EXERCISE WHEN

There is no reason not to do this exercise.

WHAT YOU NEED

- Writing paper
- Markers, crayons, or colored pencils

INSTRUCTIONS

Part I: Brainstorm a list of feelings that group members have about their sexual abuse. Add your own ideas to the list during the brainstorming session. (Make sure that feeling words such as *guilty, embarrassed, happy, noticed,* and *important* are included.)

Part II: When a thorough list has been generated, help the children get to a quiet place within themselves. Begin by having them lie down on their backs, far enough from one another that they are not touching. Take the group members through progressive relaxation to help them focus inward. Invite them to take three deep breaths, and tell them that their bodies are relaxing more and more on each exhale. Then instruct them to relax each body part, beginning with the feet, moving to each leg, the bottom and pelvic area, up the torso, to the neck and head, through the shoulders and then down the arms and through the hands—let the tension simply melt away.

Then guide them to a quiet, safe place. Once they have found this place, ask them to imagine a shape of any kind. Inform them that they will be communicating with this shape. Instruct them to ask the shape about the feelings they had when they were sexually abused, and how much of each feeling they had. For instance, you might say, "Ask the shape to show you how much anger you felt. Notice and remember how much space within the shape is filled up with anger." In the same manner, go through each of the feelings brought up during the brainstorming session. Ask the children to imagine different colors to represent their different feelings. Then allow time for them to discover any other feelings that the shape knows about, and to find out how much space these feelings fill.

Slowly end the guided imagery by counting backward from 10 to 1. As you are doing so, instruct group members to become more present and connected to their surroundings. Have them notice the carpet underneath them. Have them hear the sounds of others. Encourage them to remember the shapes they envisioned, their feelings, how big the feelings were, and what colors they were. As you finish counting down to 1, tell them to slowly open their eyes and return to their seats.

Part III: Pass out paper and markers, crayons, or colored pencils to everyone, and have each child draw a picture of his feeling image. When group members have had enough time for drawing, bring them together to share their experiences. Have group members and facilitators ask questions about the pictures and the feelings they represent, such as the following:

- What do you think is the biggest feeling you have?
- Do you want to lessen that feeling?
- What could help you to lessen it?
- Is there a feeling you wish you had more of?
- What can you do to help you feel that feeling more?

HINTS

We have used this exercise near the beginning of group sessions and then again near the end. This produces concrete images in which we and group members can see any changes in feelings that occurred during the weeks of group.

We have noticed that group members often draw triangles during this exercise. The first time we did it, five out of seven kids in the group drew triangles, and since then that pattern has held. Other shapes are also used, however. For instance, Emily drew a spiral-like shape and filled the center with guilt. She left a lot of blank space toward the outer part of the spiral before she began to fill the inner portion with her feelings. Generally, Emily had a hard time getting to her feelings; there were lots of blanks before she could get there. Her core feeling was clearly guilt. We then were able to help her view her guilt as a secondary gain she was using to prevent her from having to feel other feelings. Once she felt safe enough to let go of her guilt, she was able to identify and manage the other feelings underneath.

Kara drew an outline of a human figure as her shape, and filled in the different body parts as the feelings she experienced with the abuse. Arms represented a helpless feeling, the feet and legs showed a nervous feeling, the head was timid, and the breast level was shame and embarrassment. Where her mouth would have been was the feeling of pressure, and her lower abdomen was filled with many feelings she was as yet unable to name (Kara often complained of stomaches). It would not be unusual for a child drawing such a figure to have a litany of somatic complaints, especially stomachaches. Once Kara began to identify and express her feelings, her stomachaches lessened.

If the children cannot lie still for the guided imagery, have them sit quietly in their chairs, preferably with their eyes closed. Turn out the lights if it will dim the room, but not if it throws the room into complete darkness. Darkness is very frightening for many children who have been sexually abused during the night.

Encourage the children to draw the shapes they have visualized. Try to seat them in a way that prevents them from copying from one another's papers.

As a variation on this exercise, in a later session have group members revisualize their feeling shapes. While they are doing so, have them visualize their positive feelings taking up an increasing amount of space in their shapes. Have them imagine that their positive feelings have the power to diminish some of their other feelings, such as guilt, revenge, hate, and loneliness. What power do their positive feelings have? Do they use laser guns or darts? Maybe they smother the negative feelings with hugs or envelop them in love. During the guided imagery, state that the positive feelings have more power and strength then the negative ones. Note that it is okay to have negative feelings, but that by having a higher percentage of positive ones, group members will feel more centered, clear, and happy. Tell group members that the warmth of the positive feelings will surround them and lead them to a healing place.

Sentence Completion

GOALS

To learn about internal boundaries; to build self-esteem

AGES

6 through 18

TIME

5-20 minutes

PURPOSE

This exercise helps group members to identify and express their feelings regarding the abuse, such as guilt, shame, and isolation. It can be a quick opening exercise that everyone does together in one large group to express one feeling, or it can be done in pairs to allow the focus to be more in-depth, with an emphasis on a variety of emotions.

DO THIS EXERCISE TO

- Increase the children's capacity to identify, comprehend, manage, and express thoughts and feelings appropriately.
- Decrease levels of fear, shame, and isolation.
- Identify emotions regarding the abuse.
- Have a quick lead-in or opening exercise to address a specific emotion.

DO NOT USE THIS EXERCISE WHEN

- You want to do the expanded version and there are not enough facilitators to ensure the small groups are staying on task.
- You have a group with few talkers.

WHAT YOU NEED

- Chalkboard and chalk

INSTRUCTIONS

Short version: For older children, write on the chalkboard a sentence that you want everyone to complete verbally. Some possibilities include the following:

- I feel guilty about the sexual abuse when . . .
- The thing that makes me angriest about the abuse is . . .
- My greatest concern about having been sexually abused is . . .
- I am most scared about . . .
- I feel ashamed because . . .
- When I think about the abuse I wonder . . .
- If only I had . . .
- I feel good that I . . .
- I am proud of myself because . . .
- I feel it was my fault because . . .
- The way I feel about the person who touched me is . . .
- If anyone tries to abuse me again, I . . .

Have each group member take a turn completing the sentence on the board. Repeat this process for two or three sentences. For younger children who can't read, 6-8 years old, read aloud the sentences that you want them to complete.

Longer version: Have group members choose partners. When everyone is paired off, ask the partners in each pair to designate one person *A* and the other *B*. Write the sentence to be completed on the board, and tell the group that the *A*s have 2 minutes to say the sentence over and over again to the *B*s, each time ending the sentence in a different way. For example, *A* might say, "I feel ashamed because I didn't tell anyone. I feel ashamed because this happened to me. I feel ashamed because I liked some of the touch. I feel ashamed because I accepted money from him. I feel ashamed because I knew it was happening to my sister and I didn't do anything to stop it." Instruct the *B*s to listen quietly and nod but not to talk. When the 2 minutes are up, say, "Switch." This time, the *B*s complete the sentence while the *A*s listen.

Go through this process with up to three different sentence completions at a time. Then have the pairs come together again in the larger group and discuss what came up for them. Did anyone discover anything new about themselves? How does it feel to admit some of these feelings?

HINTS

This exercise is a great way to unblock feelings. The sentences focusing on shame and self-blame can bring forth previously undisclosed information. While doing this exercise in a group of ours, 7-year-old Susie disclosed that she had touched her sister. Also, 6-year-old Jason admitted that his baby-sitter made him touch his sister. When information like this is revealed, group members become more animated and appear much less traumatized. With the children's permission, we shared the information with their individual therapists, who helped them work through the feelings even more in their individual sessions.

The hardest part of this exercise is getting the group members to stay with it. They tend to want to supply only one ending to any given sentence. Monitor the pairs closely as they do the exercise and insist that they continue to try to complete the sentences. Tell them to just say the first things that come to their minds, even if those things do not seem to make sense. Some of the sentence completions may sound off-the-wall, but by continuing to try, the children may eventually reveal some real feelings.

Clay Faces

GOAL

To learn about internal boundaries

AGES

3 through 8

TIME

15-20 minutes

PURPOSE

This exercise helps group members to express their anger. It uses a physical and visual way to help group members identify and express their emotions appropriately.

DO THIS EXERCISE TO

- Increase the children's ability to identify, comprehend, manage, and express thoughts and feelings appropriately.
- Introduce the concept that thoughts and feelings create an internal interpretation of reality that affects behavior.
- Help group members articulate feelings they have toward their offenders.

DO NOT USE THIS EXERCISE WHEN

- Out-of-control members might hurt others by throwing clay.

- Clay may be a problem to remove from carpets or other parts of the room.
- Any group member's anger tends to escalate rather than is released when expressed physically.
- You do not feel confident in helping a child who may be heavily triggered. Be aware that sometimes children can be triggered by the feel of the clay, the movements of shaping the clay, or the actual forms they create, which sometimes remind them of penises or other objects connected to the abuse. Be attentive to trigger responses and help anyone who starts to withdraw or become too aggressive to verbalize her feelings.

WHAT YOU NEED

- Warm modeling clay that is pliable for little hands
- A large sheet of butcher paper or other protective covering for the floor
- Paper towels to wipe hands

INSTRUCTIONS

Part I: Set up a work space and seat the group members around that area. Hand each child a lump of clay. Begin by taking a piece of clay of your own and making a face with it. When you have made your clay face, ask the group members to tell you what emotion is depicted on the face. Then have them make their own clay faces showing emotions. If they need more structure, you can suggest emotions they might show, such as sad, happy, surprised, or angry.

Part II: Instruct group members to make three faces that show feelings they had when they were touched. Then have them make three faces showing the feelings they have now about the touch.

Part III: Talk with the group members about the feelings they have toward their offenders. Tell them they can make anything they want out of their clay that shows how they feel about the person who abused them. Explain that they may have a combination of feelings, like love, sadness, and anger, and that all of the feelings they have toward their offenders are fine.

Notice and make comments or ask questions about what they are making. Encourage them to show their feelings by modeling examples. Make a sad clay face and, using your voice, express the sadness you feel by saying, "I feel sad you touched me because my life has felt so different ever since you did." Then add tears to your clay face or tear it up to show what you want to do with the sadness. This gives the children permission to do the same. By going first, you make such actions less embarrassing for them.

Many group members will express anger, so be sure to talk with them about anger before they leave the day's session:

- Help them clarify who they are angry with and how to express their anger in appropriate ways.
- Ask group members for examples of how to be angry without hurting anyone, including themselves.
- Find out who they go to when they feel angry. Sometimes a child only feels comfortable enough to be consoled by a pet or a stuffed animal. Help each child identify one adult or friend she can talk to.

HINTS

We have had a lot of success with this exercise, especially with children who are developmentally unable to verbally express their feelings. It is especially important to give these children plenty of time with the clay and lots of encouragement for using their voices as part of their expression.

For younger children, it can be helpful if the facilitators roll out a bunch of "snakes" for the kids to use as mouths and round balls to use as eyes.

One warning (especially with boys): The children may want to throw the clay. This can get out of hand very quickly. Therefore, allow smashing, squashing, flattening, and pounding, but no throwing.

If any child is showing a lot of negative emotions when describing how she feels about the abuse now, talk to her about whether she feels stronger now. Help her try to find one positive aspect to the aftermath of the abuse. For example, maybe it has helped her to have a closer relationship with a caretaker. Be sure to end the day's session with a positive, uplifting exercise or game.

Target of the Offender

GOAL

To learn about internal boundaries

AGES

4 through 18

TIME

10-15 minutes

PURPOSE

This exercise helps to reduce excessive anger, express repressed anger, and guide misdirected anger. It is useful to reduce feelings of shame and internalization of feelings.

DO THIS EXERCISE TO

- Encourage group members to identify, manage, and express anger appropriately.

DO NOT USE THIS EXERCISE WHEN

- Any group members are in nonsupportive environments that could result in severe repercussions for expressing anger.
- There is not enough time to process the exercise fully in group.

- Any child in group feels no anger toward the offender and would feel a need to pretend anger to feel included by other members.

WHAT YOU NEED

- Paper
- Markers or crayons
- Clay or water balloons
- Large stuffed dolls or pillows

INSTRUCTIONS

Part I: Have group members use paper and markers or crayons to make any kinds of targets they want to represent their offenders. A target might be a picture that looks like the person who touched the child, or it might be silly or scary. Whatever each child wants to draw is fine, as long as it represents the offender.

When all group members have finished making their targets, set up the target range. Before any throwing or hitting of the targets begins, be sure that everyone understands where to stand so as not to get hurt by the other children's exuberance.

Encourage the children to use their voices to help them express their anger as they throw lumps of clay or water balloons at their targets. Let them know they can yell anything, except for swear words.

If you are using dolls or pillows to hold the targets, have group members take turns. One at a time, have each person start by pinning or taping her target picture onto a doll or pillow. Then she can say or do anything she wants to the offender target.

Part II: Following the target practice, ask group members the following questions:

- Do you feel different?
- Did it help you to get some of your anger out?
- Are you feeling less angry or more angry now?
- How do each of you express or show you are angry? (Answers to this question may provide you with new information about some of the group members and how they may or may not need help dealing with their anger.)
- What happens at home when you show your anger?

End the exercise by talking about healthy ways of expressing anger. Share with the children some ideas for ways they can express their anger that won't hurt themselves or others. Suggest some of the things that you do when you are angry.

Part III: For homework, ask group members to pick one idea to try when they get mad in the next week. Forewarn the members' parents about this homework and instruct them to encourage their children to express their anger in safe ways. They may want to allow their children to say that they are angry, or to ask for a time-out to calm down. Help the parents to understand that it is not safe for their children to express their anger through swearing or hitting. Be sure to follow up on this assignment at the next group session.

HINTS

Clear limits are important for everyone's safety, as well as for fairness, when you do this exercise. Some children will keep to the limits without any reminders, but others will test the limits. Give any child who breaks the rules one reminder and then remove her from the exercise if she cannot follow the directions in a safe manner. When the child says that she feels she can act appropriately, allow her back in.

If there is a nearby park, or even a fence in back of the building, this can serve as a good environment. Children really like using water balloons for this target exercise. They are proud when they hit their targets. Many times, group members have pointed out how they really got their offenders when their balloons blurred the colors, messed up the images, and tore the paper. A sense of satisfaction and empowerment really comes through. If using water balloons, we usually do this activity on a warm day, just in case anyone get splattered with water. We haven't had any mishaps because we heavily emphasize waiting until everyone is out of the way and ready with a new balloon before throwing begins.

A variation on this exercise is to use balloons filled with air as the targets. Have the group members draw the faces of their offenders on the balloons. They can then bat them around or pin or tape the balloons on a large board and throw darts at them. When the children are allowed to draw whatever faces they want, many choose to draw the looks their offenders had on their faces during the abuse.

When you are using a large soft doll or pillow to hold the targets, make sure that you have the children stand in a line on one side of the room. Then have them take turns, on the opposite side of the room, running up to the pillow and kicking, smashing, throwing, or hitting it. Be sure that whatever they do is done well away from those in line, so that other children do not get hurt.

We have found, through our error, that it is best to let the parents of group members know ahead of time when we will be doing anger work. This applies in both group and individual therapy. There have been a couple of times when children have gone home after one of these sessions with a lot of anger, and their parents were taken by surprise. Needless to say, we heard about it later. We modified the situation by giving parents several warnings.

Animal Boundaries

GOALS

To learn about internal and external boundaries; to learn to manage triggers

AGES

4 through 10

TIME

15-20 minutes

PURPOSE

This is a fun and nonthreatening technique to teach children that their thoughts, feelings, and sensations affect their behavior. When they understand this concept, children recognize they have more choice and control over their actions.

DO THIS EXERCISE TO

- Increase the children's ability to identify and express feelings appropriately.
- Increase the children's ability to identify sensations in the body and to begin understanding what the sensations mean.
- Teach how feelings and thoughts affect behavior.

DO NOT USE THIS EXERCISE WHEN

There is no reason not to do this exercise.

WHAT YOU NEED

A large, comfortable room

INSTRUCTIONS

Part I: Instruct group members to close their eyes and imagine being an animal. Ask the following questions, telling the children not to answer them aloud, but to picture the answers silently in their mind's eyes.

- How big is the animal?
- Is it generally a mean or friendly animal?
- What are some of the animal's strengths?
- What does its body feel like on the outside? Is it soft? Hard? Scaly?
- Does it have big ears or little ears?
- What do its face, eyes, and mouth look like?

Part II: Ask each child in turn to model with his body how his animal would react to the following situations. Act the situations out by having one child play a person and the other play the animal he has imagined. The child acting as a person should only pretend to touch the "animal." Ask the child acting as the animal to show how he would react if each of the following happened:

- Your fur was rubbed the wrong way?
- Someone stepped on your tail?
- Someone petted you nicely?
- You were scared? Lonely? Happy? Hungry? Angry? Excited? Ashamed? Goofy?

Make sure that you end the questioning on a positive feeling.

Part III: With the group as a whole, discuss the concept that how we feel on the inside affects how we act on the outside. Ask group members how they act in each of the following situations:

- They are super hungry and haven't gotten to eat yet. (Are they whiny, cranky, mean?)

Grotsky, Camerer, and Damiano, *Group Work With Sexually Abused Children*. Copyright 2000, Sage Publications, Inc.

- They are tired but don't really want to go to bed.
- They feel embarrassed about something that just happened. (An example might be that a friend just said, "You buttoned your shirt all wrong!")

Then discuss boundaries by explaining that we use our words and bodies to express our boundaries to others. Ask questions such as the following:

- How did [group member] Mary's animal tell the person she did not want to be petted? Did she hiss, or pull away, or try to scratch?
- How about when [group member] Tommy's tail was stepped on?
- How would you show your boundary if someone hugged you and you did not want to be hugged right then? What words would you use? What would you do with your body to show that you did not want to be hugged?

Now have everybody stand up and, all together, pretend that someone is hugging them when they don't want to be hugged. Have everybody act out at the same time what they would do.

HINTS

Children love this exercise, but you have to keep it moving and active. Do not spend too much time talking, or you will lose them. Follow this exercise with the "Boundary Line" or "Life Vest" exercise.

Remind the children that when they are acting out their animals, they need to keep their animals in control. Some may use the play to get too aggressive toward the persons who are "stepping on their tails." This is a concrete way to remind them that they are in control of their actions. If someone does get too rough after having been instructed not to, play the animal for that child and let him play the person. After role modeling how the animal can react in a safe fashion, have the child try being the animal again. If the animal is still too rough, let him know that this is not a game he can play because others could get hurt. He is welcome to watch and get ideas from others on how to respond in a less harmful way. After group, inform the child's individual therapist so that therapist and child can work together to address the child's aggression.

Familiar Feelings

GOALS

To learn about internal boundaries; to build self-esteem

AGES

9 through 18

TIME

5-10 minutes (or assign as homework)

PURPOSE

Many children do not know how to identify their feelings. Often they know only two feelings, "good" and "bad." This exercise gives children a vocabulary of feelings so that they can better express themselves.

DO THIS EXERCISE TO

- Increase group members' ability to identify, comprehend, manage, and express thoughts and feelings appropriately.

DO NOT USE THIS EXERCISE WHEN

- Members of the group are not able to read at a fourth-grade level or above.

WHAT YOU NEED

- "Feelings" checklists
- Pens or pencils

INSTRUCTIONS

Pass out copies of the "Feelings" checklist to all group members. Take a few minutes for each child to fill out her own checklist by putting check marks by all the feelings she has had today. With the whole group, discuss the feelings each person has had. Then ask some of the following questions:

- Did anyone express these feelings to others? If so, how?
- Was that an appropriate way?
- If not, what are some other ways to express those feelings more appropriately?

HINTS

This exercise is brief and works best when it is repeated three to four times over the length of the group session. It is also a great opening exercise, because it gets people talking about their lives.

You may want to pick one emotion that a group member has expressed and ask for further details. For example, if someone has marked that she has felt fearful, you could ask, "Can you tell us what you were fearful about?"

Copies of the checklist can also be sent home as homework. You can have the group members fill out the checklists on three different days and bring them back in the following week. This way, you can see if there are patterns to the feelings that individual children express.

Feelings

Keep track of how you are feeling by noting which of the following emotions you experience each day.

_____ Aggressive	_____ Frightened	_____ Premenstrual
_____ Agonized	_____ Frustrated	_____ Pressured
_____ Amused	_____ Gossipy	_____ Prudish
_____ Angry	_____ Greedy	_____ Puzzled
_____ Apathetic	_____ Grieving	_____ Regretful
_____ Apologetic	_____ Guilty	_____ Relieved
_____ Arrogant	_____ Happy	_____ Resentful
_____ Ashamed	_____ Helpful	_____ Sad
_____ Bashful	_____ Homesick	_____ Satisfied
_____ Blissful	_____ Hopeful	_____ Scheming
_____ Boastful	_____ Horrified	_____ Seductive
_____ Bored	_____ Hot	_____ Sheepish
_____ Cautious	_____ Hungover	_____ Shocked
_____ Cold	_____ Hurt	_____ Sick
_____ Competitive	_____ Hysterical	_____ Skeptical
_____ Concentrating	_____ Idiotic	_____ Smug
_____ Confident	_____ Impressed	_____ Sophisticated
_____ Confused	_____ Indifferent	_____ Sorry
_____ Conniving	_____ Infatuated	_____ Successful
_____ Contemptuous	_____ Innocent	_____ Sulky
_____ Contented	_____ Interested	_____ Surly
_____ Cranky	_____ Insecure	_____ Surprised
_____ Creative	_____ Insignificant	_____ Suspicious
_____ Curious	_____ Inspired	_____ Sympathetic
_____ Delighted	_____ Jealous	_____ Talkative
_____ Demure	_____ Kind	_____ Tempted
_____ Depressed	_____ Lazy	_____ Tender
_____ Determined	_____ Loaded	_____ Thoughtful
_____ Disappointed	_____ Lonely	_____ Threatened
_____ Disapproving	_____ Lovable	_____ Timid
_____ Disbelieving	_____ Love-struck	_____ Tired
_____ Disgusted	_____ Lustful	_____ Transcendent
_____ Distasteful	_____ Martyred	_____ Triumphant
_____ Domineering	_____ Meditative	_____ Turned on
_____ Eager	_____ Mellow	_____ Two-faced
_____ Eavesdropping	_____ Mischievous	_____ Undecided
_____ Ecstatic	_____ Miserable	_____ Vulnerable
_____ Efficient	_____ Nauseated	_____ Withdrawn
_____ Egotistical	_____ Negative	_____ Worried
_____ Embarrassed	_____ Nervous	
_____ Enraged	_____ Noble	
_____ Enthusiastic	_____ Nonchalant	
_____ Envious	_____ Nostalgic	
_____ Exasperated	_____ Obstinate	
_____ Exercised	_____ Optimistic	
_____ Exhausted	_____ Overworked	
_____ Expectant	_____ Pained	
_____ Fiendish	_____ Paranoid	
_____ Forgetful	_____ Passive	
_____ Frazzled	_____ Perplexed	

Talking to the
Offender Psychodrama
(Therapy Group Only)

GOALS

To learn about internal boundaries; to build self-esteem and self-protection skills

AGES

5 through 18

TIME

20-30 minutes minimum (An hour or more can be spent on this exercise when group members really get involved in it.)

PURPOSE

This exercise allows group members to voice unspoken thoughts and feelings about their offenders without fear of retribution. It also helps them to feel safe and shows them that they can think about their abusers without feeling afraid.

DO THIS EXERCISE TO

- Help group members appropriately direct repressed or displaced anger.
- Increase the children's capacity to separate the self from the abuser.
- Increase the children's capacity to place responsibility and accountability for the abuse on the appropriate persons.

- Increase the children's ability to identify, comprehend, manage, and express thoughts and feelings appropriately.
- Reduce feelings of guilt and self-blame.

DO NOT USE THIS EXERCISE WHEN

- Any group member has a strong tendency to dissociate.
- Trust is not well established in the group.
- There are too many group members who will disrupt the exercise by cracking jokes, making noises, or not taking others seriously.
- There is not enough time to complete the exercise.

WHAT YOU NEED

For younger children, use props such as the following:
- Tape recorder with blank tapes
- Dress-up clothes
- Full-length mirror
- Dolls, puppets
- Photographs or drawings of offenders
- Toy telephones

(Not all of these materials are necessary, but children enjoy having some choices.)

INSTRUCTIONS

Part I: Have group members sit in a circle, and ask them to imagine talking to their offenders in a safe and comfortable situation. Suggest some ways to make the situation safe and comfortable, including imagining that:

- The offender is in jail.
- There is a policeman watching.
- The offender is locked in a room where he can only hear you and cannot see you.

- You are invisible and magic, so you can get away if he tries anything.

When everyone has imagined a safe setting, give group members a choice of how they want to talk their offenders in the group. Tape recorders, dolls or puppets, and dress-up clothes are especially useful for younger children. Children of all ages can role-play talking to an empty chair, a doll offender, a facilitator playing the offender, a picture of the person who abused them, or an offender on the telephone.

Before starting the dramas, set some ground rules. Let the group members know that everyone will have a turn, and that no one is allowed to interrupt, unless they are asked to help. This structure helps everyone to be more attentive. Ask for a volunteer to begin talking to the offender in whatever way she chooses. Have each person begin by describing the setting. For example:

- Are you outside or inside?
- Are you alone or with others?
- Is the offender standing or sitting?
- What is his posture like?
- What is the look on his face?
- What does his voice sound like?
- How far away is the offender in relation to you?
- What helps you know you are safe while doing this exercise?

Ask the group member to express her feelings and to tell the offender what she wants from him, if anything. If she wishes, she can choose someone to play the offender. She can then instruct the person chosen on how to respond as the offender and can demonstrate how the offender stands or sits, how he sounds, his manner-isms, and the like. The group member should then describe what she would like from the offender—for example, the tone of voice he should use, if he should apologize, whether he should be angry or conciliatory, and so on.

There may not be enough time for each child to talk to her offender in one group session. If this is the situation, set aside time in the next session for the remainder of the group members to take their turns.

We give group members paper and crayons or markers to draw pictures of their offenders, then other pictures of their choice, while they wait for their turns.

HINTS

Although we recommend this exercise for children ages 5 and older, we have used it with 3- and 4-year-olds and had them dress up their offenders. During the role model presented by the facilitators, the offender apologized to his victim. One of the kids started clapping, and her face showed relief; everyone else then joined in the clapping. In another group, a girl told the offender what she really thought of him: "This guy is such a jerk."

This exercise offers material for some profound changes when used with teenagers. One teenager who was talking to her offender was getting caught in a power struggle until the offender began to soften. Then her defenses fell away and she sobbed.

Be aware that there may be times when you will have to stop the scenario and take a child aside to help further process feelings that come up during this exercise. Once, a teenager froze during this exercise and dissociated so severely that one of us spent 15 minutes softly talking to her to help her feel safe enough to return, while the other facilitator explained to the group about dissociation. When we were sure she was ready, the other group members took over her role-play so she could observe it from the outside rather than being so involved in it.

We have also used the technique of "doubling" when a group member has not felt strong enough to stand up for herself. The "double" stands beside the group member and states the feelings or thoughts that she thinks the member might want to say to the offender. The member then repeats aloud any statements the double makes that fit for her. If that is too frightening, she simply lets the double do all the talking for her.

Take note of children who have difficulty choosing situations in which they would feel safe talking to their offenders. When a child has fears, take him aside and encourage him to talk about these feelings. Help him discover what he can do to feel safer. If he is able to articulate his needs and feelings clearly, this could become a group discussion. On the other hand, he may need to explore these fears in individual therapy.

Notice, too, what situations children feel safe in and question them if those situations don't seem safe to you. For example, a child may imagine herself approaching the offender's home alone or carrying a knife with her. She needs to realize this is fine to do in a role-play, but in real life this could be a dangerous way to approach him. If she approaches him alone she may be harmed further, either verbally or physically.

We take time to brainstorm safe situations with the whole group, which teaches them to ask for help and to trust that others can assist them in solving problems.

My Own BASK Book
(Therapy Group Only)

GOALS

To understand the dynamics of sexual abuse; to learn about internal and external boundaries

AGES

6 through 18

TIME

60-80 minutes (This exercise may be done over two sessions.)

PURPOSE

This exercise helps children express their experiences with abuse at all levels. Using the BASK (behavior, affect, sensation, and knowledge) model, it helps group members understand their own reactions and begins the process of shifting the responsibility of the abuse to the offender.

DO THIS EXERCISE TO

- Increase the children's capacity to separate the self from the abuse/abuser.
- Introduce the concept that thoughts and feelings create an internal interpretation of reality that affects behavior.

DO NOT USE THIS EXERCISE WHEN

- There is not enough time to do it thoroughly.
- There are not enough facilitators to give some focused time to each group member.

WHAT YOU NEED

- Copies of "My Book" pages
- Markers, pens, and/or crayons

INSTRUCTIONS

Part I: Show the group members the different pages to "My Book" and pass the pages out one at a time. For example, give everybody the first page, "When I was touched, I thought in my head," and have them write on that page whatever thoughts they had back when they were being abused. Give a few examples:

- I'm bad.
- No one will like me.
- I hate him.
- He thinks I'm special.

Have each person work on her own page. As the children work, check on what each group member is doing and give assistance as needed. Some children may need help with ideas about what they thought. Others will need help with writing. Make sure that each child writes down many thoughts, not just one or two.

As the children complete the first page of the book, pass out the next page, and so on. Using the BASK model, the head is for thoughts or knowledge, the heart is for the affect or feelings, the stomach is for sensations or bodily feelings, and the outline of the person represents behavior or action. Finally, the last page is used to identify the beliefs the child has developed about herself, such as "I'm unlovable," "I'll never be safe," or "I'm bad" (these are core negative beliefs).

When the children have finished their books, give them paper they can draw on to make covers.

Part II: Have each person take a turn sharing her book. Make sure that everyone gives lots of praise! Encourage the children to share their books with their parents or other caregivers.

HINTS

Have group members work with some space between them, otherwise they tend to copy each other. If you have a group in which the members are hesitant to tell their own stories, you can do this same exercise with them by having them guess how Elizabeth was feeling instead (see the exercise "Elizabeth's Triggers," in Chapter 10).

Often we choose to add pages to the BASK book. The books the children just completed become their "Then" books, and we add the "Now" books, which include pages such as the following:

- Now that I have told I think . . .
- Now when I think about the abuse I feel . . .
- Now when I remember the touch, the places I feel it in my body are . . .
- If anyone tried to touch me again, I would . . .
- Now that I understand more about the abuse, I think that I am a _____ person. [Use many different adjectives.]
- The good things that have come out of all this are . . .

Give the children a lot of time to work on this exercise. When the books are finished, it is worthwhile to try to bind them or put them in really nice report folders. The children are very proud of their books. It is most effective to do this exercise toward the last two-thirds of group. This work is likely to be a major step in the children's recovery, and they will be able to look at their books time and time again.

THE WHEN I WAS TOUCHED BOOK BY:

WHEN I WAS TOUCHED, I THOUGHT IN MY HEAD

I FELT IN MY HEART...

THE SENSATIONS I FELT IN MY BODY WERE...

WHAT I DID WAS...

AND I DECIDED I WAS...

Lean on Me

GOAL

To learn about internal boundaries

AGES

9 through 18

TIME

10-20 minutes

PURPOSE

This exercise helps group members identify and define appropriate boundaries in friendships and in romantic relationships. It helps them recognize how "healthy" relationships include give-and-take by both parties involved. They learn how exhausting and limiting a heavily dependent relationship can be.

DO THIS EXERCISE TO

- Teach group members how to identify and practice healthy boundaries.
- Assess the boundaries that group participants currently have.
- Demonstrate a concrete way of understanding dynamics in past and present relationships.
- Increase the children's ability to make conscious behavioral choices.

DO NOT USE THIS EXERCISE WHEN

- Any group member is truly terrified of touch.
- Someone in the group is on crutches or in leg braces and could be physically hurt easily. (You can modify the exercise by doing it sitting down.)

WHAT YOU NEED

A clear, open space

INSTRUCTIONS

Part I: Have group members choose partners, then have each pair decide which member is *A* and which is *B*. Have the *A*s stand close behind the *B*s, facing their partners' backs. Ask the pairs to imagine that they are sweeties and then have the *A*s wrap their arms around the *B*s while the *B*s remain still. Ask the *B*s how this position feels, both physically and emotionally. Is there any discomfort or sense of uneasiness for anyone? Does anyone feel comfortable in this position? Ask the *A*s the same questions.

Part II: While the pairs are in the same position, instruct the *A*s to begin to lean on their partners. Instruct them to gradually lean more and more, until the *B*s are holding as much weight as they can. Then have them stop and return to the original position of standing behind their partners. Ask the *B*s:

- Was the leaning okay?
- Did they feel needed because their partners were leaning on them?
- Do they feel strong enough to support another person fully?
- What would it mean to support someone fully—physically, emotionally, and financially?
- Has anyone ever had this experience? What did it feel like?
- What would have happened to *A* if *B* had tried to move?

Now ask the *A*s:

- How did it feel to lean so heavily on someone else?
- Were you comfortable with it? Why or why not?

Grotsky, Camerer, and Damiano, *Group Work With Sexually Abused Children.* Copyright 2000, Sage Publications, Inc.

- Would you want to be in a position like this in a relationship?
- Have you ever been in this position before? If so, how was that for you?

Part III: Have the partners stand facing each other. Instruct the *B*s to reach out and take their partners' arms and pull them toward them. Ask:

- How did that feel for the *A*s?
- Did you resist? Why?
- How do the *B*s feel about the *A*s' responses to their pull?

Part IV: Gather the *A*s around you and privately instruct them to resist *B*s pull. Return to *A*s and *B*s facing each other and again have *B* pull *A*'s arm. Ask:

- What happens when *A* resists? Does *B* pull harder?
- What happens if *B* pulls harder?
- What does this pulling exercise feel like for you?

Part V: Have the partners stand back to back and gently lean on each other. Now ask:

- How is your partner affected when you move?
- What do you have to do to remain standing if your partner moves?
- [Directed to partners who moved first] How did it feel to move first?
- [To the other partner] How did it feel to have to move in response to your partner's move?

Part VI: Return to a circle as a whole group and discuss how these exercises are alike and different from relationships the group members have been in. Discuss what makes a relationship work. Is it really possible to have a healthy, happy relationship if one person is always leaning on the other for support but cannot give any back? How does it feel to always be giving all the support? How much can one person carry, and for how long?

HINTS

This can be a very powerful exercise. Be sure to set safety guidelines in the beginning so that no one gets hurt. The number one guideline is that when someone says "Stop," *you stop!*

Following the exercise, take time to discuss relationships. Our teens have been open to talking about their boyfriends and girlfriends. We often brainstorm lists of how they might know if the people they are attracted to can both give and take support.

We had one group in which several girls did not mind having someone hanging on them heavily. They kept saying that it helped them to feel loved and comfortable. It was not until we had them partner up again and told them to try to move and get things done while this dead weight was hanging on them that they began to understand how such dependency can affect them and their partners.

We asked them to imagine a couple of scenarios: (a) There is an imaginary ball and chain locked to their leg, or (b) they are so dependent on someone else that they can no longer make their own decisions regarding where to go, what to eat, or who their friends are. We then discussed the following questions:

- How does it feel to be in this situation?
- What would happen to you if your partner got tired of all that weight and found a way to unlock the ball and chain and walk away? How would you feel then?

We discussed with them how untreated survivors of sexual abuse tend to be either overly responsible or irresponsible. In relationship situations, past victims often will become consumed by the fantasy of the ultimate relationship and play out the role of either superwife or helpless victim. Neither is healthy. Those who act helpless often end up in battering relationships, and those who play the superwife, the woman who can do it all, often end up feeling resentful and unable to be truly intimate or vulnerable with other persons. Both miss out on true love and connection with other human beings.

If You're Angry
and You Know It

GOALS

To learn about internal and external boundaries; to build self-esteem

AGES

4 through 9

TIME

10-15 minutes

PURPOSE

This exercise encourages children to recognize and express their anger in healthy ways.

DO THIS EXERCISE TO

- Increase the children's capacity to value self and others.
- Increase the children's capacity to exert their will and desire effectively and appropriately.
- Teach group members new ways to express their anger that won't hurt them or anyone else.

DO NOT USE THIS EXERCISE WHEN

There is no reason not to do this exercise.

WHAT YOU NEED

No special materials needed

INSTRUCTIONS

Part I: Have group members stand in a large circle with a fair amount of space between them. Teach them the words to the song:

If you're angry and you know it, clap your hands. [clap hands twice]

If you're angry and you know it, clap your hands. [clap hands twice]

If you're angry and you know it, then your face will surely show it.

If you're angry and you know it, clap your hands. [clap hands twice]

The song is sung to the same tune as "If You're Happy and You Know It," which is based on the traditional hymn "Watch Your Eyes." (If you aren't familiar with "If You're Happy and You Know It," you can find it on Bob McGrath's album *Sing Along With Bob* and on Marcy Marxer's *Jump Children.* Or ask around—someone you know probably knows the tune.)

Sing the song through once to the group and then a second time with the group joining in. Now give each group member a chance to share a safe way of expressing his anger. When a child does not have an idea, move on to someone else and come back to the first child when he is ready.

As everyone sings the song, have them act out the ideas. For example, one child might sing, "If you're angry and you know it, stomp your feet." Start stomping around the room and encourage everyone else to do the same while singing. Continue the song by inserting other words that describe and demonstrate ways of expressing anger. For example:

- Punch a pillow.
- Say "I'm *mad!*"

- Go for a bike ride.
- Take the dog for a walk.

Part II: When everyone has had a turn giving suggestions in the song, ask them to choose some new ways to express anger in the upcoming week. Talk about what things make kids angry, such as the sexual abuse, not getting their way, and/or a sister, brother, or friend not sharing toys. Find out what group members do and who they go to when they feel angry.

HINTS

This song can be used to express any feeling–happy, sad, scared, or whatever. We most often use it to help children learn to express their anger in safe ways. It goes well with other exercises that allow them to express anger, such as "Target of the Offender" and "Clay Faces."

---

chapter 9

DYNAMICS OF
SEXUAL ABUSE EXERCISES

The dynamics of sexual abuse explain the emotional, psychological, and physical impact of abuse on victims and, secondarily, on the lives of their families. What occurs between an abuser and a victim is not a mutual or consensual act. It is, instead, a personal transgression in which the abuser steps beyond personal boundaries, ignoring the inner and outer reality of the person against whom he or she is offending.

Victims are children and adults, who are very definitely influenced and changed by their experiences of abuse, often in very painful and negative ways and sometimes for life. The dynamics of sexual abuse are very confusing to children. They need help to understand what happened, how they coped with their experiences, and how to deal with those experiences now. The group facilitator's fundamental and ongoing task is to help children understand, define, and challenge the core dynamics of sexual abuse, such as self blame and minimization or denial of their feelings about the abuse. "The Alligator River Story" and "Sexual Assault Continuum" are effective exercises to use for this purpose.

Once the ambivalence and minimization have lessened, victims often question why abusers abuse. Children's distorted thoughts about the abuse may become obvious to facilitators at this point and generate discussion. For young children, it is easiest to explain that abusers have a touching problem for which they need help. They cannot stop it themselves. It is such a big problem that they touch even when they know that the person they are touching feels terrible and does not want to be touched. All they can think about is themselves, and no one else. It is helpful to praise the children at this point in the explanation, to assist them in gaining an understanding that because they told, their offenders may learn how to stop abusing others. Older children and their parents can be given a more thorough explanation of how abusers are disconnected from their own tender emotions and unable to connect with the experience of others. In futile and compulsive attempts to overcome the emptiness and rage of disconnection, abusers use others for emotional ransom. Abusers experience and treat others as objects that will gratify, obstruct, or threaten their needs and impulses. The checklist in the exercise "Why People Sexually Abuse Kids" can help older children to understand the dynamics of abuse.

The next step in helping children to understand the dynamics of abuse is to teach them about the "grooming" process. By learning about grooming, children begin to understand the feelings they have toward themselves, their offenders, and their non-offending caregivers. Most child abuse is committed by someone known to the child: an immediate family member or other relative, a caregiver, or a family friend. In most instances of sexual abuse, a process of grooming occurs (Leberg, 1997; Way & Spieker, 1997, chap. 3). To groom is, by definition, "to train for a particular purpose" (*Webster's New World Dictionary*, 1974). Children are groomed by abusers to gratify the offenders' own wishes. The grooming process usually begins with special attention or seduction. A child is flattered and made to feel special by the abuser's attention, or is enticed with an age-appropriate lure, which could be anything from candy to beer. These enticements are then used to manipulate the child into performing some act for the abuser. For example, the abuser may say to the child, "I won't tell your mother you drank beer tonight if you give me a kiss." The child feels trapped and confused by the request, but, fearing punishment, may concede. The abuser's demands increase over time, and when seduction no longer works, the abuser will manipulate with threats. For instance, "If your mother finds out about what you are doing with me, she will never forgive you." Or "She will make me go to jail and I'll kill myself and it will be all your fault." Seduction, deception, manipulation, and fear are the training tools used by the abuser. Some of the exercises we use that teach about the grooming process are "The Butterfly and the Spider," "Magic Tricks," and "Letter From Angie." Another exercise that helps children identify how they were tricked or groomed by their offenders is "The Trick Hat."

The process of grooming leads many victims to believe that they were willing participants in the touch. Therefore, they believe that the abuse was their fault. Abusers act shamelessly, leaving victims to carry shame that does not belong to them. Many victims live their lives covered in this cloud of shame. They need help removing it and returning it to the abuser. Exercises that address these issues include "Revised Cookie Jar Tune," "Letter/Video to the Offender," and "Talking to the Offender Psychodrama."

Children also have confusion and strong feelings regarding the roles their nonoffending parents have played in relation to the abuse. Some parents knew the abuse was happening. Others were engaged in abusive relationships where the abuser was violating both the parent and the child. Some parents were abusing drugs and/or alcohol. Other parents were unaware of the abuse, but the children were told otherwise by the offender. Sometimes children believe that their parents should have known and should have protected them.

One exercise used in our therapy groups, "Letter/Video to Nonoffending Parent(s)," is a dramatic and powerful recovery tool when combined with a letter of response from the parent to the child. In the response letter, the parent takes appropriate responsibility for the protection of the child, alleviating many of the child's feelings and concerns. The response letter is written in the parent's therapy group and is processed with the child in a family therapy session.

All of the group exercises in this chapter are designed to help children discover and articulate what happened to them, how they were tricked or manipulated, and who is responsible for the abuse. Helping children gain separation from the abuse allows them to gain perspective and shift their belief from "I am the bad thing that happened" to "I am me," "Abuse happened to me," "Here is how it happened," and "It is one of many experiences I will have in my life."

Letter From Angie

GOALS

To understand the dynamics of sexual abuse; to build feelings of trust and safety

AGES

8 through 10

TIME

10-20 minutes

PURPOSE

This exercise acts as a useful introduction and exploration of the grooming process. It allows the group members to understand the concepts of grooming before applying them directly to themselves. We would like to thank Patricia Godleman for bringing this exercise to us.

DO THIS EXERCISE TO

- Increase the children's capacity to separate the self from the abuse/abuser.
- Increase the children's capacity to place responsibility and accountability appropriately.
- Increase the children's capacity to be vulnerable and to interact authentically.
- Increase the children's ability to put experiences and events in proper perspective, without minimizing or maximizing them.

DO NOT USE THIS EXERCISE WHEN

There is no reason not to do this exercise.

WHAT YOU NEED

- Copy of "Letter From Angie"
- Copies of the list of questions about the letter
- Pencils or pens

INSTRUCTIONS

Part I: Have the group sit together in a circle and explain that you are going to read a letter today that is from a girl who is just finishing therapy. She wanted to write a letter to them and asks that they listen to her words with their hearts and not just their heads. Read Angie's letter aloud to the group.

Part II: Pass out the questionnaires about the letter and ask the group members to answer the questions individually.

Part III: Invite everyone to come back together as a group and share their responses to the questions.

HINTS

This exercise can be done at any time during the exploration of the grooming process. Group members are usually genuinely curious about "Angie" and are interested in knowing how she is doing at the end of her therapy. They seem to identify with her story and are quick at picking out the ways she was tricked and trapped. Using the experiences of another person (as in this exercise) adds distance and safety, allowing for quicker application of the lessons to themselves.

As the children discuss their answers to the questions about Angie, they begin applying the same questions to their own situations without much, if any, encouragement. Of course, not all groups do this smoothly, so consider some possible questions to help direct the group members' thinking toward themselves. For example, you might ask:

- How were you tricked?
- How was your family tricked?
- Who was responsible for the tricking?
- What made it hard for you to tell?
- How did someone find out about you being touched?

Letter From Angie

January 25, 1996

Hi, my name is Angie and I am 13 years old and I want to tell you how I got over feeling bad about being molested.

It all started when I was about 6 years old. I had an older brother, Brian, who lived with his mom. He came to stay for about a week in the summer two times. At first it was okay. He did things like climb a tree and throw me and my little brother cherries. But one day he took me into my bedroom and started touching me in my private parts. I was really confused. I didn't know what was happening. One day when he was touching me in my bedroom, my grandma came in to say that dinner was ready. When he heard her footsteps coming, he got up from behind the bed, put me on the bed and pretended to be reading me stories. I think nearly getting caught scared him and the touching stopped.

From that time on I was afraid to be around him and I didn't tell because I wanted to protect my Mom and Dad from feeling bad. A couple of years later someone from my church took advantage of me by touching me in my private parts at my house again. I still couldn't tell, but later that year I finally told my Mom.

She said, "Why didn't you tell me?" I thought she was real mad at me for not telling but then I realized she was mad because I had been touched.

After that I went to counseling and learned that it's never your fault if you get touched. It is always the person who decided to do the touching. I drew, wrote stories, did this thing called eye movement therapy, and used talking to understand my feelings. Then I met a bunch of other girls who had been touched and we talked about what happened and realized it wasn't our fault. We also learned how to protect ourselves. Now I've finished therapy and I have put the memories behind me. In many ways I am a stronger person who can tell my parents anything, stand up for myself at school, and now I have a lot of great friends.

My wish for you, is for you to know that there is no reason to ever be ashamed of what happened and that the bad memories, dreams, and feelings will go away when you can talk about them. Always remember that you will never be alone.

From Angie, a fellow survivor

Questions Regarding Angie's Letter

How was Angie tricked?

_____

_____

_____

How was her family tricked?

_____

_____

_____

Who was responsible for the tricking?

_____

_____

_____

Why do you think Angie didn't tell her grandmother what had just happened to her?

_____

_____

_____

What do you think helped Angie to tell her mom about being abused?

_____

_____

_____

What do you think Angie was thinking when she was being touched?

_____

_____

_____

How do you think Angie felt when she was being touched?

_____

_____

_____

The Butterfly and the Spider

GOAL

To understand the dynamics of sexual abuse

AGES

8 through 12

TIME

30 minutes

PURPOSE

This story can be used as a tool at many different points during discussion of the abuse dynamics of grooming and responsibility for the abuse.

DO THIS EXERCISE TO

- Help group members understand and articulate the particular grooming dynamics used by their offenders.
- Increase the children's capacity to place responsibility and accountability appropriately.
- Increase the children's capacity to separate the self from the abuse/abuser.

DO NOT USE THIS EXERCISE WHEN

There is no reason not to do this exercise.

WHAT YOU NEED

- Copy of "The Butterfly and the Spider"
- Optional: writing paper and pens or pencils

INSTRUCTIONS

Before you read "The Butterfly and the Spider" to the group, gather the members together and ask them to listen to the story with their hearts and not just their heads. Then read the story aloud. Afterward, have the children answer some questions about the story, either by writing their responses to or by answering verbally. (If the group members write their responses, follow this with a discussion.) For example, you might ask:

- What tricks did the spider use?
- How did the spider trap the butterfly?
- Who was responsible for her getting stuck in the web?
- What is one way the offender tricked you?
- What is one way the offender tricked your family?

Think about the group dynamics before deciding which way you want to do this exercise. Some groups do better writing responses to questions, whereas others are fine responding verbally. If you have a larger group, or any shy children in group, having them write their responses initially can help balance the participation.

HINTS

This exercise can be tension producing, which often winds group members up. Make sure that there is time to do other winding-down activities after the story and discussion. The "Personal Butterfly" exercise is a great follow-up. With a boys' group, you may need a more physical activity, such as "Let It All Out/Sound Train" (see Chapter 6).

The Butterfly and the Spider
(adapted by Patricia Godleman, MA, from a story in Davis, 1990)

Once upon a time there was a spider. As spiders do, this spider built a very big web. He was determined to catch any unsuspecting flying thing—butterflies or other insects unlucky enough to come within reach. Now, the spider knew that insects need nectar from flowers, so he spun his web between two flowering bushes. He then settled back to wait for something appealing to come by looking for the sweet juicy nectar in the purple and pink flowers. He knew that he had created a good trap.

The web was invisible to the eyes of most insects unless it was covered with raindrops or morning dew; then it sparkled like jewels in the light. This made the web even more dangerous, because unsuspecting insects would not see the trap and the destruction it represented until it was too late. Sometimes insects would see the spider, but, not understanding how spiders like to eat insects, would fly directly into the trap of the web. Now, spiders wrap up their victims and keep them alive until they are ready to use them, and this spider was no different. He was proud of his web and felt no guilt at all about the way he lived his life.

One day, a beautiful young butterfly happened by, flying from one colorful flowering bush to another. The unsuspecting butterfly was attracted by the glistening web that sparkled in the sunlight, and suddenly was caught fast in the spider's trap. Terrified, the butterfly tried to free herself, pulling and twisting and fighting, but the more she moved, the tighter she was caught. The spider counted on the terror of those he caught to make the prison of the web even tighter.

Now a wise little red-and-black ladybug, who had learned about spiders from experience, saw the trapped butterfly and decided to help her escape. The spider, busily spinning on the other end of the web, was so sure that the butterfly was helplessly trapped that he did not even hurry over to make sure that she could not get away. Carefully, the ladybug flew near the butterfly and whispered, "Stop fighting the web. That will only make it a tighter prison than ever."

"But I am so scared, and I feel so stupid. I don't believe I will ever be able to get out of this sticky web," cried the butterfly.

"Then use your fear to give you power," the ladybug explained. "Understand how the spider has tricked you and the web has trapped you and use your mouth to free yourself. *You have the power to be free.*"

So the butterfly took a few deep breaths, calmed herself down, and stopped struggling against the web. Concentrating on what the ladybug had said, she thought about how she had been trapped and the best way to free herself. She used her creative brain, her clever mouth, and her whole body to escape. Once she was free, she noticed that her wings were torn from being trapped in the web. She worried that they would never heal and that everyone who saw her

(continued)

The Butterfly and the Spider *(continued)*
(adapted by Patricia Godleman, MA, from a story in Davis, 1990)

wings would know that she had been caught in the spider's web. She felt ashamed and embarrassed and thought that all the other insects would blame her for the spider's deceit. She even wondered if her family would be angry at her for being tricked. But as she confided these feelings to the ladybug and was able to talk things over with the wise old insect, she realized that she was innocent and blameless. The ladybug reminded her that all butterflies need to gather pollen to live and that spiders use that knowledge to trick and trap unsuspecting insects.

As time went by, the butterfly was able to find a way to heal the hurt that she had experienced because of the spider. Soon she was once again a strong, beautiful butterfly who loved to fly from flower to flower to gather nectar. But now as she flew she was aware of spiders and their traps, and she was proud of her awareness, and in this way she continued to be free.

Personal Butterfly

GOALS

To understand the dynamics of sexual abuse; to build self-esteem; to build feelings of safety and trust

AGES

6 through 12

TIME

15-20 minutes

PURPOSE

This exercise helps group members to put their abuse in perspective and empowers them. It is a perfect follow-up to "The Butterfly and the Spider."

DO THIS EXERCISE TO

- Increase the children's capacity to separate the self from the abuser.
- Increase the children's capacity to desire, believe in, and hold hope for a positive future.
- Increase the children's ability to put experiences and events in proper perspective, without minimizing or maximizing them.

DO NOT USE THIS EXERCISE WHEN

There is no reason not to do this exercise.

WHAT YOU NEED

- Folded pieces of paper, each with half a butterfly drawn on it (so when the paper is cut along the outline and then opened, it has the shape of a full butterfly)
- Blank paper
- Finger paints or watercolors
- Glitter (optional)
- Newsprint or newspapers to protect the floor
- Paper towels

INSTRUCTIONS

Part I: If you are *not* doing this exercise as a follow-up to "The Butterfly and the Spider," begin with a discussion about butterflies. (If you have just finished "The Butterfly and the Spider," go on to Part II.) Ask group members what they know about the metamorphosis process of the butterfly. Discuss the many changes a butterfly goes through. It starts out as a larva, becomes a caterpillar, builds a cocoon, and then finally emerges from that cocoon as a beautiful, spirited butterfly who lives and flies freely. Each growth experience affects the butterfly and makes it stronger, forming it into the wonderful spirit it is.

Part II: Before starting this part of the exercise, spread newsprint or newspapers to protect the floor in the area where you will be working. Have each child choose a butterfly picture, or let them each draw half of a butterfly on a blank piece of paper. When everyone has a butterfly, have the children fold their papers in half so that the fold is where the middle of the butterfly would be and the half butterfly is showing.

Have the children paint the half of the butterfly that is showing with multiple colors. When they have painted that side, have them fold their papers over so that the paint is transferred to the other half of the butterfly also. Have them gently press the halves together, then carefully pull the sides apart to reveal the whole butterfly.

They can add more paint after they open the butterfly up if they choose. Before the paint dries, glitter can be added as well.

Part III: While the butterflies are drying, have each group member describe, in the first person, how she is like the butterfly. For example, "I am like the butterfly because I am beautiful and I have changed a lot in my lifetime."

When the butterflies are dry, hang them up in the room so everyone can view them. The following week, at the close of group, send them home with the children who made them.

HINTS

Making the butterflies is a bonding experience that provides a good resolution to the exercise "The Butterfly and the Spider." This will help the children ease their tension after talking about their personal abuse issues.

When the children describe themselves as the butterfly, they probably will forget to make their statements in the first person. Insist that they do so—it makes the exercise much more powerful when they describe themselves using the same positive attributes that they assign to the butterfly.

Bring extra copies of the sheets with half butterflies drawn on them and extra blank paper. Usually there is at least one group member who wants to try drawing her own half of a butterfly. However, if you are short on time you may not want to allow this. Some "artists" are perfectionists and take a long time to get their drawings just right.

It is nice for group members to have the option of completely creating their own butterflies. This increases the potential for this exercise to build group members' capacity to value themselves and others. Often, the children encourage and compliment one another on the creativity and uniqueness that is expressed in their artwork.

Magic Tricks

GOAL

To understand the dynamics of sexual abuse

AGES

4 through 10

TIME

15-20 minutes

PURPOSE

This exercise is designed to help children gain an understanding of the dynamics of sexual abuse. Because of the element of magic and surprise, it is a very effective teaching tool for young children. This exercise was brought to us by a most magical intern, Margaret Vest.

DO THIS EXERCISE TO

- Increase the children's ability to separate the self from the abuse/abuser.
- Help group members understand and articulate the particular grooming dynamics used by their offenders.
- Teach about the role of tricking and grooming in the dynamics of sexual abuse.
- Increase the children's capacity to place responsibility and accountability appropriately.

DO NOT USE THIS EXERCISE WHEN

- The abuse histories of any group members involve magic tricks.

WHAT YOU NEED

- Three or four simple magic tricks or card tricks (can be purchased at most toy stores for $2.00-$4.00)
- "Invisible pen" set (optional)

INSTRUCTIONS

Before you do this exercise in group, read through the directions for the magic tricks you have purchased and practice the tricks enough times so that your magic will be really believable when you do it for the children.

Part I: Perform the card/magic tricks with one child assisting you while other group members observe. Have him guess the card, point to things—whatever the trick requires. Repeat each trick as requested. Usually, we perform the tricks with each group member, so that everyone can have the experience of being tricked.

Part II: After you have performed the tricks several times, explain in detail how each one works. Use language that clearly shows how, in performing the tricks, you had information that the group members did not have. Then briefly discuss tricks more generally. Begin by talking about how the tricks you have performed were harmless and fun. Explain how tricks fool people (note that tricksters have information and skills that others do not have, that tricksters may have to practice and train to pull off their tricks, and so on). Introduce the idea that there are other kinds of tricks that are not fun and can hurt people. Talk about how people who have been sexually abused have been tricked, and how the people who tricked them are the ones who are responsible. Tricksters know what they are doing.

Part III (optional): When the previous portion of the exercise is complete, you can use an "invisible pen" set to draw pictures with invisible ink. (Such pen sets are available at many toy stores. The most common one is called Ghost Writer.) Have the group members decode the pictures by using the companion marker. This provides an opportunity for group members to be in control of uncovering the trick.

Grotsky, Camerer, and Damiano, *Group Work With Sexually Abused Children.* Copyright 2000, Sage Publications, Inc.

Part IV: If there is time and your group is not too rambunctious, discuss with group members some of the ways in which they were tricked by their abusers.

HINTS

Boys' and young children's groups may have difficulty with the discussion portion of this exercise due to their relatively brief attention spans. This is a discussion that may be revisited later as part of a different activity.

Young children really love magic tricks. This exercise is an easy way to help them understand the difference between good tricks and bad tricks. Some children may even think of bad tricks that are not abuse related–for example, mean tricks like taking something away or telling someone they can have something and then saying, "No, I tricked you."

In therapy groups, this exercise can be easily followed by "The Trick Hat," which focuses on some specific ways that abusers trick children.

The Trick Hat
(Therapy Group Only)

GOAL

To understand the dynamics of sexual abuse

AGES

4 through 8

TIME

10 minutes

PURPOSE

This exercise works as an introduction to talking about grooming and as a way to begin the process of helping group members understand how their abusers tricked them.

DO THIS EXERCISE TO

- Increase the children's ability to separate the self from the abuse/abuser.
- Increase the children's capacity to place responsibility and accountability appropriately.
- Help group members understand and articulate the particular grooming dynamics used by their offenders.

DO NOT USE THIS EXERCISE WHEN

- Any group member has a sexual abuse history that involved the use of magic.

WHAT YOU NEED

- Magician's hat
- Deck of jumbo playing cards
- Colored paper
- White paper
- Scissors
- Glue
- Pen or fine-tipped marker and colored markers

INSTRUCTIONS

Before the group session, take a large-sized deck of cards and cut pieces of colored paper the size of the cards. On the pieces of paper, write some of the ways that children are tricked by sexual abusers. Some examples:

- Said my mom would get mad if I told.
- Gave me candy.
- Let me have special time.
- Bought me presents.
- Said I was his "special girl."
- Said he'd have to go away if I told.
- Said I'd get in trouble if I told.
- Said he would hurt my dog.

When you have about 15 ways that children are tricked written on the colored pieces of paper, glue each of the pieces over the face of a playing card. (Be sure to write the tricks first, and then glue them on. If you make a mistake writing a trick, it is easier to start over with another piece of paper than to have to cover the card again or peel off the mistake.)

Part I: In group, place the cards you have created in the magician's hat. Have each group member take a turn drawing out a card, and have a facilitator read it aloud. After each trick is read, ask if anyone in the group was tricked that way. Give the group members a chance to respond either verbally or with a show of hands. Leave the card out of the hat and go on to the next group member. Continue taking turns picking cards out of the hat until all the cards have been read.

Part II: Pass out markers and paper to everyone. Instruct the group members to draw pictures of how they were tricked. When their pictures are completed, have everyone come back into a circle and share what they have drawn.

Write down what the group members describe about their pictures on the pictures themselves, because it may be difficult to tell what they are trying to communicate simply by looking at their pictures. They will often talk about abstract things that are right on target. For example, one child said that her picture was about a giraffe who got tricked by an icky jellyfish that hurt and lied to the giraffe. She was telling us how she was hurt and was lied to.

HINTS

Be sure to review the files of group members and cull any information they reveal about grooming techniques that are specific to your group. For example, if you know that one of the group members didn't tell about the abuse because she was worried her brother would have to move away, use a similar scenario as one of the tricks on your cards.

When writing up the tricks, keep in mind the age of your audience. Although perpetrators can be quite explicit in their descriptions of how they will kill children's pets or how they will be sent away, be sure to avoid including graphic details on your cards.

Questions and Answers Box

GOALS

To build safety and trust; to understand the dynamics of sexual abuse

AGES

9 through 18

TIME

10 minutes to most of the group session (Time will vary depending on how you set up the exercise. Allow time to answer all the questions over the entire length of an 8-15 week group.)

PURPOSE

This exercise gives children a chance to ask embarrassing questions anonymously while encouraging discussion. This helps reduce feelings of shame and isolation.

DO THIS EXERCISE TO

- Correct misinformed beliefs regarding sexuality.
- Answer questions group members may have regarding the many new systems that have affected their lives since their abuse was disclosed (may include questions regarding the court system, supervised visitation, schools, and more).

- Further assess the collective needs and direction of the group.
- Reduce levels of fear, shame, and isolation.
- Increase the children's capacity to place responsibility and accountability appropriately.

DO NOT USE THIS EXERCISE WHEN

- Group members are unable to sit still long enough for at least a 5-minute discussion.

WHAT YOU NEED

- A shoe box or similar container
- Pencils
- Paper (all pieces should be identical to protect anonymity)

INSTRUCTIONS

Part I: Set up the box for group members' questions ahead of time. Pass out pencils and uniform pieces of paper so that questions can remain anonymous when they are being discussed later. Ask everyone to think of a couple of questions they have about sexual abuse, about the group, or about anything that relates to sexuality.

When everyone has finished writing their questions, have them deposit them in the box. Explain that time will be taken each week to discuss the questions in the box and that new questions can be added during the following weeks.

Immediately after introducing this exercise, you may want to take some time to discuss a few of the questions, so that group members understand how the process works. This may encourage them to think about additional questions for future weeks. The timetable for answering the questions is up to you. We have begun group with one question from the box each week. In other groups we have set time aside at the end of every two or three sessions to discuss some of the questions.

Part II: Choose someone to draw a question from the box and read it aloud. Ask others what they think in response to the question. Encourage them to express their opinions and to be supportive of others' ideas.

HINTS

When we first began doing this exercise we made the mistake of not limiting the questions to sexual assault or group process. We had many questions relating to movies and more esoteric questions, like "What is time anyway?" By limiting the questions to topics related to sexuality, sexual abuse, and systems, we got questions such as "Could I have AIDS?" and "Am I sick if I liked the abuse?"

Revised Cookie Jar Tune

GOALS

To understand the dynamics of sexual abuse; to build self-esteem

AGES

3 through 8

TIME

4-10 minutes

PURPOSE

This exercise helps group members begin talking in a fun, safe way about being touched. It is a first step toward placing responsibility for the abuse on the perpetrator.

DO THIS EXERCISE TO

- Reduce self-blame for the abuse.
- Build self-esteem and group cohesiveness.
- Encourage disclosure.
- Reduce feelings of isolation and lessen the children's sense of being different.

DO NOT USE THIS EXERCISE WHEN

There is no reason not to do this exercise, as long as you let group members "pass" if they want to.

WHAT YOU NEED

No special materials needed

INSTRUCTIONS

This exercise uses a revised version of the hand-clap song "Who Stole the Cookie From the Cookie Jar?" which goes like this:

Who stole the cookie from the cookie jar?

Joe stole the cookie from the cookie jar.

Who, me?

Yes, you.

Couldn't be.

Then who?

Mary stole the cookie from the cookie jar.

And so on. In this version, we have altered the words.

Have everyone sit in a circle. Start by demonstrating the hand motions before adding the words. We use three beats: On the first beat everyone slaps their laps, on the second beat all clap their hands, and on the third beat everyone snaps their fingers. Continue the sequence. Once the children have the hand motions down, sing the song using the following words:

Facilitator: Who touched [child's name] in her private parts?

Child: My [abuser's name or relationship; for example, my brother, my dad, my uncle, or John] touched me in my private parts.

Group: Your [abuser's name or relationship] shouldn't have!

Facilitator: Who's fault was it when he [she] touched you that way?

Child: Not mine!

Group: Not yours!

Facilitator: Then whose?

Group and child together: Her/my [abuser's name or relationship] that's who!

Take turns so that each person in the group gets to sing (at least once) who touched her. When the kids know the words well, they tend to just say them on their own without help from a facilitator.

HINTS

Children greatly enjoy this exercise, as it helps them to feel powerful. They get the whole group in unison making their offenders responsible for the abuse. Usually they are clamoring for a turn, saying, "My turn, my turn next," or "My brother touched me too, so can I have two turns?" Young children love repetition, so repeat this exercise several times throughout the group sessions.

Some children have been forced to touch but were not touched themselves. Change the words to fit the situation–for example, "Who made Sammy touch him on his private parts?"

Younger children probably cannot snap their fingers or keep the rhythm very well. For children 4 and 5 years old, have everyone hold hands and swing their arms back and forth, or just clap to the beat.

Under special circumstances a child will occasionally join a group a week or two after it has started. We had a 5-year-old girl in group who felt out of place and was disruptive after joining 2 weeks late. A few weeks later we did this exercise. When it came to her turn to say who touched her, she began to giggle and couldn't stop. Pretty soon she had all of us laughing hysterically. Once the laughter subsided, she proudly took her turn. She actively participated in and enjoyed group activities through the remainder of the group sessions.

Another little girl who had been sexually abused by her mother learned this song in group. Little Miranda's mother would never admit to the abuse, but that didn't stop Miranda from singing this song during supervised visits with her mother.

The children in group will want the facilitators to sing the song about themselves, and to share the names of the persons who touched them. Facilitators who do not have sexual abuse histories should try to think of situations that involved uncomfortable touching so that they can join in also.

Why People Sexually Abuse Kids

GOAL

To understand the dynamics of sexual abuse

AGES

7 through 18

TIME

20 minutes

PURPOSE

This exercise provides children with an opportunity to explore possible reasons their offenders sexually abused them. This lessens their feelings of responsibility, self-blame, and shame, reverting accountability to the offender.

DO THIS EXERCISE TO

- Reduce the children's self-blame for their abuse.
- Further assess the children's perspectives regarding their abuse.
- Help group members better understand why they were sexually abused.

DO NOT USE THIS EXERCISE WHEN

- Group members cannot read.

WHAT YOU NEED

- Copies of the "Why People Sexually Abuse Kids" Checklist
- Pens or pencils

INSTRUCTIONS

Explain to the group that you want to know why they think people sexually abuse children. Pass out copies of the checklist and encourage the children to take time to fill them out with their own ideas about why adults sexually abuse children. The only rule is that no one may write or say that the sexual assault happened because of something he, the child, did. We instituted this rule to encourage group members to take the first step toward realizing they did nothing to cause the abuse.

When everyone has finished filling out the checklists, bring the group back together in a semicircle. Go over the items on the checklist one item at a time to find out how each child responded. Ask for a show of hands after you read each statement, then talk with the children about why they did or did not agree with that particular choice.

Group members often suggest some motivations not included on the checklist. Be sure to ask them to share their ideas with the rest of the group. These can often generate good group discussions.

HINTS

To date, studies have revealed no single reason for sexual abuse. Many of the items on our checklist come from ideas suggested by the children themselves. You may choose to have your group members create their own checklist instead of making copies of this one. Either way, be sure to keep complete records of all the children's responses, so that you can refer to them throughout your work with the group.

From this exercise we learn a lot about how group members' perceptions affect their coping styles. We have often seen this exercise help group members to move beyond self-blame, allowing them to hold their offenders accountable for the abuse.

Grotsky, Camerer, and Damiano, *Group Work With Sexually Abused Children*. Copyright 2000, Sage Publications, Inc.

When a child consistently feels responsible for her abuse, it is important to explore why she needs to hold on to these feelings so strongly. Possibly, it is her only sense of control. Maybe she feels it is too hard to believe that someone she loves would deliberately hurt her. The group process can be used to slowly chip away at these self-destructive beliefs. Because the child has already established identification and trust with other group members, the similar nature of the others' experiences and their empathy reflected back to the child may allow her a sense of relief from the burden of guilt.

Why People Sexually Abuse Kids

Below is a list of reasons some adults sexually abuse children. Check as many reasons as you think are true for the person who sexually abused you. Fill out one checklist for each person who sexually abused you. Use the back if you need more space.

_____ Because he/she wanted some fun out of me.

_____ He/she is going crazy.

_____ He/she might want to hurt kids.

_____ He/she is always drunk.

_____ He/she had been smoking marijuana and taking drugs.

_____ It's what his/her family did when he/she was young.

_____ He/she doesn't have any friends.

_____ He/she was sexually abused when he/she was a kid.

_____ He/she doesn't think sexual abuse is wrong.

_____ He/she can do what he/she wants to kids because he/she is bigger and stronger.

_____ He/she is out of control.

_____ He/she thought it was the way to teach me about sex.

_____ He/she thought this was the way to show me he/she loves me.

_____ He/she did it to punish me.

_____ I don't know.

Write any other reasons you think you were sexually abused below.

_____

_____

_____

_____

_____

_____

_____

_____

_____

_____

_____

Letter/Video to the Offender

GOAL

To understand the dynamics of sexual abuse

AGES

5 through 18

TIME

One to two group sessions

PURPOSE

This exercise gives group members a safe place to express freely their emotions about being abused. Hearing how others feel helps group members to admit many of their own "secret" emotions. Expect feelings of anger and the first lessening of guilt.

DO THIS EXERCISE TO

- Increase the children's capacity to separate the self from the abuse/abuser.
- Increase the children's ability to value self and others.
- Help the children to focus on identifying and expressing their emotions appropriately.
- Increase the children's capacity to place responsibility and accountability appropriately.
- Increase the children's ability to define and express personal needs.

DO NOT USE THIS EXERCISE WHEN

- You believe a group member or a family member may want to send the letter or video produced to get "revenge" or in hopes of getting an apology back. The letters and videos produced in this exercise are not to be sent.

WHAT YOU NEED

- Pens or pencils
- Writing paper

Or

- Video camera

INSTRUCTIONS

Part I: Ask group members to write letters to their offenders. Explain that the letters will not be mailed, so they can write whatever comes to mind without worrying about spelling or grammar. The letters can be any length. (*Note:* This part of the exercise can be done as a homework assignment or in the group session. The homework assignment works well for children 12 years old or under, but teenagers are more likely to get their letters written if you use group time. If the letters are written in the group session, have the children sit widely separated from each other and write for 20 minutes.)

Children younger than 9 often prefer to videotape their letters. If you do not have access to a video camera, consider letting each child speak his letter into a tape recorder and then you can transcribe it. We have also divided into small groups and had facilitators take dictation from one child at a time while the other children drew pictures to illustrate their letters. If children 9 and older are having difficulty writing their letters, you may want to give them the questions below as a guide.

If you are videotaping letters, do a practice run one week and then do the final letters the next. The second time around, the letters will be far superior because the children are more familiar with the questions and the camera. It is best when videotaping to ask some open-ended questions to help the children along. If they have difficulty answering these questions, ask more specific ones. The younger the child, the simpler the questions need to be. Some sample questions are as follows:

- If you knew you would be totally safe and could say anything you wanted to the person who touched you, what would you want to say?
- What were the feelings you felt when you were being touched?
- What were you thinking when you were being touched?
- What would you like to happen to the person who touched you?
- If you saw the person who touched you again, what would you like to do or say to him or her?
- Is there anything you wish the person who touched you would say to you?
- Do you have any questions you would like to ask the person who touched you?
- Is there anything else you would like to say?

Part II: Have the letters read aloud in group, either by their authors or by individuals they choose to read for them. We also show the videos in group if time allows. After each letter, allow time for group hugs, comments, or whatever is needed. Always acknowledge the strength it takes to write such a letter.

THERAPY GROUP ONLY: Video letters to offenders often have huge impacts on nonoffending parents if the children are willing to have them see the videos. In these cases, we show the videos during family therapy sessions and only to nonoffending parents who we know to be supportive of their children and also strong enough to hear what the children have to say.

Other versions: Group members can also write letters to their nonoffending parents or other caregivers. Many children who have been abused are angry at their moms or other adults who they feel did not protect them. This is often true whether these adults knew the abuse was happening or not (see the exercise "Letter/Video to Nonoffending Parent[s]").

Group members can also write to themselves. This is another version of the exercise "The Parent Within" (see Chapter 7).

HINTS

Teenagers will often ask if they can swear in their letters. We tell them they can in their first drafts, but then they need to do second drafts that have minimal swearing. Children need to learn how to express their strong emotions in effective and appropriate ways so that others can hear what they have to say. We found that without this rule, group members can get into a swearing competition and the true meaning of the letter can be lost.

Do not send any of these letters. Usually, abused children have many unresolved issues with their offenders, and the sending of such letters may involve hidden agendas and hurtful expectations. These letters can also be used in other damaging ways. Once, a letter that a child wrote in one of our groups was sent to her offender, her father, in the midst of a major custody battle between her parents. The letter ended up in court as an example, according to the father, of the "hatred, anger, and lies that Mom and the therapists were trying to put into the daughter's head." Luckily, his argument was not accepted and he did not win custody.

Parents and other caregivers may also find letter writing to be very helpful. During the parent meetings, we often encourage adults to do this exercise on their own. We tell them that we will read what they write if they want us to. When appropriate, we recommend that they read their letters to their children during family therapy sessions.

Samples of Letters to Group Members' Offenders

Cody,

I am writing this letter to you about what you did to me. I didn't appreciate it. When it happened you made me feel guilty, like it was my fault. I was scared too. I don't want you to get in trouble but if that's what happens you'll have to suffer the consequences. But now I know it's not my fault and I feel better, although I am glad you don't live with me.

Sincerely,
Ellen [age 11]

Dear Steve,

I hate you for what you did to me and you are a dummy, and a scum and you are a chicken and I love you for a brother. And hate you for what you done to me. Steve, you need help. Steve, I hate you for what you done and you need to be punished. Steve, I hate you. Steve, you hurt me.

Love,
Abigail [age 11]

Dear Daddy,

I hate you very much. I don't love you anymore. I felt sad and not comfortable and more things. I don't like you anymore. I have more fun here. I don't eat a lot of candy. I have new clothes that I picked out myself. I visit Grampa every Thursday. You are a nincompoop. I do hate you very much. I have more friends here. And I felt like jumping out the window when you abused me. I hope you have fun in jail! You are a SON OF A BITCH! I hate you because you touched me in my privates. And I felt mad. I know what you did to my sister, you molested her. Don't do it anymore. You are a geek and you are a A-Hole.

Hate,
Susan [age 10]

Dear Joe,

I felt like it was my fault and it wasn't my fault 'cause you were the one who was touching me. And I didn't like it at all and I told Mom and Dad because it was a bad thing to do. And when you did that it made me mad.

Donald [age 7]

Sexual Assault Continuum
(Therapy Group Only)

GOALS

To learn to manage triggers; to understand the dynamics of sexual abuse

AGES

10 through 18

TIME

45-60 minutes

PURPOSE

This exercise helps to desensitize group members so that they are not alarmed or triggered by other participants' disclosures. Simultaneously, it gives participants permission to disclose details about their abuse that they may not otherwise be willing to reveal. It also educates them to the "grooming process" (a subtler, more covert form of abuse) and describes how some offenders progressively desensitize children and slowly increase their control over them. Be sure that group members have learned the "Centering" exercise (in Chapter 10) before doing this one.

DO THIS EXERCISE TO

- Help group members understand the covert and overt forms of sexual abuse and how one form may not be greater or lesser than the other in terms of how it affects the victim.

- Begin to decrease and desensitize trigger reactivity.
- Create a sense of safety that encourages disclosure of details of the abuse, rather than keeping them hidden by a veil of shame.
- Help group members begin to manage trigger responses.

DO NOT USE THIS EXERCISE WHEN

- Group members are under 10 years old. It is too triggering for them and they may learn about sexual acts way beyond their previous experience.
- Any group member is triggered quite easily and has already displayed an inability to manage triggers well.
- There is not enough time to process the continuum during the same day's session.
- Group members have not yet learned the "Centering" exercise.

WHAT YOU NEED

- A chalkboard and chalk or a large piece of paper and a marker

INSTRUCTIONS

Part I: Ask group members to generate a list of all the things they think are sexual abuse, from the subtlest to the most overt. List all the things they say on the chalkboard or on a large piece of paper.

Part II: When the brainstorming winds down, explain that the group will be ranking all the different types of abuse from the subtlest to the most overt. Draw a long horizontal line across a clean writing surface and, using the brainstormed list, ask the children which form of abuse mentioned is the subtlest. Write the answer on the far left end of the line on a diagonal, leaving plenty of room for the other answers. Now ask the group to choose the most overt form of sexual abuse, and write that answer on the far right end of the line. All the rest of the answers will fall in between. If the group cannot agree on the placement of a specific form of abuse, put it in two or three different areas, showing that there are no right or wrong answers.

Group members may need some help in coming up with some of the subtler forms of sexual abuse. Some of these are not sexual abuse in and of themselves, but they are forms of abuse if they have sexual overtones and if the recipients experience discomfort and disrespect. A continuum might include the following abuses, from subtlest to most overt:

- Tickling someone and not stopping when asked
- Walking into the bathroom without knocking
- Making lewd comments about another's body
- Nude exposure that brings on discomfort
- Forcing someone to view pornography or pornographic movies
- Forcing someone to pose in the nude for photos or videos
- Forcing someone to watch a person masturbate
- Forcing someone to watch people being sexual
- Forcing someone to touch someone else's private parts
- Touching a person on his/her private parts, making that person feel uncomfortable
- Forced kissing using the tongue
- Forced oral sex
- Forced vaginal penetration (digital or penile)
- Forced anal penetration (digital or penile)
- Penetration with other objects (vegetable, bottles, sticks)
- Penetration with a weapon
- Forced sex by threatening with a weapon
- Gang rape
- Homicide after sexual abuse
- Suicide because of sexual abuse by victim or offender

While doing this exercise, pay close attention to each group member. If anyone seems to be dissociating or being triggered, attend to her immediately by telling her what you are noticing in her actions or looks and asking her to talk about how she is feeling. Do not move on until you feel she is okay and able to focus in the present time or is receiving one-on-one private attention from another facilitator.

Part III: Do the "Centering" exercise to ensure that everyone is in the present time and able to be focused in the room after hearing the different forms of abuse. Afterward, ask group members the following questions:

- What feelings surfaced while we were doing the continuum?
- What thoughts and feelings surfaced in relation to your own abuse?
- Was anyone in the group groomed by an abuser who started with a subtle form of abuse and slowly built to more overt forms?
- Were some of the subtler forms of abuse harder to deal with than the more overt? If so, why?
- Is there anything else you learned from doing this exercise?

HINTS

Make sure that the continuum includes the act of forcing someone to watch or participate in making photographs, videotapes, and/or pornography. It is not unusual for children who have been forced to be involved in such things not to admit it.

Following this exercise, you may want to have each group member individually draw the continuum of her own abuse. If you do so, then end that exercise either by doing a guided imagery of a safe place or by having each child physically put her continuum in a box marked "Then." Then have each draw a picture of her safe person or place and put that picture in a box marked "Now." This serves as a reminder that the abuse is in the past and that the child is safe now.

We have found it interesting that many children find French kissing by their abusers to be the most invasive aspect of the abuse. For some, that made them feel more vulnerable then vaginal penetration.

The Alligator River Story

GOALS

To build self-esteem; to understand the dynamics of sexual abuse

AGES

9 through 18

TIME

30-40 minutes

PURPOSE

This exercise leads to fascinating discussions that illustrate how pervasive blaming the victim is in our society. Children, especially teenagers, see life as black-and-white, with no shades of gray. This exercise helps them see the other shades. In addition, it encourages individuals to work cooperatively as a group. It teaches them to speak up for their own beliefs, yet listen to others and together come up with solutions that feel comfortable to all. The origins of this exercise are unknown; we do know that it has been passed on for years from one rape crisis center to another in the training of volunteers.

DO THIS EXERCISE TO

- Decrease feelings of self-blame and shame.
- Increase the children's ability to define and express personal safety needs.
- Increase the children's capacity to place accountability and responsibility appropriately.

DO NOT USE THIS EXERCISE WHEN

- There is not enough time for a full discussion.
- There is so much competition among group members that cooperation is unlikely.

WHAT YOU NEED

- Copies of "The Alligator River Story" with instructions for ranking
- Pens or pencils

INSTRUCTIONS

Part I: Pass out copies of "The Alligator River Story" to group members. Instruct them to read it to themselves and then individually rank the characters from 1 to 5, with 1 being the most objectionable.

Part II: When group members have completed their individual rankings, divide the large group into smaller groups of 3-4 people. Ask the members of the small groups to share their individual rankings, and then together reach an acceptable group ranking. Encouraging discussion during this process can help individuals explain their reasons for their rankings.

Part III: Return to the larger group and ask everyone to explain what rankings their small groups agreed upon and why.

Part IV: Encourage further discussion by asking questions such as the following:

- What if the situation were different and Abigail lived in a city and was hitchhiking?
- What if Abigail had been wearing a turtleneck and jeans?
- What if Abigail had been really drunk?
- Was Abigail tricked or manipulated in any way? Does that change how you feel about her?
- Does Abigail have a right to be sexy and to choose who she wants to have sex with?

HINTS

Abigail is rarely last in the rankings and often comes in second. If, after the discussion, group members still blame Abigail, chances are they still blame themselves. This was illustrated for us by a 10-year-old group member who consistently expressed few effects from the sexual abuse. During this exercise she was adamant that the assault was Abigail's fault. After much arguing from other group members, two issues became very clear. First, this girl blamed herself for the abuse she had suffered. Second, she held on to the belief that sexual assault was the victim's fault so that she could maintain the belief that she could prevent it from happening to her again. This cognitive distortion functioned as a false sense of protection for her. By being nice, not standing up for yourself, and not recognizing your right to protect yourself, you can end up being revictimized.

Female group members are often confused by gender roles (e.g., the female role expectation that females are viable only if they are always being nice). Therefore, many have a hard time accepting Abigail's laughter over Gregory's being beaten up. Facilitate a discussion about the ways people sometimes respond in the heat of crisis, which can include laughter to release tension. Help them to remember or imagine what it feels like not to be believed. Remind them that rape and molestation occur when someone is manipulated or coerced into doing something sexual against her will or consent. Discuss what differences there are, if any, between Abigail's sexual abuse and theirs.

The Alligator River Story

After you read this story, privately rank the five characters from the most offensive to the least objectionable.

Once upon a time, there was a woman named Abigail who was in love with a man named Gregory. Gregory lived on the shore of the river. Abigail lived on the opposite shore of the river. The river that separated the two lovers was teeming with man-eating alligators. Abigail wanted to cross the river to be with Gregory. Unfortunately, the bridge had been washed out, so she went to ask Sinbad, a ferryboat captain, to take her across.

She was wearing a tight skirt and a low-cut blouse, because she wanted to look sexy for Gregory. Sinbad said that he would take her across; however, the look in his eyes frightened Abigail. So she went to her friend Ivan and explained her plight to him. Ivan did not want to be involved at all in the situation. Abigail felt that her only alternative was to take the ferry, even though she did not trust Sinbad.

After the ferry left the shore, Sinbad told Abigail that he couldn't control himself and had to go to bed with her. When Abigail refused, he threatened to throw her overboard. He also said that if she complied he would deliver her safely to the other side. Abigail was afraid of being eaten alive by the alligators, and she didn't see any other alternative, so she did not resist Sinbad. Sinbad delivered her to the shore where Gregory lived.

When Abigail told Gregory what had happened to her, he viewed her as asking for it because of the way she was dressed. He saw her as unclean and cast her aside with disdain. Heartsick and dejected, she turned to Slug, who was a black belt in karate. Slug felt anger toward Gregory and compassion for Abigail. He sought out Gregory and beat him brutally. Abigail was overjoyed at the sight of Gregory getting his due. As the sun set on the horizon, Abigail laughed at Gregory's fate.

Rank the five characters, making the most objectionable number 1:

1. _____

2. _____

3. _____

4. _____

5. _____

Letter/Video to Nonoffending Parent(s) (Therapy Group Only)

GOALS

To understand the dynamics of abuse; to build self-esteem; to recognize boundaries; to learn to manage triggers; to build self-protection and feelings of safety and trust

AGES

4 through 18

TIME

30 minutes in the first session; 20-30 minutes in the following session (Parts III and IV are done in individual therapy.)

PURPOSE

This exercise allows group members to express what the abuse experience was like for them and what they need from their nonoffending parents or other caregivers for further protection. It helps group members to begin to place accountability and responsibility for the abuse with the appropriate persons. This exercise helps to both heal and improve relationships between abused children and their nonoffending parents. The parents will work with their own therapists on letters to their children.

Grotsky, Camerer, and Damiano, *Group Work With Sexually Abused Children.* Copyright 2000, Sage Publications, Inc.

DO THIS EXERCISE TO

- Reduce levels of fear, shame, and isolation.
- Increase the children's capacity to be vulnerable and to interact authentically.
- Increase the children's capacity to desire, believe in, and hold hope for a positive future.
- Increase the children's capacity to separate the self from the abuse/abuser.
- Increase the children's capacity to place responsibility and accountability appropriately.
- Increase the children's ability to define and express personal safety needs.

DO NOT USE THIS EXERCISE WHEN

- Any of the nonoffending parents or other caregivers are not receiving group or individual therapy.
- Any parents or other caregivers are unable to write their own letters to their children in therapy and therefore will probably be unable to be supportive of their children.

WHAT YOU NEED

- Copy of "Questions for Children to Answer Before Writing to Their Nonoffending Parents/Caregivers"
- Paper and pens
- Video camera if desired (especially useful for young children's groups)

INSTRUCTIONS

Part I: Pass out pencils and paper. Go through the items on the "Questions for Children" list one by one, having members write down their answers as you ask the questions. After each question, ask one or two members to share what they have written so that you are sure they are understanding the questions. Ask more clarifying questions if necessary. As the children finish, give them a choice (as a group) whether they want to put their answers into letter form for their parents or if they would prefer to videotape their answers. Instruct them to spend the next week thinking about anything else they want their parents to know about the abuse or about their feelings or thoughts regarding it.

If the children in the group are too young to write, have them answer the questions orally. Simplify the questions so that they can understand them.

Part II: Do not do Part II until the following week. If you are videotaping the children's letters, have the group members all on one side of the room with the video camera and a chair set up on the other side. One by one, have each member sit in the chair and answer the questions while you videotape him. Because the children thought about their answers the week before, they should be able to answer the questions easily. If a child leaves something out that he mentioned the week before, you may want to prompt him. Instruct those waiting their turns to sit quietly and to be attentive. You may want to let them color while they are waiting so they do not get too restless. After each person finishes, applaud his efforts and allow the group to share any positive comments.

For older children who have chosen to write letters, have them use their answers from the previous week to compose letters to their parents or other caregivers. Give them at least 20 minutes to do this. When everyone is finished, have each child read his letter aloud to the group.

Part III: Give a copy of each child's letter or video to the individual and/or group therapist working with the child's parent. We always have each parent view the letter or video once in therapy without the child being present. This way the parent has time to react authentically without worrying about how her reaction will affect the child. The therapist can help the parent decide what she would like to say to the child later. Naturally, the parent should receive help to process any feelings the letter or video brings up.

Part IV: This part is done with both the parent's and the child's individual therapists. The parent brings her letter to the child to the session, and the child's letter or video is also brought in. The child usually goes first and either reads his letter or shows his video. The child can choose to have someone else read his letter if he wishes, but the letter must be read aloud. After this is completed, the parent responds to the child, commenting on specifics in the letter and asking any clarifying questions. This needs to be a very supportive interaction. Then the parent reads her letter to the child. Afterward, the child gets to ask any further questions or to clarify anything he is confused about. The session ends with the parent agreeing to the ways she can help reduce the child's trigger responses and/or concrete things she can do to keep him safe.

Grotsky, Camerer, and Damiano, *Group Work With Sexually Abused Children.* Copyright 2000, Sage Publications, Inc.

HINTS

This is probably the most powerful and healing exercise we do. It is done when children are far enough along in therapy that they are able to express themselves. The parents must be willing to look at themselves and at the life choices they make that affect their children. Parents often take on either all the blame and guilt for the abuse or none of it at all. Children often do not express their needs and overprotect their parents or blame the nonoffending parents for everything. This exercise helps put the accountability and responsibility where it belongs and breaks down the barriers that may have been built between the child and parent.

Questions for Children to Answer Before Writing
to Their Nonoffending Parents/Caregivers

When asking the following questions, use group members' answers as springboards to other questions. For example, if a child answers the question, "What stopped you from telling your parents?" with "I didn't think I would be believed," probe further, asking, "Why not?" and "Had you not been believed about other things before?"

1. How did it become known that you were being sexually abused?

2. What stopped you from telling your parent (or other caregiver) about the abuse?

3. Had you tried to tell your parent before? If yes, what happened then?

4. Did your not telling have anything to do with feelings or thoughts you had about yourself? Feelings or thoughts about the person touching you? Feelings or thoughts about the parent who wasn't touching you? Can you describe those feelings and thoughts?

5. When your parent did find out, what did she or he do that was helpful to you?

6. What did your parent do that was not helpful?

7. Did your parent believe you when you told?

8. Is there anything else you wish your parent had said or done?

9. Do you feel safe now? If not, what is it that makes you feel unsafe?

10. Is there anything your parent could do differently to help you feel safer? Do you believe your parent is protective of you?

11. What are some of your triggers? How can your parent help you reduce how you react to those triggers?

12. Would you tell your parent if something like this happened again? Why or why not?

13. If some sort of abuse happened to you again, do you think your parent could handle it in a supportive manner?

14. Is there anything else you have not said or that you think your parent should know?

Samples of Letters Written to Nonoffending Parents

Dear Mom [Stepmom] and Dad,

We are getting to tell you some things and it might be hard for you to hear this but I will need you to get ahold of it and listen. (I'm not being mean.) I felt if I told you, you would just tell me to stop lying to you. Stephanie and I felt if we told anyone we would get in trouble, and not Bobby. Now I know that isn't true and I know how I can tell you how I feel and I won't get in trouble.

I don't think it was you and I don't want to hurt you, but I thought that it was all my fault and not Bobby's for drinking. But now I know that it was Bobby who did it, not me.

I thank you for telling me that I didn't do it, but I still think it was my fault. Thank you for being there for me. Here is some more about how I feel: I think I feel safer around you than I would around anyone. I think of everything you have done and I don't think I need anything anymore. I might need some time with just you and Dad or just you or just Dad. I love you a lot.

This trigger doesn't have anything to do with you but I will like you to hear this: It's when my mother doesn't give me any attention and you and Dad were there for me in the summer. And when my mother asked me the question about my braces and not say "hi" or even give me a hug. I felt she hated me.

If this would happen again, I would tell you because I would know to and not hold it in anymore. And if this happened again, I think that I could handle it again because you have already been through it.

I love you and I am sorry that my own mother couldn't be there for me and she was there for him. I love you and thank you.

Jordan [age 10]

Dear Mom,

Mom it was hard for me to tell you because I thought you and "you know who," Jerry, would get in a fight. Mom, you helped me after I told you. Mom, you and Bill and Jane helped me. Thank you. Mom, I wish you had gone to the police or called them at least. Mom, to be safe now, I need you to help me. I am so scared that he is coming back to get me and my brother and you. If I tell you it's important, I need you to listen and give me attention if you aren't busy, and understand. I still get scared.

Sincerely,
Terry [age 12]

Dear Mom and John [Stepdad],

Hello. This is a letter to tell you two about things I need to tell you. (Mom), the reason I didn't tell you right away is that I thought you wouldn't believe me, get mad at me, or be very upset and not have time to sit down with me and make sure I'm okay because you were so busy being happy and letting me do

Samples of Letters Written to Nonoffending Parents *(continued)*

anything I wanted. Also, I didn't tell you because I thought it was going to hurt you a lot more and that I wasn't special enough to be listened to. The things that you did was to let me stay out of school for 2 weeks with you. And also you paid attention to me and I felt you were guarding me from all fears and enemies.

(John) The things that you didn't help me with is you two yelled at me. I didn't feel trusted, protected, very insecure and like I just abused somebody instead of them doing that to me.

(Mom and John) The things that I wish you never said or did was to yell at me, put me down, and killing my ego, and self-esteem/confidence.

I don't want this letter to put down either John or Mom because I love you both and now I'm happy, safe, secure, and still know that I can tell you guys anything, most of the time.

(Mom) I do feel safe now. Thank you for believing me that this was going on. The only triggers I have is seeing my offenders or somebody like them.

(John, Mom) I don't like to hear their names at all or anything about them. So please don't ask questions, or say anything in my presence.

(Mom, John) If I was being abused again I wouldn't tell because how you two acted with Mitchell,* and I don't want to lose any trust or feel different about the way you two see me now. I don't think that I could go through this again because I think I won't be supported.

All you two need to know is to not to say, or talk about my offenders in front of me, and I would tell you two if I was being abused but you two yelled at me and so now my whole opinion has been changed. Sorry.

Always,
Kaylee [age 15]
*Mitchell was someone Kaylee recently met who was "making advances towards her." When she told her parents, they yelled at her.

Sample of a Letter Written by a Group (instead of individual letters)

Dear Mom, Dad, Grandma, Poppa, Aunt, Uncle, and Foster Mom,
We are writing this letter to tell you how we all felt about being touched, what helped us, what was hard, and what we need from you to feel safe.
What made it hard to tell was:

1. I was blackmailed by my offender.
2. I was afraid my mom would be mad.
3. I was ashamed to tell the details of how he did it.
4. I felt icky and gross.
5. I was threatened not to tell.
6. My offender said he would tell my mom that I lied.

(continued)

Grotsky, Camerer, and Damiano, *Group Work With Sexually Abused Children.* Copyright 2000, Sage Publications, Inc.

Samples of Letters Written to Nonoffending Parents *(continued)*

What helped me to tell was:

1. I didn't feel safe and I wanted to feel safe.
2. My heart helped me listen to my inner voice.
3. I just needed to tell because it bothered me.
4. My real dad called.
5. Me saying to my mom that my dad touched me in my private parts and I said he scared me badly so I told on him.

How my family helped me after I told was:

1. She told the whole family and said it wasn't my fault.
2. My family helped me by sending me to counseling.
3. I got into counseling.
4. I got to ride in a police car and go to a foster home.
5. My mom told me how to tell on somebody if they touch me bad or if they treated me meanly, I could say "NO!" and walk away, or tell an adult and scream loudly.

What I wish my family had done differently was:

1. Not go upstairs so my brother would not do that.
2. Called the judge so we could talk.
3. I wished they would keep me away from the person who did it to me.
4. I wish the *whole* family had helped me.
5. Been with me and gave me security and safety and I could have been safer at the time, and scared my dad away from me.

What I need from my family to be safe now is:

1. Lots of love and lots of protection.
2. I wish they would keep me safe and stay by me.
3. Security doors and know who the people who are coming in the house. Get hard windows so nobody can break the window open and steal me. Mom check in with me every 30 minutes. If there are people around me that she doesn't know, only let safe people be around me.
4. To care for me more.
5. A security bubble that won't pop, and my dad being in jail.

chapter 10

TRIGGER RESPONSE EXERCISES

Sexually abused children often experience negative trigger responses. A trigger is any thought, feeling, or bodily sensation activated by a stimulus, causing a temporary loss of current reality. This stimulus is a reminder of the abuse. Often a stimulus is a sound, smell, sight, touch, or taste. Triggers usually happen so fast that the child is not conscious of what is going on. Suddenly the child feels unsafe or anxious but is not sure why. Children often respond dissociatively when triggered, therefore most of the trigger exercises should be done in **therapy groups only.**

All people experience triggers, and triggers can be either positive or negative. For example, imagine sitting in a car repair shop waiting for your car to be serviced when a customer enters carrying a box of freshly baked cookies. With one sniff, you suddenly feel warm and happy. You may or may not know why. You might recognize the smell as chocolate chip cookies and suddenly have a memory of sitting in your grandmother's kitchen. For a few seconds you may feel like you are actually there. You may not have noticed the smell of cookies on a conscious level, but still you were transported momentarily to your grandmother's kitchen. This is a positive trigger response.

A negative or traumatic trigger evokes responses that are mentally, emotionally, or physically distressing. Children who have been sexually abused sometimes experience traumatic trigger responses in the form of vivid intrusive thoughts, images, and sensations. These interpretations and responses are symbolic reminders of the abuse.

When children are triggered by something that represents an aspect of the abuse, they can temporarily lose touch with their present reality. They often feel as if the abusive events are actually taking place in present time. They react to triggers in a conditioned manner and usually have no conscious control over their responses. For instance, imagine a child who was often abused by an alcoholic father. Drunk and out of control, he would stumble into her room, slamming the door closed behind him. With the abuser behind bars, the child has been safe for 2 years. One day, she is coloring quite contentedly on the living room floor when she hears the sound of a door banging shut. Suddenly, she is running out of the living room straight to her bedroom to hide beneath her bed. This child just experienced a negative trigger response. The sound of the slamming door caused her to lose touch with time and reexperience the feelings of terror she felt while being abused.

Due to the intrusive and disintegrating nature of traumatic triggering, children develop defensive coping mechanisms to deal with the recurrence of such experiences. Often they cope by avoiding thoughts and feelings that relate specifically to the abuse. However, these defensive measures often compound the issues rather than resolve them and create more problems than they solve. It is not unusual for some children to try to protect themselves against traumatic thoughts and feelings by regressing to earlier behaviors, such as thumb sucking, clinging, or wanting to be cradled in a parent's lap. Other children may exhibit fearful or phobic behaviors, such as throwing themselves on the floor and screaming to avoid going outside to the backyard, where the abuse occurred. One child we worked with had been abused while watching the TV show *Barney*. He anxiously avoided watching the program and would rip up any advertising he saw of Barney products. For some children the feeling of anxiety alone is an unconscious reminder of abuse. At the slightest hint of anxiety, children may act out, using harmful coping strategies to avoid these feelings. Still other children may act out aggressively, fighting with their siblings at home or with their peers at school. Childrens' particular coping strategies may vary, but the goal is the same. They want to feel safe and secure and to avoid feelings of powerlessness, fear, and anxiety.

The group exercises in this chapter are designed to help children regain a sense of control and safety over the involuntary and intrusive nature of trigger responses. Utilizing the BASK concept (see the introduction to this volume as well as Chapter 8) with the exercises in this chapter, children can be taught what triggers are ("101 Dalmatians"), how to identify their own triggers ("Triggered Memories"), and how to manage experiencing triggers by bringing themselves into present reality ("Centering").

101 Dalmatians

GOAL

To learn about triggers

AGES

4 through 12

TIME

20 minutes

PURPOSE

This exercise is an introduction to the definition of triggers. It is done in a nonthreatening way with a story that most children already know. Again, we would like to thank Patricia Godleman, who recognized *101 Dalmatians* as the perfect story to use when introducing the concept of triggers.

DO THIS EXERCISE TO

- Increase the children's understanding and articulation of trigger reactions.
- Continue to identify and express the internal and external triggers that result in reactive coping behaviors.

DO NOT USE THIS EXERCISE WHEN

There is no reason not to do this exercise.

WHAT YOU NEED

- A short, well-illustrated picture-book version of *101 Dalmatians*
- Paper
- Pens and pencils

INSTRUCTIONS

Part I: Explain to the group what a trigger is (see the example in Part I of "Elizabeth's Triggers"). Then read *101 Dalmatians* aloud to the group, showing the illustrations as you go.

Part II: When you finish the story, pass out paper and pencils and ask the group members to write down anything they think might trigger the puppies after their bad experiences with Cruella DeVille. Remind them to think of triggers the puppies might feel, see, hear, or smell. For example:

- Black and white hair
- Fur coats
- Smell of smoke
- Feel of cold snow
- Sound of moving trucks
- Sound of the TV

Part III: Have each child share the triggers she thought of with the group. Then ask the group members to guess:

- How do the puppies feel when they are being triggered?
- What thoughts go through the puppies' heads when they are being triggered?

Part IV: Ask the group members to write down some things they think might help comfort the puppies when they are being triggered. Some examples:

- Tell their mom or dad.
- Tell their nanny.
- Lie in their puppy baskets.

- Listen to Roger play piano music.
- Notice they are now safe.
- Cuddle with the other puppies.

Ask the group members to share their answers with each other.

HINTS

Obviously, younger children are not able to do the writing part of this exercise, but they will happily express their ideas aloud in response to questions. Young children have a hard time grasping the concept of triggers. They may confuse a trigger response with being tricked. Help them understand how to be conscious of their feelings by listening to their bodies and minds. Explain that their bodies and their minds let them know when they are being triggered. For example, "When my mom says we get to go to the toy store, I want to burst with happiness and then scream and yell and jump up and down. That's because I remember that I had so much fun there the last time. My memory of going there triggers all these feelings and thoughts inside me. These are nice triggers." Or: "When my mother says we're going to fly on the airplane, I can feel the pressure in my ears, and I think, 'Oh, I might not be safe,' and then I feel all sleepy because I was so bored the last time we flew. This time when Mommy told me about flying, memories and thoughts were triggered and I didn't feel that great."

This exercise is a good introduction to triggers. Because it does not involve the abuse that the children experienced, it allows them to more fully understand the concept of triggers. When doing this exercise, do not ask the group members about how they were triggered when they were abused. Leave that discussion for another week, or they will be too overwhelmed.

Elizabeth's Triggers
(Therapy Group Only)

GOAL

To learn about triggers

AGES

6 through 12

TIME

15-20 minutes

PURPOSE

This exercise helps group members begin to look at triggers by using a third-person perspective. The children learn to name Elizabeth's triggers and, by doing so, begin to identify their own.

DO THIS EXERCISE TO

- Begin to identify personal triggers.
- Increase the children's understanding and articulation of trigger reactions.
- Help the children identify and express the internal and external triggers that result in reactive coping behaviors.

DO NOT USE THIS EXERCISE WHEN

- There are any vulnerable children in group who may adopt Elizabeth's story as their own.

WHAT YOU NEED

- Copy of "Elizabeth's Story"
- Copies of "Elizabeth's Triggers" worksheet
- Pens or pencils

INSTRUCTIONS

Part I: Begin by explaining to the group what triggers are: They are reminders of experiences. Note that when we are reminded of experiences, this sometimes brings back old thoughts or feelings. Give an example of a good trigger, such as the following:

Imagine your mom tells you that you get to buy a new puppy. Imagine you go to someone's house and there is a box of puppies there. One little brown furry puppy jumps right out of the box and comes over to you and gives you a big kiss on the face. Two years later, when your puppy has grown big, you still might get triggered from that time you picked her up. These positive triggers remind you of thoughts and feelings you had when you first met her. For example, whenever you see a little puppy it reminds you of that first time you saw your puppy and you feel all warm inside. That is a positive trigger. Or every time you get a wet lick on your face you remember the first time she kissed you. Again, maybe it gives you a tingly feeling on your face and the feeling makes you want to hug someone. The kiss is the trigger and your feelings and behaviors are how you react to that trigger. Maybe whenever an animal comes to you, you might think, "I'm nice, animals like me." You then had a positive thought pop into your head because of being triggered by a good memory.

Then give an example of a negative trigger, such as the following:

Imagine that you have the flu and are lying on the couch. You have a fever and feel terrible. You are watching TV and a commercial comes on and shows a big greasy hamburger with lots of cheese. You look at it and you have to go throw up. Now, it is possible that a year or two later, you may see that same commercial and feel nauseated, like you want to throw up. It is not that you are sick now. It is simply that without realizing it, you have been triggered and your body and mind are reminded of those old feelings that never got healed inside you. Until they are healed, this trigger might keep happening. Recognizing a trigger can help you to have a choice about how to take care of yourself when you feel or remember the abuse.

Part II: Read "Elizabeth's Story" aloud to the group and ask group members to be aware of what might trigger Elizabeth. Instruct them to think about what feelings and thoughts might get triggered for her later in life.

Part III: After you finish the story, pass out copies of the "Elizabeth's Triggers" worksheet and have group members write down individually any triggers they think Elizabeth might have from Uncle Tim's actions. Have them include the feelings and thoughts she might have as she is being triggered.

Part IV: Also on the worksheet, have them write down anything that might comfort Elizabeth when she is being triggered.

Part V: Have the children come back together as a group and have each member share the triggers she wrote down and the ways she thinks that Elizabeth can comfort herself.

HINTS

Pay close attention to each member's thoughts and feelings about Elizabeth's story, because they will probably express what most fits the child's own. Group members will probably have a hard time coming up with thoughts, so you may need to help them with this. Ask them what Elizabeth might have been thinking about herself when her uncle was touching her. Was it "I am so stupid" or "I wish I could make him stop"? (In other words, "I'm helpless"?) The thoughts mentioned will help you to identify the core beliefs of each group member, and thus help you to understand what coping mechanisms each uses to try to make her core beliefs a reality.

After doing this exercise, group members usually have a much easier time identifying their own triggers.

Elizabeth's Story

Seven-year-old Elizabeth had lots of friends and loved school. Her mom and dad worked during the day but they spent lots of time with her at night and on Saturdays and Sundays. Once in a while, when they went out, her mom and dad would invite Uncle Tim to baby-sit Elizabeth. Uncle Tim was not really her uncle, but the family had known him since Elizabeth was just 2 years old. He lived near them and he loved kids. He taught Elizabeth how to ride her bike and taught her how to roller-skate down at the roller rink.

Elizabeth's mom and dad used to tell all their friends how lucky they were to have Uncle Tim around. They felt good knowing that there was another adult in Elizabeth's life. She loved him and loved talking to him. He was like a member of their family and joined them for all their holidays, including birthdays. Once a year, Elizabeth's mom and dad would go away for two or three days and Uncle Tim would take care of Elizabeth.

When Elizabeth turned 7, Uncle Tim started acting kind of weird. He hugged Elizabeth in a way that made her feel yucky. He kept wanting her to sit on his lap when he read her stories, but she did not like the way he touched her chest while he was reading. One time he tried to kiss her on her lips. She remembered he had this faraway look in his eyes and his breath smelled liked peppermint. She turned her head really quickly and so he kissed her cheek instead. It was a really wet kiss.

Sometimes, Uncle Tim acted just like he used to. He would be really goofy and lots of fun. But one day something really weird happened. Elizabeth's mom and dad had gone to the movies and Uncle Tim was taking care of her. She went to sleep and woke up feeling someone touching her back and forth on her private parts. She knew it was Uncle Tim because her night-light was on and when she opened her eyes a tiny bit she could see his flannel shirt. She felt really scared and didn't know what to do, so she kept her eyes shut and pretended she was sleeping. She was hoping that if she didn't move, he would go away. Then he kissed her cheek and she could feel his mustache tickling her. Still pretending she was asleep, she turned around and curled up into a little ball. He got up then, but right before he left the room he said, "You're my special girl. Don't tell anyone, this is our special secret."

The next day, when she woke up, she thought maybe she had been dreaming. She didn't see Uncle Tim for a few days, but when she did her stomach started to hurt. He baby-sat her one more time and came into her room again. Once more she pretended she was asleep. She hated the sound of his breathing and couldn't stand how he kept shaking the bed.

The next day she told her parents about Uncle Tim. Her mom started to cry, but she also hugged Elizabeth and told her she was glad she had told. Her mom and dad told her that Uncle Tim would never baby-sit for them again and that they would not even let him in the house again.

(continued)

Elizabeth's Story *(continued)*

This confused Elizabeth a little bit because she really liked Uncle Tim most of the time. She just didn't like him doing that touching stuff. But then she was kind of relieved she didn't have to see him because she knew if she did, then her stomach would start feeling weird again.

She didn't tell many of her friends what happened because she was kind of embarrassed by it. Then she got to be in a group with all these other kids who all had similar things happen to them. She was so glad she wasn't the only one! The group was super fun and it lasted for lots of weeks. When it was over she didn't feel so bad anymore.

She still isn't positive why Uncle Tim did what he did. She is glad he won't be able to do it to her anymore.

In the columns below, write down Elizabeth's triggers, her feelings and thoughts when she has the triggers and how she can find comfort when she is triggered.

Elizabeth's Triggers		
Triggers	*Feelings and Thoughts*	*Comforts*

Centering

GOALS

To learn about internal boundaries; to learn to manage triggers; to build self-protection skills

AGES

5 through 18

TIME

10 minutes

PURPOSE

This exercise presents a technique that is essential for all sexually abused children to learn. It teaches children how to bring themselves back to present time when they are being triggered or experiencing flashbacks in relation to the abuse.

DO THIS EXERCISE TO

- Decrease dissociative behavior when abuse is mentioned.
- Help the children identify and express the internal and external triggers that result in reactive coping behaviors.
- Decrease trigger reactivity.
- Increase the children's ability to manage trigger responses.

DO NOT USE THIS EXERCISE WHEN

There is no reason not to do this exercise. However, if anyone in the group has a cold or is feeling ill, use a different past experience then one of remembering an illness.

WHAT YOU NEED

No special materials needed

INSTRUCTIONS

Part I: Have group members sit in a circle, and explain to them that this exercise can be used anytime and anyplace. Tell them that you are going to teach them how to keep themselves aware, focused, and in the "here and now" when they want to be. Ask them if they daydream often, or suddenly have bad memories about the abuse and feel like they are reexperiencing it. This simple exercise will help them better manage those times.

Part II: Have everyone close their eyes and think about a time they had the flu or a really bad cold. Tell them to remember how they felt, saying, "For a few moments let yourself feel the illness." Then ask:

- Is your head full or stuffy?
- How does your stomach feel?
- Do you have a fever?

Now tell them you are going to bring them back to present time. All they need to do is keep their eyes closed and follow your instructions. They are to answer your questions in their heads, not aloud. Say the following to them:

- I want you to say in your head, "I am not sick. I am remembering a time that was long ago. I am safe and healthy now."
- Notice your body. Feel your feet on the floor. Notice the weight of your arms and what your arms are touching. Notice your back and bottom. Feel the parts of the chair, floor, or pillow your body has contact with.

- What are the sounds you hear? Do you hear the sound of birds outside or the rustling movement of your friends near you?
- Notice the temperature. Do you feel warm or cool?
- Do you feel any sensations on your body, like a cool breeze or the soft feel of your shirt?
- Open your eyes and look around. What colors do you see? What pictures or drawings are on the wall? Notice the room you are in and who is around you.
- Again, say to yourself, "I am safe and healthy. I am not sick. I was remembering a time when I was sick but now I am not. That was then and this is now."
- Now take a deep breath and really feel yourself being present in this room.

Part III: Discuss what this experience was like for everybody to do. Were they able to come back to the here and now? Explain that when they are reexperiencing the abuse, they can do this exercise to bring themselves to the present. The main things they need to remember to tell themselves are these:

- I am safe now.
- That was then, this is now.
- I can use all of my senses—sight, sound, smell, touch, and taste—to bring myself back to the here and now.
- I am safe.

Part IV: As homework, have group members practice centering during the next week. Follow up in the next group session to support and encourage them in practicing centering.

HINTS

Once you have introduced this exercise, use it often in group. Whenever you notice a child withdrawing or dissociating, use it. Use it if the children are becoming very distracted or inattentive. The more practice they have with centering, the greater the likelihood that they will use it automatically. If they begin to use this technique daily, they will have a much easier time managing triggers; they will be able to experience the world as it happens and participate in it more fully.

Drawing Where Molested
(Therapy Group Only)

GOALS

To learn to manage triggers; to build feelings of safety and trust; to learn about internal boundaries

AGES

5 through 12

TIME

15-20 minutes

PURPOSE

Drawing the locations where they were molested can help to desensitize group members and make it easier for them to talk about their abuse. The drawings also help the facilitators as well as group members begin to identify some of the children's trigger points regarding the abuse.

DO THIS EXERCISE TO

- Reduce levels of fear, shame, and isolation.
- Begin to increase the children's ability to identify and manage trigger responses.

DO NOT USE THIS EXERCISE WHEN

- There has been no previous discussion of management and containment of triggers. Many children will be triggered by doing this exercise. Do one of the earlier trigger exercises first, so they understand the concept.

WHAT YOU NEED

- Drawing paper
- Markers, crayons, or colored pencils

INSTRUCTIONS

Part I: Have group members find comfortable places in the room where they will not be disturbed or distracted. They can lie down and you can lower the lights as long as it is not too dark. Tell them that you will be leading them in a guided imagery exercise. Have them close their eyes and begin to focus on their breathing. Lead them through a brief progressive relaxation and then ask them to remember a place where they were sexually abused. Remind them that they are safe, that this is only a memory and nothing can hurt them here in this room.

Tell them, when they can imagine the place where they were sexually abused, to let themselves continue to relax and notice what that place looks like. Ask questions such as the following:

- What is it like there?
- Is it inside or outside?
- Are there any furnishings or other objects around?
- Are there people or animals there?
- What time of day is it?
- If the place is inside, are there any windows or doors? If so, can you see outside?
- What else can you see?
- Is it hot or cold out?
- Do you notice any smells or noises?

Continue to remind them that no one is going to hurt them, that the memories are from the past and they are safe now. Reassure them that if they do not feel safe now, you will do everything you can to help them feel safe. Encourage them to remember everything they can about the places where their abuse happened. Ask them to come back to the group room with as much of this memory as they can.

Part II: As group members return from the guided imagery exercise, have them immediately start drawing the places where they were abused, and include any sensory descriptions. For example, a child might draw his bedroom in the dark with snow outside of the house. As group members complete this task, invite them to come back into a circle to discuss their drawings with the group. While they share their drawings, have group members state what objects or sensory memories they have drawn in their pictures trigger them now. You may need to ask some very specific questions to elicit this information. For example, you might say, "I notice you drew a spider in the corner. Do you have any big feelings or thoughts when you see spiders now?"

Part III: End the day's session with a centering exercise. Have the children notice the colors in the room, feel their bodies touching the floor or their chairs, notice the air in the room and how it smells. Have the group members say to themselves, "I am safe now. I was abused back then, but this is now. I am safe now." This will help them stay in the present and not get lost in the memories triggered by their drawings.

HINTS

It is important to take notes about the children's triggers during the discussion part of this exercise so that you can help them identify when they are being triggered in the future. Give group members the power to decide how much they feel comfortable sharing about their abuse. Ask each group member's permission before you allow other participants to ask him questions about his abuse and where it took place.

The places the children remember while doing this exercise may be where they were abused once or repeatedly. Their reactions to these memories can vary greatly. Pay close attention to how the children describe these places and what occurred there. Ask them how thinking about these memories again makes them feel. Be certain they feel all right before they leave the group setting. With older children, encourage them to exchange phone numbers. Make certain that younger children have some adult to talk to at home if the need arises. Also, inform the children's

---

parents or other caregivers about this exercise so they can be supportive after the children leave the safety of the group setting.

In a recent teen group, two members drew pictures and described their triggers in the following ways. Jody drew an open field behind a school and car exhaust at night. She said she had her eyes closed or looked at the stars. She reported not remembering any sounds, except the voice of the man who raped her. She mentioned these images and memories, saying that they brought up more and more anger. She commented that she is "realizing it is wrong and he's responsible." She stated she doesn't feel sad anymore, just angry at "the system" (which let him go). Beth drew pictures of two houses she had lived in. She reported that the abuse took place in "every room of the house." She stated that she is bothered when she sees others with hair or a similar walk or run as her brother. Beth remembers the cologne he wore. In her old house, there was always someone else at home when she was abused. She would crawl out her window onto a roof, and her brother would come and get her there and abuse her. She said that now she is afraid of heights.

Triggered Memories
(Therapy Group Only)

GOALS

To learn to manage triggers; to learn about internal and external boundaries

AGES

4 through 18

TIME

20-30 minutes

PURPOSE

Sexual abuse survivors often have memories of their abuse restimulated or triggered by something in their environments. Suddenly they are reliving the experience, but they don't know why. By learning to identify the triggers, survivors learn ways to increase their ability to manage these automatic responses. For example, they learn to stay in the present time and consciously recognize the stimulus that has triggered them.

DO THIS EXERCISE TO

- Decrease dissociative behavior when abuse is mentioned.
- Help the children identify and express the internal and external triggers that result in reactive coping behaviors.
- Decrease trigger reactivity.

- Increase the children's ability to manage trigger responses.

DO NOT USE THIS EXERCISE WHEN

- The group has not had lengthy discussions of triggers and has not done previous exercises concerning triggers. (Group members must already understand that triggers can be positive and negative.)
- The group has not previously done the exercises "101 Dalmatians," "Elizabeth's Triggers," and/or "Drawing Where Molested."
- Group members dissociate to such a degree when they are triggered that it is difficult to bring them back to the present.

WHAT YOU NEED

- Drawing paper
- Crayons or markers

INSTRUCTIONS

Part I: Review with the group what triggers are and have group members share a few examples to make sure they understand the concept. Then ask all the children to draw on their own pieces of paper all the things that trigger memories of the abuse for them. Remind them to include sights, smells, objects, feelings, touches, and tastes.

Part II: Have each person share her drawing with the group and talk about each of her triggers. Find out if there are any triggers that can be taken care of immediately. In other words, if a child's trigger is a teddy bear or a pillow, you can talk to the parents about getting rid of such objects so they do not act as constant reminders of the abuse. Maybe the child should be moved to a different bedroom, or an award that says she is "special" removed from the wall. Most triggers are not taken care of so easily, however; they can include such things as colors and odors (such as the smell of cigarettes).

Part III: Do a guided imagery with the children. With older groups, you can have them lie on the floor, close their eyes, and relax. With younger children you might want to have them stay in their chairs with their eyes shut. Have them take three deep breaths to relax themselves. Ask them to imagine all of the tension leaving their bodies each time they exhale. Do not spend a lot of time on relaxation, as you want them to stay somewhat in the here and now.

Have them imagine one of their triggers. Ask them to respond to the following questions and instructions in silence:

- How do you feel as you experience this trigger?
- How does your body feel?
- Is any part of your body tight?
- How is your breathing? Now breathe slow and easy. [Lead them by saying, slowly, "In, out, and again, in, out." Do this two or three times.] Keep breathing slowly while experiencing the trigger. Relax your body even while you see the trigger in your mind. You can relax every muscle in your body. Keep breathing and relaxing.
- Now look at that trigger and know it can't hurt you.
- Say to yourself, "You can't hurt me. I am okay. I am strong. I am not being sexually abused now. I am right here in a room with other people and I am safe. I am all right. I am breathing, I am relaxed, and I am safe."
- Know that you can do this anytime you see or feel a trigger. Just breathe, relax, and stay in the present.
- Be aware of where you are and tell yourself over and over again that you are okay.

Slowly bring them back to the room, telling them, in sequence:

- Feel the carpet underneath you.
- Notice what parts of your body are touching the floor.
- Hear the sounds in the room.
- Feel the air temperature.
- When you are ready, open your eyes and look around the room.

Part IV: Tell them that their homework assignment is to practice this exercise during the week. Whenever they feel scared, or "triggered," they are to talk to themselves about being in the present and tell themselves that they are okay. Ideally, they'll be in situations where they can do the entire imagery.

HINTS

A good follow-up exercise to this one is "My Safety and Comforts" (see Chapter 11).

Keep a close eye on group members while they are doing their drawings and make sure they stay in the present. If anyone appears to need help staying in the present, talk to her about what she is feeling in her body and where she is feeling it, and remind her that she is safe now. Tell her to look around and to name the different people in the room. Repeat over and over again, "The abuse was then, this is now. You are safe now. Look around. Feel yourself in the room. You are safe." (Use this technique only when you are sure the child is not currently in an abusive situation.)

While doing this exercise, 7-year-old Carrie drew the basement where her brother used to abuse her. She drew it as a very stark place with a bare lightbulb, stacks of boxes, a Ping-Pong table, spiders, and a pull-out couch. She hated to go down to the basement. After doing this exercise, she decided to reclaim the basement as her own. She went down there, added pillows and stuffed animals she liked, moved things around, and made it into a comfortable room for herself.

Sometimes the drawings of triggers give hints of ritualistic or sadistic abuse. If any child's drawing has a lot of religious symbols, masks, snakes, or animals being hurt, consider this a red flag and make sure that the child is also in individual counseling. Beth, a 4-year-old, constantly drew blood in all her pictures. Every person was bleeding and her pages would be covered with splotches and smears of red representing blood. The pictures were too frightening for the other children. In an effort to not alienate her and unduly frighten the other children, the facilitators chose not to have the children share their drawings with the entire group. Instead, they went to the children individually and had them share their drawings with the facilitators only.

Samples of Children's Triggers

Guy with long hair
Guys named Ron
His brother
His family
If anyone brings up the subject of sexual abuse
Going to group
People asking me why I have to go to counseling

Christy [age 9]

Blond hair
Yelling
A laugh like his
Thinking about it
Hearing his name mentioned
Beaded necklaces
Being under my bed
Seeing pictures or movies where people kiss or have sex

Katherine [age 10]

How We
Sabotage Ourselves

GOALS

To learn to manage triggers; to learn about internal boundaries; to build self-esteem

AGES

9 through 18

TIME

60-90 minutes

PURPOSE

Children who have been abused often engage in behaviors that result in their hurting themselves. Many of them have learned to act helpless, which can set them up to be revictimized. This exercise helps group members identify their own self-destructive behaviors and teaches them to choose healthier ones as substitutes.

DO THIS EXERCISE TO

- Increase the children's capacity to make conscious behavioral choices.
- Help the children recognize how they keep themselves in a victim's role.
- Build self-empowerment and social skills.
- Begin to decrease and manage trigger reactivity.

DO NOT USE THIS EXERCISE WHEN

- There is not enough time to complete it adequately.

WHAT YOU NEED

- Copies of the "Sabotage" checklist
- Pencils
- Chalkboard and chalk

INSTRUCTIONS

Part I: Pass out copies of the "Sabotage" checklist and have group members fill them out individually. Then ask them to go back over their checklists and put asterisks by the three sabotaging behaviors they do most often.

Part II: Have each member read her asterisked behaviors to the large group. Write down the behaviors she mentions as part of a general list on the chalkboard. Role-play two or three of the behaviors that most group members use. For example, if many members pout and whine, make up a role-play such as the following: "Mary wants to spend time with Ellen, but Ellen has already made plans to be with Jennifer." Have group members play Ellen and Mary. Have Mary ask Ellen to play with her and, when Ellen says she can't, have Mary pout and whine. Notice what Ellen does then. After the role-play, ask the child who played Ellen how she felt when Mary reacted that way. Ask the child who played Mary how she felt when she was pouting and whining. What feelings was she trying to express?

Part III: Repeat the role-play, but this time ask for volunteers to play Mary and have them come up with healthier ways to respond. For example, one person playing Mary may say, "Gee, would it be all right if I joined you and Jennifer?" Another might say, "Can we make plans to play together another day?" After each of these role-plays, have the players comment on how they were affected by the responses.

Continue the role-plays with the other two sabotaging behaviors most common to the group members.

Part IV: Ask each group member to name one behavior that she will work on changing during the next week. Instruct each to choose one behavior she would like other group members to "call her on" when they notice her doing it. Make sure that you follow up on this assignment during the next session.

HINTS

Ask group members to fill out the "Sabotage" checklists as honestly as possible. They should not talk with others while they are doing so.

During the role-plays, it may be difficult for some group members to stay in their roles. You may want to play a character in the initial role-play to help demonstrate how to play a role and how to stay in it.

This exercise can help group members take responsibility for their own behaviors. Katie, a 12-year-old, used to complain each week about how she never felt included with her friends and how they did not like her as much as they liked each other. After this exercise, she realized that whenever she walked with them she was always one or two steps behind and that she never initiated contact with them. Instead, she would wait for them to call her. Her homework assignment from this exercise was to walk right in line with them and to initiate an activity with one of her friends. She returned the following week and reported gleefully that her friends had been thrilled she initiated something, and for the first time she felt included with them.

Sabotage

Place a check mark by any of the behaviors that you do. You do not need to turn this paper in when you are done with it. We will ask you to share some of your answers with the group. Please be as honest as you can. You will not have to share anything you do not want to share.

_____ I get sick a lot.

_____ I skip out of school.

_____ I don't do my homework.

_____ I say mean things to other people.

_____ If someone is getting too close to me, I start a fight.

_____ When I am angry, I cry instead.

_____ I get high using alcohol, illegal drugs, or prescription medication.

_____ I don't stay friends with anyone very long.

_____ I feel like an outsider, like I never fit in with anyone.

_____ I feel sorry for myself a lot.

_____ I hang around people who say mean things to me and put me down a lot.

_____ I don't take anything seriously. I make jokes about everything and act like a clown.

_____ I blame other people when things don't go right for me.

_____ I'm kind of negative and criticize other people a fair amount.

_____ I always think it is my fault whenever something goes wrong.

_____ I don't let people know how I feel.

_____ I hardly ever feel angry.

_____ I skip meals almost every day.

_____ I hardly ever get enough sleep.

_____ I keep myself super busy.

_____ I'm always late for school and appointments.

_____ I sleep too much.

_____ I'm always tired.

_____ I eat a lot of junk food.

_____ When I don't get what I want, I pout and whine a lot.

_____ I act tough even when I'm feeling hurt.

_____ If I'm mad about something, I just withdraw. I go to my room or I just won't talk.

(continued)

Sabotage

_____ If I am feeling hurt or angry, I hit, kick, or punch others.

_____ I tease other people a lot.

_____ I yell a lot when I am angry or hurt.

_____ [For girls] I flirt or act really silly and giggly around boys or men.

_____ [For boys] I talk about girls all the time and try to kiss them and get sexual with them as fast as I can.

_____ [For girls] I wear clothes that look pretty sexy or that show a lot of my body.

_____ I eat whenever I am feeling mad or hurt.

_____ I act like I don't care or like nothing bothers me, like I'll say, "No big deal," even though it might be.

_____ I have sex with others I don't really love.

_____ I don't join any clubs or groups or try to meet friends.

_____ I wait for others to come to me to say they want to be friends.

_____ I'm really stubborn and won't give in.

_____ I always seem to be in some sort of crisis.

_____ I tell lies.

_____ I spend a lot of time figuring out ways to get back at people who have hurt me or made me mad.

_____ I feel jealous a lot.

_____ Others (write them below):

_____

_____

_____

_____

_____

_____

_____

Secret Soliloquy
(Therapy Group Only)

GOALS

To learn to manage triggers; to build feelings of trust and safety; to learn about internal boundaries

AGES

9 through 18

TIME

20 minutes (if only sharing two to three secrets per week)

PURPOSE

Children who have been sexually abused often have parts of the abuse they never share because they feel so humiliated or scared about them. This psychodrama exercise attempts to set up a safe way for them to air those secrets without being identified. This helps children feel accepted by seeing that others can understand them. This in turn reduces their sense of shame and often reduces their trigger response pattern. (We adapted this very intense and powerful exercise from one that we learned at a psychodrama workshop in Eugene, Oregon, that was led by Ann Taylor.)

DO THIS EXERCISE TO

- Encourage further disclosure by group members you suspect are withholding major parts of their stories.

- Reduce levels of fear, shame, and isolation.
- Increase feelings of safety.
- Increase the children's capacity to value themselves and others.
- Further assess the safety of group members.
- Identify, manage, and reduce trigger responses.

DO NOT USE THIS EXERCISE WHEN

- You believe some group members may make fun of the secrets or badger others to reveal which secrets belong to them.
- There is not enough time to do the exercise fully.

WHAT YOU NEED

- A shoe box or similar container
- Matching paper and pens for everybody

INSTRUCTIONS

Part I: Ask the group members to take a few minutes to think about one aspect of their abuse they have never told anyone. This could be something that happened to them or something they were forced to do to somebody else. It may be a feeling they have about themselves, the abuse, or the offender. It could be that they are still being abused.

Ask them to write down their secrets about themselves or their families, but not to put their names on the papers. Emphasize to the group members that they are not to guess whose secret is whose, and explain that they are revealing these secrets so they will no longer be burdened by them. Even the most embarrassing, humiliating, shameful secret can come up here. In fact, chances are that someone else has the same secret. No one will be asked to talk about his own secret. Point out that everyone has the same color and size of paper and the same color pens, so they can't identify whose secret is whose. Ask all group members to fold their papers in the same way, and demonstrate exactly how you want the papers folded.

Give the group 2 minutes to write down their secrets. Tell them to write clearly, so that someone else can easily read what they have written. Have each person write only one secret. When they are done, have them place their folded papers in a box with everyone else's.

Part II: Mix up all the folded papers and have each person pick one out of the container. If anyone picks his own secret, have him put it back and pick another one. (If the last person picks his own, have the group return all the secrets to the container and start the process over again.)

Ask for a volunteer who is willing to start. The volunteer is to read the secret he has picked from the box as if it were his own. Then he is to "soliloquize"—that is, talk about how he feels regarding this secret. For example, the secret John has picked says, "My father put his penis in my mouth and made me suck on it." John reads that aloud and then continues, "It was really gross. I wanted to throw up. I feel so ashamed, I can't believe I did that. . . ." Thus John talks as if the secret happened to him.

If anyone gets stuck, a facilitator or another member of the group can "double" for him. The double can stand behind him and act like the secret happened to him and begin to soliloquize. If the group gets a good feel for how to double, then anyone can double for the person soliloquizing at any time (say his feelings and then sit down). This encourages a lot of members to share how it feels to have a particular secret. In addition, through doubling, the person whose secret it is may feel safe enough to talk about it anonymously. Through this exercise, each person also gets to see how commonly shared his feelings are.

If the secrets are quite heavy, you may want to do only two or three in a session. After every two or three soliloquized secrets, stop to process the feelings in the group. Ask:

- Are there any comments?
- Do any of you feel like this too?
- Did any of these secrets particularly hit home for you?

Part III: Tell group members that they are welcome to share their secrets in future group sessions, but no one is expected to.

HINTS

If anyone starts trying to guess whose secrets are whose, even jokingly, intervene immediately. Remind him that this is a safe place, and part of feeling safe means knowing that you will not be laughed at, put down, judged, or identified against your will.

Once during this exercise we discovered that one of the teens in our group was suicidal. Just talking about her secret relieved some of the pressure for her.

Usually, this exercise reveals further details of the children's abuse. You may have group members who say they do not have any secrets. Stress to them that virtually everyone has at least one thought or feeling he has never shared. It may be "I don't like the way my body looks," or "I think most girls are ugly." Everyone has at least one thought or feeling that he has not shared with others. Tell them they must come up with something.

chapter **11**

HEALTHY BODY IMAGE AND SELF-PROTECTION EXERCISES

A body can become a frightening, dangerous, and powerful reality for a sexually abused child. Because it is "the body" that seems to attract the abuser's attention (threats, touches, tricks, violations, and manipulations), it is "the body" that a child learns to fear and wishes to escape, control, or use to defend against the abuse.

Children's developing ideas and images about themselves and others are shaped largely by their relationships. Abusive relationships confuse and distort a child's self-image. The dynamics of sexual abuse often negatively influence children's ideas about who they are, how they look and feel, and how others view them.

Healthy body image and self-protection exercises are used to correct these distorted images and to give children a better sense of their bodies and themselves. These exercises are designed to help children create self-images that are not defined solely in relation to their sexual abuse. This requires guidance, support, and encouragement.

The reality of abuse forces many children to choose coping behaviors that, over time, can cause further harm to them and keep them isolated from others. Not all children respond in the same ways to being sexually abused. In our experience, some of the ways sexually abused children cope with their negative body images include the following:

- *Developing strong contempt for their bodies:* Children who view their bodies with contempt see their bodies as having betrayed them, especially if they became aroused during their abuse experiences. They may blame themselves for the abuse and believe it is the fault of their bodies' shape or allure. These children may physically harm themselves by being very accident-prone or by cutting on themselves. As they get older, they may develop

243

eating disorders. They may try to hide their bodies with layers of clothes or try to blend into the background by constricting their activities and participation in social situations.

- *Dissociating from the reality of their bodies:* Many sexually abused children basically feel numb from the neck down. Often they will not feel pleasure or pain. They may ignore parts of their bodies that feel too threatening. These children may not be very physically active. As they get older, they may be asexual, simply having little or no sexual desire.

- *Acting out sexually and aggressively toward others:* In an attempt to master their feelings of vulnerability and powerlessness, some children may try to control and overpower others.

- *Exhibiting seductive behavior in an attempt to increase their desirability to others:* Sexually abused children who act seductively believe they are objects of desire and display learned exhibitionistic and sexualized behavior with peers and adults. These children may be confused by the negative responses they receive for their behavior. Sexualized children often seek attention and admiration in place of intimacy.

Most children who have been sexually abused on an ongoing basis fear intimacy because it increases the possibility of exposure and vulnerability. When children who have been abused learn to separate what happened to them from how they coped and who they are, their true nature and potential may be developed.

Through their introduction to the "Body Bill of Rights," sexually abused children learn their most basic rights and responsibilities concerning their bodies. For many of these children, these are brand-new concepts.

It is important for sexually abused children to develop clearer and more realistic views of their bodies. Exercises that can help them do this include "Body Rights and Responsibilities" and "Body Tracing."

Once the children have more realistic views of themselves, they recognize their rights to physical and emotional protection. This enables them to assert their boundaries with strength and conviction. It is then much easier for them to learn and practice self-protection skills and to believe that they have a right and responsibility to express their needs in a clear and direct manner.

Body Rights
and Responsibilities

GOALS

To build self-protection skills and healthy sexuality; to learn about internal boundaries

AGES

9 through 12

TIME

20-40 minutes (depending on the size of the group)

PURPOSE

This exercise helps children identify ways they can nurture and comfort themselves. It also reinforces the concept that they have the right to protect and care for their bodies.

DO THIS EXERCISE TO

- Introduce the concept of the rights and responsibilities of having a body to protect and nurture.
- Introduce the concept that thoughts and feelings create an internal interpretation of reality that affects behavior.
- Increase the children's ability to make conscious behavioral choices.
- Increase the children's ability to define and express personal needs.

DO NOT USE THIS EXERCISE WHEN

There is no reason not to do this exercise.

WHAT YOU NEED

- Copies of the "Body Bill of Rights"
- Paper
- Pens or pencils
- Colored markers

INSTRUCTIONS

Part I: Have everyone sit together in a circle for a brainstorm and discussion of what it means to have a body and what rights and responsibilities go with having a body.

Part II: Pass out copies of the "Body Bill of Rights" to all group members, along with blank paper and pens or pencils. Review each right and responsibility on the "Body Bill of Rights," and then ask the group members to make lists of the personal things they do to take care of their bodies. For example, in response to the right to decide who can and cannot touch your body, Susie could write down that she uses her voice to say, "No! I don't want you to touch me." In response to the right to feel bodily sensations such as pain, sexual arousal, and comfort, Anna might write, "I laugh when my little brother tickles me" or "I cried when I fell off my bike and hurt my knee last week." Regarding the responsibility to understand your body's basic needs for a healthy diet, good hygiene, exercise, and safe sex, David may write, "I eat cereal and bananas for breakfast because it feels good in my tummy."

Part III: Have each child draw a picture, using the markers, that illustrates one of the things from her list that she does or has done. Tell the children to think of specific examples that are in response to one of the rights on the "Body Bill of Rights."

Part IV: When everyone has completed their tasks, invite the group to come back into a circle. In turn, have all group members share their drawings and their personal lists.

HINTS

Often, one or more group members will have difficulty thinking of specific ways they take care of their bodies. You can make suggestions or ask them questions to help stimulate ideas.

This exercise can help children begin to recognize and regain a sense of personal power and awareness of their own bodies.

Body Bill of Rights

Having a body means there are rights and responsibilities that go with it:

- The right to exist and occupy space

- The right to decide who can and cannot touch your body

- The right to determine how your body can be touched

- The right to change your mind about by whom, how, and when your body may be touched

- The right to protect and defend your body against harm

- The right to feel bodily reactions such as pain, sexual arousal, and comfort

- The responsibility to express directly your needs and wants regarding your body

- The responsibility to understand your body's basic needs for a healthy diet, good hygiene, exercise, and safe sex

My Safety and Comforts

GOALS

To build self-protection skills and healthy body image; to learn about internal boundaries

AGES

5 through 12

TIME

20-40 minutes (depending on group size)

PURPOSE

This exercise encourages children to develop self-soothing behavior; to increase a feeling of safety in their lives. Sexually abused children often live in a constant state of fear, vulnerability, and/or anxiety. This exercise begins to replace negative stimuli associated with the abuse with positive stimuli that induce thoughts of safety and protection.

DO THIS EXERCISE TO

- Introduce the concept that thoughts and feelings create an internal interpretation of reality that affects behavior.
- Increase the children's ability to identify, comprehend, manage, and express thoughts and feelings appropriately.
- Increase the children's ability to define and express personal safety needs.

DO NOT USE THIS EXERCISE WHEN

There is no reason not to do this exercise.

WHAT YOU NEED

- Copies of the "Things That Make Me Feel Safe" worksheet
- Pens or pencils

INSTRUCTIONS

Explain to the group that each of them will be making his own list of things that help him feel safe in his life. Pass out copies of the "Things That Make Me Feel Safe" worksheet, along with pens or pencils, so the children can write their answers.

Go around the circle and allow all group members to fill in each blank on the worksheet. Encourage the children to write down (or, for those who are younger, to draw) their endings to the statements. Items that make them feel safe might include certain clothes, favorite books, or animals. Animals can include pets or stuffed or imaginary animals. Things they can look at to help them feel safe may include a picture of someone they love and trust or a sunset. If you have extra time, let group members ask some of their own questions. For example, "What [person, place, or thing] makes you feel safe?"

HINTS

In one of our girls' groups, Jody asked the question, "What food makes you feel safe?" We added this to the list. This gave us an opportunity to talk about the drawback of relying on food for comfort. In such a discussion it is important to go back to the "Body Bill of Rights" and emphasize that eating food is part of the body's basic needs for health and nutrition, not for gaining emotional comfort. Other questions you can ask group members to promote further discussion about this topic include the following:

- Have you used food for comfort?
- What were the circumstances?
- How do you feel after eating for comfort?
- What else could to do to comfort yourself?

Be sure to include the children's completed "Things That Make Me Feel Safe" worksheets in their final group packets at closure. Unless their offenders have been sentenced to serve time in prison, many children who have been abused have difficulty feeling safe. Encourage them, with their parents or other caregivers, to gather some of the safe things from their lists and keep them in their rooms to enable them to sleep more restfully.

This exercise can be modified and used with younger children. It is fun to be creative in imagining what helps the children feel safe. A few of the ideas that we have tried include the following:

- Different smelly things to pass around for them to smell (e.g., vanilla extract, suntan lotion, chalk)
- Recordings of different sounds for them to listen to (e.g., someone singing, the sound of a flute, children's voices, laughter)
- Various materials for them to touch (e.g., suede, cotton blanket, velveteen)

Usually, young children can tell you places that make them feel safe or animals that help them feel safe. Have them draw pictures using one color that makes them feel safe. Or have them draw pictures of people, places, or things that they could look at and feel safe.

Samples of Some Things That Help Children Feel Safe

Smell: Perfume

Safe activity: Talk on the phone

Sound: Listening to the radio

Taste: Taco salad

Touch: White cotton sweater

Colors: Blue and white

See: Pictures of friends

Lisa [age 9]

Smell: Ocean air

Taste: Chocolate

Touch: My fuzzy teddy bear

Sound: Little kids laughing

Sight: Woods

Colors: Green and purple

Place: Anywhere with friends

Janine [age 13]

Things That Make Me Feel Safe

The place that makes me feel safe is:

_____

_____

The smell that makes me feel safe is:

_____

_____

The animal that makes me feel safe is:

_____

_____

The sound that makes me feel safe is:

_____

_____

The thing that I can touch that makes me feel safe is:

_____

_____

The color that makes me feel safe is:

_____

_____

The thing that I can look at that makes me feel safe is:

_____

_____

The food that makes me feel safe is:

_____

_____

Healing Image

GOALS

To build self-protection skills and healthy sexuality; to learn about external boundaries; to build self-esteem

AGES

9 through 18

TIME

30-40 minutes

PURPOSE

This exercise gives participants a sense of power and hope that assists them in their recovery work from the sexual abuse. It is adapted from an imagery exercise in Marty Rossman's book *Healing Yourself: A Step-by-Step Program for Better Health Through Imagery* (1987).

DO THIS EXERCISE TO

- Give participants a sense of inner strength and a stronger core self-image.
- Create an image of what it looks like and feels like to be healthy again.
- Reduce and desensitize trigger reactivity.

DO NOT DO THIS EXERCISE WHEN

- There are group members who dissociate easily and would have difficulty maintaining awareness and attachment to their present surroundings following the exercise.

WHAT YOU NEED

- Paper
- Pastels, paints and paintbrushes, or markers

INSTRUCTIONS

Tell the group you will do a guided imagery exercise with them, and explain that imagery is not the same for any two people. Tell them, "It's easy enough. All you have to do is use your imaginations." Have group members spread out in the room and ask them to get comfortable where they will not be distracted by anyone else.

Begin with a progressive relaxation to help group members focus inward. Then lead them to an inner place of deep relaxation and healing. Here is an example of a healing imagery exercise:

To become more relaxed, go to a place in your mind that's filled with great beauty, peacefulness, and security . . . a place that feels safe and beautiful and healing to you. It may be a place that's real or imagined. Take a few moments to look around this place and feel more comfortable here. Find a spot where you feel most relaxed, centered, and quiet in this place. . . . Become calm and comfortable here.

When you are ready, notice any problem you are having because of the sexual assault. . . . It might be how you feel or how your body feels. . . . Simply put your attention there, staying completely calm, no need to worry . . . you are safe now. . . . Allow an image to come to you that represents this problem. . . . It might be different from what you expect or it might be familiar. . . . Just allow it to be whatever comes up. . . . Let it become clearer and clearer. . . . Observe it carefully.

Explore this image from as close or as far away as you feel comfortable. . . . Try observing it carefully from different perspectives. . . . Don't try to change it . . . just notice what catches your attention.

What seems to be the matter with this image? . . . How does this image symbolize the problem? . . . When you know this, let another image appear that represents the solution, the healing of this problem. . . . Again, let the image arise without any effort . . . and allow it to become clearer and clearer. . . . Watch it closely from different angles. . . . How does this image represent healing?

Hold this image in your mind . . . now recall the first image next to it. . . . How do they differ? . . . How do they relate to each other? . . . Observe them carefully.

Now make one image . . . the healing image. . . . Let the healing image take up more and more space. . . . Let it change the other image of the problem into the healing image. . . . Do this in whatever way works for you. . . . Stay relaxed and comfortable. Hold the healing image in your mind and know that you can have this image anytime you think about it. . . . Each time you imagine this healing image you become stronger and healthier. . . . You can remember it anytime.

Now imagine yourself slowly coming back to this room. Begin coming back one step at a time . . . as I count from one to ten. . . . Stay in a relaxed state. . . . One, two . . . just beginning to move, . . . three, . . . feeling comfortable, . . . four, five, . . . halfway to the room, . . . six, . . . remembering what was important to you from this imagery, . . . seven, . . . feeling more awake, . . . eight, . . . your eyelids might be feeling lighter, . . . nine, . . . feeling better than before, . . . ten, . . . fully awake, opening your eyes, and back in this room.

Have group members immediately get drawing or painting materials and begin creating the healing images they had. When all have completed their images, come back together as a group and talk about the images. Ask each person, as the group members share, what kinds of feelings she had with each of the images and how she is feeling now. Give group members a chance to ask one another questions.

HINTS

Generally, children are able to use their imaginations and visualize images very easily. There are times, however, when children's fears make it difficult for them to feel comfortable enough to close their eyes. In these cases, take time and explain the imagery process step by step. Have any children who feel scared choose places in the room near friends or a facilitator. Encourage them to try closing their eyes, and if it still feels too hard, give them permission to open their eyes at any time. Encourage them to do the imagery even if they need to keep their eyes open.

In the past, we have used the image of going down some stairs as a way of deepening relaxation to assist in creating healing imagery. We stopped doing this, however, when a little girl in group was triggered by the image of the bottom of the stairs. She had been abused in the downstairs of a house when she was very young. We now try to limit and use only very general image suggestions when children have difficulty imagining a safe place. For example, you might suggest that they imagine their favorite place or what their favorite place might look like, or a place that they have always wanted to go.

The images that get created during this exercise can be used throughout the remainder of the group sessions. You may also want to repeat this exercise in a later group session, especially if anyone has difficulty creating a healing image. This exercise also provides a good baseline for assessing how victimized the group members still feel from the sexual assault.

In one of our girls' groups, Jessica's healing image was of talking with her offender and asking him why he had abused her. She held this image in her mind, and though she had difficulty confronting him in group role-plays, she was finally able to confront him in individual therapy a year later.

Andrea's healing image was an image of her body as a chalice overflowing. This contrasted greatly to the emptiness and loss she felt after finally realizing her perpetrator had manipulated her into believing that she was his girlfriend. This was a long process for Andrea, and this healing image helped to reinforce her strength.

Body Tracing

GOALS

To build self-protection skills, healthy sexuality, and good body image

AGES

4 through 6

TIME

20-30 minutes

PURPOSE

This exercise helps to introduce group members to the concepts of identifying personal boundaries, being aware of their own bodies and bodily sensations, while learning to express themselves regarding touch they like and do not like.

DO THIS EXERCISE TO

- Continue to reinforce the children's ability to define and express personal safety needs.
- Define age-appropriate sexual behavior.
- Introduce the concept of the rights and responsibilities of having a body to protect and nurture.

DO NOT USE THIS EXERCISE WHEN

- Any child in the group is hypersensitive to any form of touch. For such a child, you can modify the exercise: Let her know her body won't be touched at all. If she still feels too uncomfortable, give her the option of drawing an outline of her body freehand. This way she does not have to lie on the paper, which may be too vulnerable a position for her.

WHAT YOU NEED

- Roll end of newsprint (available at most newspaper printing offices)
- Colored markers

INSTRUCTIONS

Before group starts, measure and cut newsprint in lengths that are as long as the tallest group member.

Part I: Let group members know that you will be tracing around their bodies. Have each child decide what feels most comfortable to her, either lying down on the newsprint with her face toward the ceiling or standing with her back against newsprint that is hanging on the wall. Also, encourage each child to choose her favorite color for you to trace with.

While you make a tracing on the newsprint around each child's body, talk to her to be sure she is comfortable. Ask her to tell you to stop if the marker is tickling her or if she doesn't want you to trace around any part of her. Do not trace close to the child's genital area. Draw to slightly above her knees on the inside of her legs, and later, after her body is fully traced and she is off the paper, you can fill this part in freehand. By talking to the child during the tracing and encouraging her to state how she is feeling, you help her to focus her awareness on her body and her personal safety needs.

Part II: Explain to the group members that they will be using a color code to indicate their personal safety needs related to the different areas of their bodies. Have them color the tracings of their bodies with green, red, yellow, and blue according to the following key:

- *Green:* All areas that I like to be touched.
- *Red:* All parts of my body I don't like to be touched.
- *Yellow:* The parts of my body that I don't care if I am touched.
- *Blue:* The parts of my body only I can touch.

Hang the tracings on the wall and have the children color them according to the color key. As they work on their drawings, talk with them about the specific areas they like or don't like to have touched and why.

HINTS

It is helpful with children in this age group to remind them what the different colors mean, because they will just keep coloring with whatever color they are using if you don't provide some gentle nudging.

Often, we follow this exercise with a hand or foot massage that children do together in pairs. This helps reinforce appropriate touch and a gentle approach to nurturing their bodies. If you decide to do such massage and you are using hand lotion, have a facilitator put it in the group members' hands or supervise it very closely. Many young children will get too much lotion if they are allowed to squeeze it into their hands themselves. Naturally, you should not use lotions or oils if any kinds of lubricants were used during the abuse of any of the children in group.

Safety Plan

GOALS

To build self-protection skills and healthy sexuality; to learn about internal boundaries

AGES

6 through 12

TIME

15 minutes

PURPOSE

This exercise helps children think about their safety and actively identify adults they can confide in. It also encourages them to ask for help when they need it.

DO THIS EXERCISE TO

- Reinforce the concept of the rights and responsibilities of having a body to protect and nurture.
- Increase the children's ability to make conscious behavioral choices.
- Increase the children's ability to define and express personal safety needs.

DO NOT USE THIS EXERCISE WHEN

There is no reason not to do this exercise.

WHAT YOU NEED

- Paper
- Pencils or pens

INSTRUCTIONS

Part I: As a group, discuss what the children would do if they needed help and did not feel safe. Ask them to think of three things they could do. Give them a few minutes to come up with their own ideas about ways they could get help. Here are some suggestions that came from some of our group members:

- Go to the neighbor's house.
- Call the police.
- Go into a store.
- Call a friend.
- Call your parents.
- Go to the school counselor.
- Call your counselor.
- Talk to your teacher.

Part II: Have each child write down the names of three people he would go to if he needed help. If a child cannot come up with three names, contact his individual counselor so that the child can also work on safety issues in his individual sessions.

HINTS

The trauma of sexual abuse often leaves children feeling unsafe, which can put them at further risk. This very simple and straightforward exercise takes only a few minutes to do in a group, yet it gives tremendous strength in resources and ideas to children in need. Talking about what to do when they need help gets them thinking and feeling confident enough to choose consciously to protect themselves.

During this discussion, consider whether you believe that the children in the group would really do what they are suggesting. To help strengthen their self-protective skills, you may wish to follow this exercise with "Prevention Skits." When children seem less capable of self-protection (e.g., they have difficulty knowing what to do if

---

they need help, or who to ask for help, or they hesitate to believe that anyone would help them), practice prevention skills repeatedly with them. Encourage them by recognizing their strengths and their uniqueness. Help educate the other adults in their lives to praise and encourage them as well. This allows the children more chances to feel stronger and more confident about themselves. We also suggest to the parents of group members that their children need to feel strong in their bodies as well as their minds. Various activities—such as ballet, gymnastics, and martial arts—can help create this feeling, depending upon the child's interests.

After doing this exercise we often assign homework for the children to do before the next week's group. We instruct them to ask someone for help during the week and report back about it in group next week. Usually group members do the homework or during group they think of something that happened where they needed to ask for help.

Simon Says and I Say

GOALS

To build self-protection skills; to build self-esteem

AGES

5 through 11

TIME

5-15 minutes

PURPOSE

In this exercise, group members play Simon Says with an assertive twist added. Children learn that it is okay to say no even when playing a fun game.

DO THIS EXERCISE TO

- Increase the children's capacity to value self.
- Increase the children's capacity to assert their will and desire appropriately and effectively.
- Decrease restlessness in the group.

DO NOT DO THIS EXERCISE WHEN

- Some group members are not respectful of others' boundaries, so they will not accept "no."

- Too many of the group members will play only if they can be Simon and would refuse to follow other Simons.

WHAT YOU NEED

No special materials needed

INSTRUCTIONS

Explain that the group is going to play a version of Simon Says that is played just like the original, but with one exception: When Simon asks you to do something that you do not want to, you can say no, and you don't have to do it.

To begin, pick a group member to play Simon. Instruct everyone else in the group to follow what Simon tells them to do as long as he says, "Simon says." If he tells you to do something without preceding his command with "Simon says," then you are not to do anything. If you do what he says and he hasn't said "Simon says," then you are out. The last person left wins.

HINTS

When we play this game in group, we often say no to one of Simon's commands early in the game to model being assertive. Group members soon follow our lead.

We have had children in groups who will participate only if they can lead. To help such children move from a place of control, make it clear that the first one to lead will be the one who is quiet and paying attention. The next one to lead will be the one who wins the first game, so you must be playing in order to get a chance to be Simon. If someone wins more than once, we have her choose somebody else who hasn't had a turn yet and who is participating. She can then have the control of choosing whether she wants to play or not.

Maddie, a 6-year-old, was not feeling comfortable in group. She appeared shy and nervous and the other children were finding it hard to get to know her. When it was her turn to be Simon, we supported and encouraged her to give it a try. She was great at it. She came up with many fun, outlandish moves and switched from one move to another so fast that she kept fooling people as Simon. Everyone was laughing and engaged. This helped build her self-esteem, and she started to be more talkative in group.

Prevention Skits
(Therapy Group Only)

GOALS

To build self-protection skills and healthy sexuality

AGES

4 through 11

TIME

45 minutes

PURPOSE

Often children who have been victimized in the past are at high risk for revictimization. It is vital to practice specific prevention techniques with them. These skits, which are divided up according to age groups, are useful for such practice.

DO THIS EXERCISE TO

- Reinforce the concept of the rights and responsibilities of having a body to protect and nurture.
- Increase the children's ability to define and express personal safety needs.
- Build the children's self-protection skills.
- Empower the children to feel confident enough to act consciously and appropriately.

DO NOT USE THIS EXERCISE WHEN

- Any group member tends to dissociate as a coping style. Stop the exercise if a child begins to dissociate or feels genuinely frightened.

WHAT YOU NEED

- Dress-up clothes (optional)

INSTRUCTIONS

Part I: Explain that everyone in group will be doing role-plays about different situations that could happen in real life. They will have a chance to practice various ways of protecting themselves. Let hem know that if at anytime anyone is feeling scared and wants the role-play to stop, she should just say so. Stay alert and attentive to how the children are doing and initiate asking others for help if you sense someone is having trouble.

Part II: Pick a role-play from some of the examples that follow. The facilitators should do one role-play first as an example for the group. As you act out the role-play and come to the point in it where you need to assert yourself for self-protection, turn to the group members and ask them for suggestions on what you could say in order to stay safe. When the group members have a sense of the exercise, choose a small group to act out the same or a different prevention skit. Take turns so that each group member has several chances to practice defining and expressing her personal safety needs in the skits. When someone doing a role-play gets stuck, have her ask the rest of the group for ideas to help her. If you run short of role-plays, ask the group members for some of their ideas.

Vary the role-plays according to the ages of the group members. Following are some prevention skit ideas grouped for children ages 4-5, 5-7, and 8-11. (Some skits for teenagers are described in the exercise "Date Rape.")

Some examples of role-plays for 4- to 5-year-olds:

- You are at the park with your friend. A stranger comes up to you and wants you to help him find his dog. What do you do?

- You are at the park with a friend and her older brother. Someone offers you candy to come with him. What do you do?
- You and your friend's brother are playing together. He wants to touch you in the private parts. You really like him and you want him to be your friend. What do you do?
- You are at child care and are playing house. A child asks you to pull down your pants. What do you do?

With little children (4-5 years old), you act out more fantasy than simple role-plays. For example, everyone would pretend to be kids playing in the park and one of the therapists would approach the group to try and trick a child. The other therapist and other group members would help that child stay safe.

Some examples of role-plays for 5- to 7-year-olds:

- You just had a special dinner that your mom made for her favorite brother, your Uncle Tim. When your mom tells you it's time for bed, Uncle Tim volunteers to tell you a bedtime story. As Uncle Tim is telling the story, he is also playing tickle. At first it's fun, but then Uncle Tim tries to tickle you down your pants. What do you do?
- You are 7 and your friend Jason is 9. Today you are playing in your room. Jason wants to play doctor, and he tells you to take off all your clothes, so he can see if you are sick. You say no. He calls you a baby and says he doesn't want to play with you anymore. What do you do?
- You go to the corner store with a friend to buy some candy. You see her slip some into her pocket. What do you do?

The following role-play, also suitable for 5- to 7-year-olds, is done in two parts. In the first part children learn that they need to ask their parents or other caregivers for permission to go to someone's house. In the second part, they learn what to do when someone starts playing a game that they do not like.

- (a) Mr. Garrison is your school bus driver. All the kids like him. Sometimes he gives special treats and even invites some kids over to see his new puppies. Today he invites you over and you love puppies. What do you do? (b) After you get permission, you go to Mr. Garrison's house. You're holding a puppy and Mr. Garrison pretends he is a puppy and playfully tries to lick your face. Then he acts like he has a puppy paw and he touches you in your private parts. He says that this is a very special game and that he may even give you a puppy after the game is over. What do you do?

Some examples of role-plays for 8- to 11-year-olds:

- You get home and your mom isn't there. You don't have a key and a strange man is lurking around your neighbor's yard. What do you do?
- You are sitting at a bus stop and a cute boy, who is the older brother of a classmate, stops by in his car and asks you to go for a ride with him. What do you do?
- You are at the mall and someone keeps standing too close to you. When you back up they get closer. What do you do?
- You are staying the night at a friend's house and she wants you to drink some alcohol with her. You see her take it out of her parents' liquor cabinet, and when you say no she keeps pressuring you. What do you do?
- A friend of your parents' keeps putting his arm around and you don't like it. What do you do?
- Your sister came home drunk and wants you to lie to your parents and says she'll get in trouble if you don't keep the secret. What do you do?

Part III: Return to the large group to discuss what worked and what did not work in the role-plays. Have each person tell what she did before when she was touched, then have her state what she would do now if someone tried to manipulate her.

HINTS

When acting out the role-plays, be especially sensitive to how the children are responding. If anyone is having a particularly difficult time, or appears to be shutting down, pull her out of the role-play immediately. She may be getting triggered and so may be reexperiencing her own abuse.

The most effective tools we can teach children in doing these role-plays is to say, "No!" and "I am going to tell." These responses need to be stressed over and over again. Studies have shown that offenders will not hurt children who they believe will tell on them. For children who have disclosed their abuse in the past and haven't been believed, strongly encourage them to keep telling. Ask them to make lists of the people they trust and could tell if they weren't believed by the first person they told.

Another effective way for children to avoid victimization is to scream. Screaming "Fire!" catches people's attention and they usually respond quickly. If a child screams, "Help, this stranger is hurting me," others are more likely to get involved, because the person threatening the child is a stranger, not a family member. Naturally, encouraging children to run away from potential offenders is important. And of course you should be sure they know how to call 911.

When doing these skits with younger children, we often alter some of the role-plays so that the touch is good. This helps them learn to discern between safe and unsafe touch. For example, a baby-sitter may ask a child if he would like to sit on her lap while she reads him a story. The baby-sitter may put her arm gently around the child's waist or lightly touch his arm. No "bad" touch is intended. When the children are acting this skit out, keep checking with them to see if they feel comfortable or if they are feeling "uh-oh" feelings.

Date Rape

GOAL

To build self-protection skills

AGES

12 through 18

TIME

60-90 minutes

PURPOSE

Acquaintance or date rape is extremely common, and children who have been previously abused are even more susceptible to this form of victimization. The focus on date rape in this exercise is intended to prevent further abuse and to help teens recognize whether they have been exploited in their own dating experiences.

DO THIS EXERCISE TO

- Reinforce the concept of the rights and responsibilities of having a body to protect and nurture.
- Increase the children's ability to define and express personal safety needs.
- Build group members' self-protection skills.
- Empower the children to feel confident enough to act consciously and appropriately.

DO NOT USE THIS EXERCISE WHEN

- You suspect someone in the group has recently been date raped. (Instead of doing this as a group exercise, discuss your concerns with the group member's individual therapist.)

WHAT YOU NEED

- *No Easy Answers* videotape (optional; available from the Illusion Theater, 528 Hennepin Ave., Ste. 704, Minneapolis, MN 55403)

INSTRUCTIONS

Part I: Have group members brainstorm the definition of rape or sexual molestation. When summarizing, make sure the final explanation includes "being coerced or manipulating into doing something sexual that makes you feel uncomfortable."

Part II: Have group members brainstorm situations in which they have felt they were manipulated sexually. Ask them what sort of "lines" or "tricks" were used.

Part III: Discuss the following questions with the group:

- How do you feel when you are being manipulated?
- What are the feelings inside you?
- Where do you feel it in your body?
- What thoughts go through your head when you are being manipulated?

Part IV: The facilitators now role-play a potentially dangerous situation. We like using this one, which we have adapted from the *No Easy Answers* video (see above). One facilitator plays Frank and the other is Susan. The facilitators set the scene: Frank and Susan are on their first date. They just went to dinner and a movie. Frank paid for both of their dinners. They have been having a really good time. They now decide to drive around and talk for a while. Frank takes Susan to "his favorite spot" and parks the car. They are fairly isolated from any main roads, although there are a couple of other cars parked around there too.

Now begin the role-play. Frank starts to "come on" to Susan. She is uncomfortable. Although she likes him, she wants to know him better before getting "involved." She doesn't even want to kiss him yet. As Frank comes on to Susan, the facilitator playing Susan asks group members for advice on what she should do. She tries out their suggestions and Frank responds to each one of them. Afterward, have a discussion as to what worked and what did not. Why did some suggestions work better than others?

Part V: Now have group members participate in role-playing. Have them think of situations they have found themselves in or are concerned about. Have them rehearse both serious and outrageous responses to give them the chance to risk something they would never do otherwise. Make sure that one of the scenarios played out includes both people being drunk or stoned.

Part VI: You may consider bringing in a self-defense instructor at this point. People who specialize in self-defense often have simple hints to give group members that will help build their confidence. One simple hint is, if you can hit your attacker in the eyes or the nose, it may give you enough time to get away. This can lead to a discussion about when it would feel okay for group members to use physical force to get away from someone. These are important questions to consider:

- Which is worse, hurting someone else or getting hurt?
- Is being forced or coerced into doing something sexual hurtful to yourself?

HINTS

One of the reasons date rape is so prevalent is that girls are afraid to make a scene and are also afraid to hurt boys' feelings. In the role-plays, have girls practice making a scene. Also, have them rehearse telling a guy, "I am not afraid to tell others that you are sexually abusive." The willingness to tell seems to be the best protection there is.

Have group members practice using the "broken record" technique rather than snappy comebacks. By not getting involved in a war of words and just repeating yourself over and over again, a person will take you seriously and know you are not willing to play any games. For example, when Frank says, "Ah, c'mon, Susan, what's the big deal? I just want to kiss you," she should respond, "But I don't want to kiss." He might then say, "Why are you acting like such a baby?" Her response: "I don't want

---

to kiss." Frank says, "C'mon, let's just practice one time." Susan's response: "I don't want to kiss."

Explain to group members that the sooner they say something in an uncomfortable situation, the easier it is to stop it. Make it clear that each of them has to decide for herself what feels comfortable and what does not. Maybe kissing Frank is fine but fondling isn't. Maybe a group member has made love before but does not want to anymore. Everyone has a right to choose who she wants to be with and what she feels comfortable doing.

Grotsky, Camerer, and Damiano, *Group Work With Sexually Abused Children.* Copyright 2000, Sage Publications, Inc.

chapter 12

Closing Exercises

Each group session and every group series ends with closure. Closure is a transitional process. It is a way to celebrate and summarize each child's efforts and achievements. It is a time to plan for the future, prepare for the next experience, and say good-bye.

Closure helps to make group a more tangible experience for children. It creates an opportunity for them to learn how to acknowledge their progress. It teaches them how to value what they have learned about themselves and how to use the skills they have acquired to ensure their future safety. To reinforce what children have learned, positive comments are often made to children during closing exercises, such as "Mickey knows who to ask and how to ask for help when he does not feel safe" and "Zac has learned what some of his triggers are and knows how to make himself present." These affirmations both support and encourage children in continuing to make healthy choices.

Summarizing the children's progress also enables them to gain perspective on their abuse. When children understand that abuse is an experience with a beginning, a middle, and an end, it is easier for them to trust in their present safety and to find hope for the future.

"Completion of Group Ceremony" is one exercise we use to acknowledge children's successes. This exercise offers the opportunity for family members to share in celebrating their children's progress and completion of group and for the children to take home concrete reminders of their accomplishments. Another closure exercise, "Debriefing and Evaluating Group," is used to review concepts often introduced to children for the first time in group. This process may be useful for revisiting and reinforcing ideas such as the rights and responsibilities of having a body to protect and nurture. This exercise also serves as a review of the entire group process, starting from the children's thoughts and feelings when they arrived the first day to their thoughts and feelings on this day of closure. This reinforces the concept of "then" and "now" and that life is an ever-changing process.

Part of group closure includes developing a plan for the future of each child. Most group members will continue to have contact with individual therapists. Some might benefit from additional group experience or from family therapy. The group facilitators' review and evaluation of a child's progress is integral to the success of the individual therapist's treatment plan. What the facilitators share about the child's progress in group will also help the individual therapist to determine the length of time and the modality of treatment most appropriate for the child.

As group draws to a close, some children will naturally become more inquisitive about when they will be finished with their therapy. The facilitators can inform them that they will contact their individual therapists and tell them about how well they did in group, which will help their therapists decide how much longer therapy will be needed. Other children who are further from completion may be anxious about group ending. They should be supported and encouraged to both recognize and rely on the resources they still have available in their lives, such as grandparents, their individual therapists, school counselors, and caseworkers. This also may be a time for children to exchange phone numbers, so that they can retain connections with one another.

For children who are not continuing in individual therapy after completing group, it is especially important that the facilitators review the resources they have available if the need arises. The facilitators can discuss with these children who they feel comfortable going to for help and what they can do if they need help feeling safe in the future. The facilitators should also make sure to offer themselves as resources, particularly to children who have few others to rely on.

Closure helps children to feel complete about what they have accomplished in group. It teaches them to contain their issues, and it helps them to make the transition back into their lives, with direction and goals for a positive future.

Wishes

GOALS

To provide closure; to build self-esteem

AGES

3 through 18

TIME

10-15 minutes

PURPOSE

This exercise helps group members to leave group with positive feelings about themselves and each other, and to hold on to a sense of future.

DO THIS EXERCISE TO

- Increase the children's capacity to desire, believe in, and hold hope for a positive future.
- End group on a positive note and leave the children feeling connected with the other members.

DO NOT USE THIS EXERCISE WHEN

There is no reason not to do this exercise.

WHAT YOU NEED

- Colorful individual sheets of paper

INSTRUCTIONS

Have the group sit in a circle and choose someone to go first. Then, going around the circle, have each member give that person a wish for the future, such as "I wish that you are safe with your brother," "I wish that you keep your great laugh," or "I wish that you can see how wonderful you are to be with." Each person then takes a turn at receiving wishes. As the wishes are spoken to each, a facilitator should write them down on a colored piece of paper for the individual to keep.

HINTS

If you let the group members know about this exercise a week in advance, they may think about their wishes ahead of time and the wishes may be more profound. This is a quick, short, positive exercise that can also be used as a filler during any other session.

Debriefing and
Evaluating Group

GOAL

To provide closure

AGES

4 through 18

TIME

10 minutes

PURPOSE

This exercise allows the group members to review and evaluate what they have learned in group over the weeks. It also encourages the transition of group members from depending on each other to meeting new people and feeling connected to the "outside" world.

DO THIS EXERCISE TO

- Review the learning and growth that have taken place in group.
- Facilitate closure of group.
- Help group members transition from group to moving on.
- Restate the children's accountability for their own behaviors, feelings, and thoughts and the offenders' responsibility for the abuse.

DO NOT USE THIS EXERCISE WHEN

There is no reason not to do this exercise (just keep it short).

WHAT YOU NEED

- Chalkboard and chalk or large piece of paper and marker

INSTRUCTIONS

Part I: Review some of the exercises you have done during the group sessions and highlight the general themes. Ask the group members:

- Do you remember when you walked into group on the first day? How did you feel?
- What were some of the games we did that first day to get to know one another?
- Did any of those games help you to feel safer in group and less nervous?
- What else did we do that helped you feel safer?
- Do you remember when we first started talking about the touch? How did you feel then?
- How do you feel now when we talk about it?
- When you first came to group, did you think the touch was your fault? Do you still think that? If not, whose fault is it?
- What else did we do in group that helped you?

THERAPY GROUP ONLY: Add these questions:

- Remember when we talked about triggers? What can you do when you are being triggered to be back here in the present time?

Part II: In all groups, brainstorm with group members:

- What was the best part of group?
- What would have made group better?
- In what ways are you different now from when you came here the first week?

HINTS

While reviewing the group exercises, include the objectives of trust and safety, understanding triggers, boundary setting, accountability for the abuse, and so on. When asking what group members learned, feel free to add your own observations; for example, "Katy, when you first came, remember how you used to hide under a pillow and would not talk to anyone? Then you learned to ask for what you needed. Instead of hiding under the pillow you learned to state, 'I would like some attention' or 'Talking about this makes me feel yucky inside.' Then we knew how to help you. I hope you keep asking for what you need so others can understand."

Keep this review short, especially for younger children. The members will be excited because it is the last day of group and you will probably be doing some form of party or celebration. Therefore, their attention spans will be short.

Completion of
Group Ceremony

GOAL

To provide closure

AGES

4 through 18

TIME

25 minutes

PURPOSE

This closing exercise highlights and honors the significance of the children's completing the group. Parents and other caregivers should also be included in the ceremony as long as each group member has someone who can attend it. (This exercise works well when preceded by "Debriefing and Evaluating Group.")

DO THIS EXERCISE TO

- Bring conscious closure to the end of group.
- Celebrate the accomplishments that the children have made in group.

DO NOT USE THIS EXERCISE WHEN

There is no reason not to do this exercise.

WHAT YOU NEED

- Preprinted personalized certificates for all group members (These certificates are made in advance after facilitators have brainstormed each member's strengths. These strengths are printed on the certificates along with general statements regarding the completion of group. Examples of some certificates follow this exercise.)

INSTRUCTIONS

Part I: Ask the children's parents or other caregivers in advance to come up with mental lists of things they are proud of about their children who are in group. Let group members know that their parents will be joining them for a few moments in this session.

Part II: Have the parents come into the room and sit next to their children. Stand up and present a summary of group and what the children have learned during the past few weeks. Then, one by one, call each child up to the front of the room to receive her certificate. As each child is called up, ask her parent to share with her the things about the child that she is proud of. Follow this by reading aloud to the group the personalized statements about the child on the child's certificate. Then hand the certificate to the child and shake her hand. Everyone then applauds as the child returns to her seat, and the process continues for the next child.

Part III: When all of the certificates have been passed out, join with the group members in the middle of the circle to do a chant. (Practice the chant before the parents come in, so group members are prepared for it.) Chants that we have used in the past include "Hey, hey we're really great!" "We feel, we think, we share, we're strong!" and "We like us!" Choose just one chant and have the group repeat it at least five times, getting louder each time. Finish by having everyone share a big round of applause. At this point, have the parents leave the room.

Part IV: To celebrate group completion further, we end the session with a party. Pizza and soda pop are usually the popular requests. (We ask the group about pizza toppings and dietary restrictions the week before.) If the parents have agreed, this is also a good time for children to exchange phone numbers.

HINTS

When making the certificates, make sure you spell the children's names correctly. We make our certificates on our computer. Most paper stores, office supply stores, and copy centers have papers with fancy borders that can be used as certificates.

Some parents have a difficult time giving compliments to their children and often will qualify everything they say. Help them to give clear positive statements. If a parent makes disparaging remarks, such as "I'm proud she got through group, I just wish she wouldn't wear those awful colors," you can protect the child and teach the parent by stating, "I think those colors look great on her. They are fun and bright. It sounds like you and your daughter have different tastes in clothing. Let's get back to other things you are proud of. Stay positive."

Teenagers may not want their parents at the celebration. Check with teen group members the week before to give them a choice of whether to have their parents at the ceremony or not. Remind them that parents will be there for only 10 or 15 minutes.

CONGRATULATIONS!!

To: _____

For successfully completing group
and for knowing how to say "no" and
"I'm gonna tell!" _____ is

_____
_____
_____
_____

WAY TO GO, _____ !!!

Signed: _____
Dated: _____

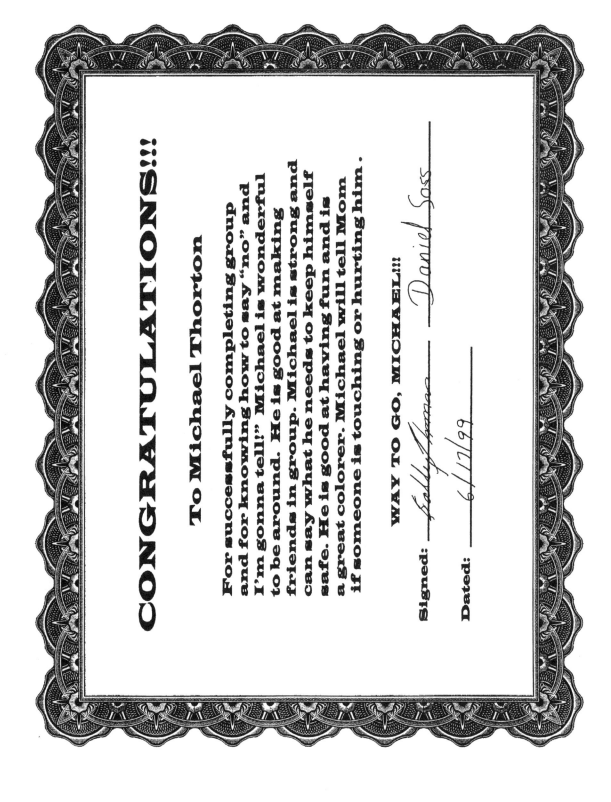

CONGRATULATIONS!!

To Michael Thorton

For successfully completing group and for knowing how to say "no" and I'm gonna tell!" Michael is wonderful to be around. He is good at making friends in group. Michael is strong and can say what he needs to keep himself safe. He is good at having fun and is a great colorer. Michael will tell Mom if someone is touching or hurting him.

WAY TO GO, MICHAEL!!!

Signed: _Kelly Thomas_

Daniel Soss

Dated: _6/17/99_

286

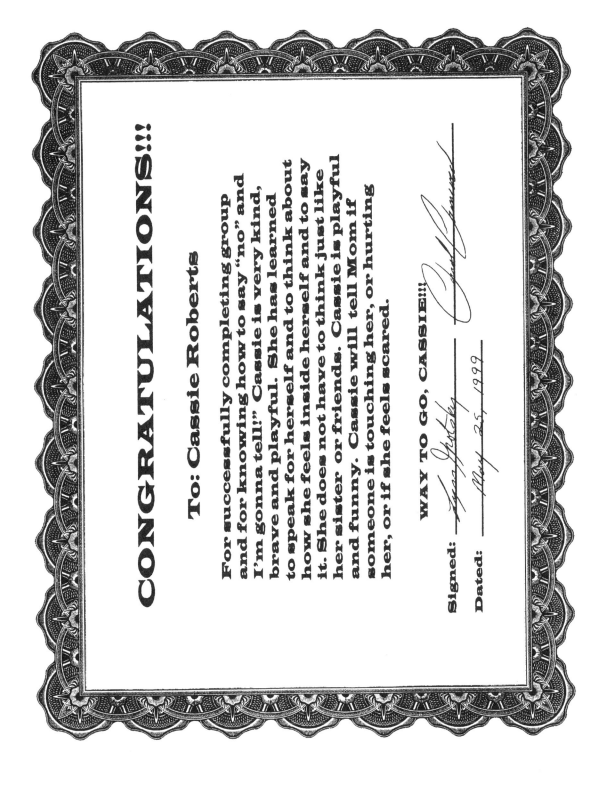

CONGRATULATIONS!!!

To: Cassie Roberts

For successfully completing group and for knowing how to say "no" and I'm gonna tell!" Cassie is very kind, brave and playful. She has learned to speak for herself and to think about how she feels inside herself and to say it. She does not have to think just like her sister or friends. Cassie is playful and funny. Cassie will tell Mom if someone is touching her, or hurting her, or if she feels scared.

WAY TO GO, CASSIE!!!

Signed: _Lynn Grotsky_

Dated: _May 25, 1999_

APPENDIX:
SAMPLE GROUP OUTLINES

Preschool Support Group
(8 weeks, 60-minute sessions)

Week 1

Goal: Safety and trust
"Ball Toss" to learn each others' names and other general information (use a teddy bear for a ball)
"Safety Rules"
"Yes/No/Maybe Continuum"
"My Own Safe Place"
A story about safety or building friendships and snack

Week 2

Goals: Safety and trust; self-esteem
"Ball Toss" to relearn names and say one thing you like about yourself
Review safety rules
"Group Mascot"
"London Bridge"
Draw a picture of yourself big and strong
Story about feeling good about yourself and snack

Week 3

Goals: Self-esteem and boundaries (identifying feelings)
"Ball Toss" using questions about general feelings
"Animal Boundaries"
"If You're Angry and You Know It" (using all feelings)
Draw pictures of feelings you feel sometimes (happy, mad, sad, confused)
Story about feelings and snack

Week 4

Goals: Boundaries (feelings about the abuse); dynamics of abuse
"Ball Toss" with questions about feelings about the abuse
"Revised Cookie Jar Tune"
"Yes/No/Maybe Continuum" with feelings about the abuse
"Magic Tricks"
Draw a picture of your feelings about being touched
Story about being tricked and snack

Week 5

Goals: Triggers; dynamics of abuse
"Ball Toss" with an explanation of triggers first; then each give an example of a positive
       and a negative trigger unrelated to abuse
Read *101 Dalmatians* (a short version)
Draw a picture of a safe place
"Revised Cookie Jar Tune"

Week 6

Goal: Boundaries (regarding feelings about the offender)
"Ball Toss" with questions about triggers they have and ways they can center themselves
"Clay Faces"
"Boundary Line"
"London Bridge"
"Let It All Out/Sound Train"

Week 7

Goals: Self-protection; healthy body image
"Ball Toss" about parts of your body you like
"Simon Says and I Say"
"Safety Plan"
Story about self-protection or body image and snack

Week 8

Goal: Closure
"Debriefing and Evaluating Group"
"Completion of Group Ceremony"
"Friendship Medals" while eating and partying

Preschool Therapy Group
(8 weeks, 60-minute sessions)

Week 1

Goal: Safety and trust
"Ball Toss" to learn each others' names and other general information (use a teddy bear for
    a ball)
"Safety Rules"
"Yes/No/Maybe Continuum"
"My Own Safe Place"
A story about safety or building friendships and snack

Week 2

Goals: Safety and trust; self-esteem
"Ball Toss" to relearn names and say one thing you like about yourself
Review safety rules
"Group Mascot"
"London Bridge"
Story about feeling good about yourself and snack

Week 3

Goals: Self-esteem; boundaries (identifying feelings)
"Ball Toss" using questions about general feelings
"Animal Boundaries"
"If You're Angry and You Know It" (using all feelings)
Draw pictures of feelings you feel sometimes (happy, mad, sad, confused)
Story about feelings and snack

Week 4

Goals: Boundaries (feelings about the abuse); dynamics of abuse
"Ball Toss" with questions about feelings about the abuse
"Revised Cookie Jar Tune"

"Yes/No/Maybe Continuum" with feelings about the abuse
"Magic Tricks"
"The Trick Hat"
Story about being tricked and snack

Week 5

Goals: Triggers; dynamics of abuse
"Ball Toss" with an explanation of triggers first, then each give an example of a positive and a negative trigger unrelated to abuse
Read *101 Dalmatians* (a short version); discuss how the puppies might be triggered later in life (eat a snack during the story)
"Drawing Where Molested"
"Centering"
"Revised Cookie Jar Tune"

Week 6

Goals: Boundaries (regarding feelings about the offender)
"Ball Toss" with questions about triggers they have and ways they can center themselves
"Clay Faces"
"Boundary Line"
"Talking to the Offender Psychodrama"
Eat a snack
"Let It All Out/Sound Train"

Week 7

Goals: Self-protection; healthy body image
"Ball Toss" about parts of your body you like
"Prevention Skits"
"Simon Says and I Say"
"Safety Plan"
Story about self-protection or body image and snack

Week 8

Goal: Closure
"Debriefing and Evaluating Group"
"Completion of Group Ceremony"
"Friendship Medals" while eating and partying

Boys' Support Group
(8 weeks, 90-minute sessions)

Week 1

Goal: Safety and trust

"Imaginary Object" to learn each others' names and other general information

"Safety Rules" (while eating snack)

"Group Mascot"

"My Own Safe Place"

Tag (if you have enough room) or Red Light/Green Light

Week 2

Goals: Safety and trust; self-esteem

"Ball Toss" to relearn names and say one thing you like about yourself

Quick review of safety rules

"Yes/No/Maybe Continuum"

Draw a picture of yourself big and strong (snack while drawing)

Discussion of the power of our thoughts (postive thoughts help us feel and be stronger)

Fun closing game, such as Telephone, Freeze Tag, or Duck, Duck, Goose

Week 3

Goals: Self-esteem; boundaries (identifying feelings)

"Ball Toss" using general questions about identifying feelings

"Yes/No/Maybe Continuum" with questions about feelings

"Sentence Completion" (with snack during the discussion)

"If You're Angry and You Know It" (using all feelings)

Draw pictures of feelings you feel sometimes (happy, mad, sad, confused)

Closing exercise such as passing a hand squeeze around the circle

Week 4

Goal: Boundaries (with a focus on anger)

"Ball Toss" with questions about different feelings they had during the week

"Target of the Offender"

"Yes/No/Maybe Continuum" with feelings about situations when they might feel angry and ways they sometimes express that anger

"Clay Faces" (and snack)

"If You're Angry and You Know It" (focusing just on anger)

Closing exercise—a fun game

Week 5

Goals: Internal boundaries; dynamics of abuse

"Ball Toss" with questions regarding feelings about the abuse

"Revised Cookie Jar Tune"

"Magic Tricks"

Write a list of three ways you were tricked by your abuser.

Using paper taped to the wall, draw a line to represent how tall the abuser was and a line showing how tall the child was. Discuss how difficult it is to stand up to someone larger than you. Do this for each child. (Serve snack during this time)

Quick discussion of why people abuse others (Include an explanation that they have a touching problem and are drawn to children. Explain that this has nothing to do with homosexuality.)

"Let It All Out/Sound Train"

Week 6

Goals: External boundaries; triggers

"Ball Toss" with questions about how their abusers tricked them

"Life Vest"

"Feelings/Thoughts Mask" (with snack)

"Centering"

"Simon Says and I Say"

Week 7

Goal: Self-protection

"Ball Toss" with questions about a time this week they used their vest and one thing they like about another person in group

"Preventions Skit"

"Safety Plan" (with snack)

"Simon Says and I Say"

Week 8

Goal: Closure

"Debriefing and Evaluating Group"

"Completion of Group Ceremony" and party

Boys' Therapy Group
(8 Weeks, 90-minute sessions)

Week 1

Goal: Safety and trust

"Imaginary Object" to learn each others' names and other general information

"Safety Rules" (while eating snack)

"Group Mascot"

Tag (if you have enough room) or Red Light/Green Light

Week 2

Goals: Safety and trust; self-esteem

"Ball Toss" to relearn names and say one thing you like about yourself

Quick review of safety rules

"Group Mascot"

"Yes/No/Maybe Continuum"

"My Own Safe Place" (snack during the exercise)

Fun closing game, such as Telephone, Freeze Tag, or Duck, Duck, Goose

Week 3

Goals: Self-esteem; boundaries (identifying feelings)

"Ball Toss" using general questions about identifying feelings

"Group Collage"

"Sentence Completion" (with snack during the discussion)

"If You're Angry and You Know It" (using all feelings)

Closing exercise such as passing a hand squeeze around the circle

Week 4

Goal: Boundaries (with a focus on anger)

"Ball Toss" with questions about different feelings they had during the week

"Target of the Offender"

"Sentence Completion" (in front of a video camera)

"If You're Angry and You Know It" (focusing just on anger)

Snack

Closing exercise—a fun game

Week 5

Goals: Internal boundaries; dynamics of abuse

"Ball Toss" with questions regarding feelings about the abuse

"Revised Cookie Jar Tune"

"Magic Tricks" (one or two tricks)

"The Trick Hat"

Using paper taped to the wall, draw a line to represent how tall the abuser was and a line showing how tall the child was. Do this for each child. (Serve snack during this time.)

Quick discussion on why people abuse others (Include an explanation that they have a touching problem and are drawn to children. Explain that this has nothing to do with homosexuality.)

Begin "My Own BASK Book"

"Let It All Out/Sound Train"

Week 6

Goals: External boundaries; triggers

"Ball Toss" with questions about how their abusers tricked them

Begin "My Own BASK Book" (while eating snack)

"Boundary Line"

"Centering"

Week 7

Goal: Self-protection

"Ball Toss" with questions about a time this week they used their personal space and one thing they like about another person in group

Finish "My Own BASK Book"

"Prevention Skits"

"Safety Plan" (with snack)

"Simon Says and I Say"

Week 8

Goal: Closure

"Debriefing and Evaluating Group"

"Completion of Group Ceremony" and party

Girls' Support Group
(14 weeks, 90-minute sessions)

Week 1

Goal: Safety and trust
"Imaginary Object" to learn each others' names and other general information
"Safety Rules"
"Group Mascot"
"Sharing Our Stories"
If there is time, Tag (if you have enough room) or Red Light/Green Light

Week 2

Goals: Safety and trust; Self-esteem
"Ball Toss" to relearn names and say one thing you like about yourself
Quick review of safety rules
"Group Collage About the Abuse"
"Yes/No/Maybe Continuum"

Week 3

Goals: Self-esteem; boundaries (identifying feelings)
"Check-In" (What thoughts or feelings did you have this week regarding the abuse?)
"Sharing Our Stories" (beginning part: Who touched you? How old were you? Are you safe now?)
Draw a picture of yourself big and strong
Closing exercise such as passing a hand squeeze around the circle

Week 4

Goals: Self-esteem; boundaries
"Check-In" (Share one great thing and one rotten thing that happened this week.)
"Yes/No/Maybe Continuum"
"Feelings/Thoughts Mask"
"Questions and Answers Box"
Group hug or hand squeeze

Week 5

Goals: Self-esteem; boundaries
"Check-In" (Share one time in the past week you showed an inside feeling to someone on the outside.)
"Friendship Medals"
"Questions and Answers Box"
Red Light/Green Light or Tag

Week 6

Goals: Boundaries
"Check-In" (Has being sexually abused changed you in any way? If so, how has it changed you?)
"Boundary Line"
"Life Vest"
Drawing of yourself wearing the life vest
"Questions and Answers Box"

Week 7

Goals: Boundaries; dynamics of abuse
"Check-In" (Share a time this week that you used your life vest.)
"Familiar Feelings"
"Sentence Completion"
"Letter From Angie"
"Let It All Out/Sound Train"

Week 8

Goal: Dynamics of abuse
"Check-In" (Is there anyone you trust? If yes, what about that person helps you to trust him or her?)
"The Butterfly and the Spider"
"Personal Butterfly"
"Questions and Answers Box"
Hot Potato with a ball (if time permits)

Week 9

Goals: Triggers; self-esteem
"Check-In" (Name three things you like about yourself.)
"101 Dalmatians"
"Centering"
"Target of the Offender"
"Questions and Answers Box"

Week 10

Goal: Boundaries
"Check-In" (Share a trigger you had this past week.)
"The Alligator River Story"
"Letter/Video to the Offender"
"Questions and Answers Box"

Week 11

Goal: Healthy body image
"Check-In" (Share one thing you like about your body.)
"Body Rights and Responsibilities"
"Body Tracing"
"Questions and Answers Box"

Week 12

Goals: Self-protection; healthy body image
"Check-In" (Name some ways you felt you used your body this week that felt good.)
Stretches (each person takes a turn leading the group in a body stretch)
"Healing Image"
"My Safety and Comforts"
"Questions and Answers Box"
"Simon Says and I Say"

Week 13

Goal: Self-protection
"Check-In" (Share one time you stood up for yourself or protected yourself this week.)
Roleplay what to do if: (1) you notice a fire; (2) a car pulls up and a driver asks you for directions; (3) you're home alone and someone comes to the door; and (4) your uncle wants you to hug him but you don't because you feel a little bit icky inside.
Draw a picture of yourself healthy and strong
"Questions and Answers Box"

Week 14

Goal: Closure
"Debriefing and Evaluating Group"
"Completion of Group Ceremony" and party

Girls' Therapy Group
(15 weeks, 90-minute sessions)

Week 1

Goal: Safety and trust
"Imaginary Object" to learn each others' names and other general information
"Safety Rules"
"Group Mascot"
"Sharing Our Stories" (first set of questions)
If there is time, Tag (if you have enough room) or Red Light/Green Light

Week 2

Goals: Safety and trust; self-esteem
"Ball Toss" to relearn names and say one thing you like about yourself
Quick review of safety rules
"Group Collage About the Abuse"
"Yes/No/Maybe Continuum"

Week 3

Goals: Self-esteem; boundaries (identifying feelings)
"Check-In" (What thoughts or feelings did you have this week regarding the abuse?)
"Sharing Our Stories" (second set of questions)
"Me, Through the Years"
Closing exercise such as passing a hand squeeze around the circle

Week 4

Goals: Self-esteem; boundaries
"Check-In" (Share one great thing and one rotten thing that happened this week.)
"Internal/External Self"
"Life Vest"
"Questions and Answers Box"
Group hug or hand squeeze

Week 5

Goal: Boundaries
"Check-In" (Share one time in the past week that you used your life vest.)
"Sentence Completion"
Begin "My Own BASK Book"
"Questions and Answers Box"

"Simon Says and I Say"

Week 6

Goal: Boundaries
"Check-In" (Has being sexually abused changed you in any way? If so, how has it changed you?)
"Why People Sexually Abuse Kids"
Continue "My Own BASK Book"
"The Trick Hat"
"Questions and Answers Box"

Week 7

Goal: Dynamic of abuse
"Check-In" (Do you think you could have stopped the sexual assault? If yes, how?)
"Letter From Angie"
"Sexual Assault Continuum"
"Sharing Our Stories" (third set of questions)
"Let It All Out/Sound Train"

Week 8

Goal: Dynamics of abuse
"Check-In" (Is there anyone you trust? If yes, what about that person helps you to trust him or her?)
Word association
"The Butterfly and the Spider"
"Personal Butterfly"
If there is time, "Questions and Answers Box"

Week 9

Goals: Dynamics of abuse; boundaries (regarding feelings about the offender)
"Check-In" (What are some of your feelings toward the abuser?)
"My Own Safe Place"
"Talking to the Offender Psychodrama"
"Letter/Video to the Offender"
"Let It All Out/Sound Train"

Week 10

Goal: Triggers
"Check-In" (Share one way your offender tricked or manipulated you.)
"Elizabeth's Triggers"

"Drawing Where Molested"
"Centering"
"Questions and Answers Box"

Week 11

Goal: Triggers
"Check-In" (Share a time this week that you were triggered. What happened?)
"Triggered Memories"
"How We Sabotage Ourselves"
"Centering"
Group cheer

Week 12

Goals: Self-protection; healthy body image
"Check-In" (Share one thing you like about your body.)
"Body Rights and Responsibilities"
"Boundary Line"
"My Safety and Comforts"
"Questions and Answers Box"

Week 13

Goal: Self-protection
"Check-In" (Share one time you stood up for yourself or protected yourself this week.)
"Prevention Skits"
"Healing Image"
"Questions and Answers Box"

Week 14

Goals: Self-protection; dynamics of abuse
"Check-In" (What do you need to feel safer in your life now?)
"Letter/Video to Nonoffending Parent(s)"
"Safety Plan"
"Questions and Answers Box"

Week 15

Goal: Closure
"Debriefing and Evaluating Group"
"Completion of Group Ceremony"
"Friendship Medals" while eating and partying

Teen Support Group
(Ages 11+) (15 weeks, 90-minute sessions)

Week 1

Goal: Safety and trust
"Check-In" (How are you feeling about being here and what do you hope to get out of the group?)
Self collage
"Safety Rules"
"Questions and Answers Box"

Week 2

Goals: Safety and trust; self-esteem
"Check-In" (What was the most outrageous thing you did this week?)
Quick review of safety rules
"Group Mascot"
"Sharing Our Stories" (first set of questions)
Hot Potato with a ball

Week 3

Goal: Self-esteem
"Check-In" (Name three things you like about yourself.)
"Group Collage About the Abuse"
"Sharing Our Stories" (second set of questions)
Closing exercise such as passing a hand squeeze around the circle

Week 4

Goal: Boundaries
"Check-In" (Share one great thing and one rotten thing that happened this week.)
"Feelings/Thoughts Mask"
"Life Vest"
Group hug or hand squeeze

Week 5

Goal: Dynamics of abuse
"Check-In" (Share one time in the past week that you used your life vest.)
"Letter From Angie"

"Sexual Assault Continuum"
"Sharing Our Stories" (third set of questions)
"Questions and Answers Box"

Week 6

Goal: Boundaries
"Check-In" (Has being sexually abused changed you in any way? If so, how has it changed you?)
"The Alligator River Story"
"Clay Faces"

Week 7

Goal: Dynamics of abuse
"Check-In" (Do you think you could have stopped the sexual assault? If yes, how?)
Checklist in "Why People Sexually Abuse Kids"
"Boundary Line"
"Lean On Me"
"Let It All Out/Sound Train"

Week 8

Goal: Dynamics of abuse
"Check-In" (Is there anyone you trust? If yes, what about that person helps you to trust him or her?)
"The Butterfly and the Spider"
"Personal Butterfly"
"Questions and Answers Box"

Week 9

Goals: Dynamics of abuse; boundaries (regarding feelings about the offender)
"Check-In" (What are some of your feelings toward the abuser?)
"My Own Safe Place"
Sentence Completion
"Questions and Answers Box"
"Let It All Out/Sound Train"

Week 10

Goal: Triggers
"Check-In" (Share one way your offender tricked or manipulated you.)
"Letter/Video to the Offender"

"Centering"
"Questions and Answers Box"

Week 11

Goal: Triggers
"Check-In" (Share a time this week that you were triggered. What happened?)
"How We Sabotage Ourselves"
"Centering"
"Questions and Answers Box"
Group cheer

Week 12

Goals: Self-protection; healthy body image
"Check-In" (Share one thing you like about your body.)
"Body Rights and Responsibilities"
"My Safety and Comforts"
"Healing Image"
"Questions and Answers Box"

Week 13

Goal: Self-protection
"Check-In" (Share one time you stood up for yourself or protected yourself this week.)
"Date Rape"
"Questions and Answers Box"

Week 14

Goals: Self-protection; dynamics of abuse
"Check-In" (What do you need to feel safer in your life now?)
"Body Tracing"
"Safety Plan"
"Questions and Answers Box"

Week 15

Goal: Closure
"Debriefing and Evaluating Group"
"Completion of Group Ceremony"
"Friendship Medals" while eating and partying

Teen Therapy Group
(Ages 11+) (15 Weeks, 90-minute sessions)

Week 1

Goal: Safety and trust
"Check-In" (How are you feeling about being here and what do you hope to get out of the group?)
Self collage
"Safety Rules"
"Questions and Answers Box"

Week 2

Goals: Safety and trust; self-esteem
"Check-In" (What was the most outrageous thing you did this week?)
Quick review of safety rules
"Group Mascot"
"Sharing Our Stories" (first set of questions)
Hot Potato with a ball

Week 3

Goal: Self-esteem
"Check-In" (Name three things you like about yourself.)
"Group Collage About the Abuse"
"Sharing Our Stories" (second set of questions)
Closing exercise such as passing a hand squeeze around the circle

Week 4

Goal: Boundaries
"Check-In" (Share one great thing and one rotten thing that happened this week.)
"Internal/External Self"
"Life Vest"
Group hug or hand squeeze

Week 5

Goal: Dynamics of abuse
"Check-In" (Share one time in the past week that you used your life vest.)
"Letter From Angie"
"Sexual Assault Continuum"
Begin "My Own BASK Book" (if there is time)

"Questions and Answers Box"

Week 6

Goal: Boundaries
"Check-In" (Has being sexually abused changed you in any way? If so, how has it changed you?)
"The Alligator River Story"
Continue "My Own BASK Book"

Week 7

Goal: Dynamics of abuse
"Check-In" (Do you think you could have stopped the sexual assault? If yes, how?)
"Boundary Line"
Continue "My Own BASK Book"
"Sharing Our Stories" (third set of questions)
"Let It All Out/Sound Train"

Week 8

Goal: Dynamics of abuse
"Check-In" (Is there anyone you trust? If yes, what about that person helps you to trust him or her?)
"Why People Sexually Abuse Kids"
"The Butterfly and the Spider"
"Personal Butterfly"
If there is time, "Questions and Answers Box"

Week 9

Goals: Dynamics of abuse; boundaries (regarding feelings about the offender)
"Check-In" (What are some of your feelings toward the abuser?)
"My Own Safe Place"
"Talking to the Offender Psychodrama"
"Let It All Out/Sound Train"

Week 10

Goal: Triggers
"Check-In" (Share one way your offender tricked or manipulated you.)
"Letter/Video to the Offender"
"Elizabeth's Triggers"
"Centering"
"Questions and Answers Box"

Week 11

Goal: Triggers
"Check-In" (Share a time this week that you were triggered. What happened?)
"Drawing Where Molested"
"Triggered Memories"
"Centering"
Group cheer

Week 12

Goals: Self-protection; healthy body image
"Check-In" (Share one thing you like about your body.)
"Body Rights and Responsibilities"
"My Safety and Comforts"
"Healing Image"
"Questions and Answers Box"

Week 13

Goal: Self-protection
"Check-In" (Share one time you stood up for yourself or protected yourself this week.)
"Date Rape"
"Questions and Answers Box"

Week 14

Goals: Self-protection; dynamics of abuse
"Check-In" (What do you need to feel safer in your life now?)
"Letter/Video to Nonoffending Parent(s)"
"Safety Plan"
"Questions and Answers Box"

Week 15

Goal: Closure
"Debriefing and Evaluating Group"
"Completion of Group Ceremony"
"Friendship Medals" while eating and partying

REFERENCES

Alexander, P. C. (1993). The differential effects of abuse characteristics and attachment in the prediction of long-term effects of sexual abuse. *Journal of Interpersonal Violence, 8,* 346-362.

Brauns, B. G. (1993). *The BASK model of dissociation.* Paper presented at the Outcome-Oriented Treatments of Choice Conference, "Psychotherapy Under Managed Care," San Francisco.

Browne, A., & Finkelhor, D. (1986). Impact of child sexual abuse: A review of the research. *Psychological Bulletin, 99,* 66-77.

Carozza, P. M., & Heirsteiner, C. L. (1982). A group art therapy model. *Clinical Social Work Journal, 10,* 165-175.

Celano, M. P. (1990). Activities and games for group psychotherapy with sexually abused children. *International Journal of Group Psychotherapy, 40,* 419-429.

Conte, J., Briere, J., & Sexton, D. (1989, August). *Mediators of long-term symptomatology in women molested as children.* Paper presented at the 97th Annual Meeting of the American Psychological Association, New Orleans.

Davis, N. (1990). *Once upon a time: Therapeutic stories to heal abused children.* Oxon Hill, MD: Psychological Association of Oxon Hill.

Deblinger, E., Hathaway, C. R., Lippman, J., & Steer, R. (1993). Psychological characteristics and correlates of symptom distress in nonoffending mothers of sexually abused children. *Journal of Interpersonal Violence, 8,* 155-168.

Deblinger, E., & Heflin, A. (1996). *Treating sexually abused children and their nonoffending parents: A cognitive behavioral approach.* Thousand Oaks, CA: Sage.

Everson, M. D., Hunter, W. M., Runyon, D. K., Edelson, G. A., & Coulter, M. L. (1989). Maternal support following disclosure of incest. *American Journal of Orthopsychiatry, 59,* 197-207.

Fluegelman, A. (1976). *The new games book.* Garden City, NY: Dolphin.

Friedrich, W., Berliner, L., Urquiza, A., & Beilke, R. (1988). Brief diagnostic group treatment of sexually abused boys. *Journal of Interpersonal Violence, 3,* 331-343.

Furniss, T. (1987). An integrated treatment approach to child sexual abuse in the family. *Children and Society, 2,* 123-135.

Gomes-Schwartz, B., Horowitz, J. M., & Cardarelli, A. P. (1990). *Child sexual abuse: The initial effects.* Newbury Park, CA: Sage.

Horney, K. (1991). *Neurosis and human growth: The struggle toward self-realization* (40th ed.). New York: W. W. Norton.

Kelley, S. J. (1990). Parental stress response to sexual abuse and ritualistic abuse of children in day care centers. *Nursing Research, 39,* 25-29.

Leberg, E. (1997). *Understanding child molesters: Taking charge.* Thousand Oaks, CA: Sage.

Linehan, M. M. (1993). *Cognitive-behavioral treatment of borderline personality disorder.* New York: Guilford.

Mandell, J., & Damon, L. (1989). *Group treatment for sexually abused children.* New York: Guilford.

McCarthy, B. W. (1990). Treatment of incest families: A cognitive-behavioral model. *Journal of Sex Education and Therapy, 16,* 101-114.

Ribordy, S. C. (1989). Treating intrafamilial sexual abuse from a systemic perspective. *Journal of Psychotherapy and the Family, 6,* 71-82.

Rossman, M. (1987). *Healing yourself: A step-by-step program for better health through imagery.* New York: Pocket Books.

Saunders, B. E., Villeponteaux, L. A., Lipovsky, J. A., Kilpatrick, D. G., & Veronen, L. J. (1992). Child sexual assault as a risk factor for mental disorders among women: A community survey. *Journal of Interpersonal Violence, 7,* 189-204.

Sgroi, S. M., & Dana, N. T. (1982). Individual and group treatment of mothers of incest victims. In S. M. Sgroi (Ed.), *Handbook of clinical interventions in child sexual abuse* (pp. 191-214). Lexington, MA: Lexington.

Way, I. F., & Spieker, S. D. (1997). *The cycle of offense: A framework for treating adolescent sexual offenders.* Notre Dame, IN: Jalice.

Zaidi, L., & Gutierrez-Kovner, V. (1995). Group treatment of sexually abused latency-age girls. *Journal of Interpersonal Violence, 10,* 215-227.

ABOUT THE AUTHORS

Lynn Grotsky, MSW, CSW, began working with traumatized and abused children in 1979. Through the years, she has combined her background in hospice, play therapy, feminist theory, trauma work, and child development in forming her theories and practice for her work with children. She strongly believes in the importance of advocating for children, and therefore serves on numerous committees and works on policy and legislative changes to benefit children and their families. She is also a trainer and consultant as well as a presenter at conferences throughout Washington State and the nation on such subjects as group work with sexually abused children, the dynamics of sexual abuse, sibling incest, and the mental health professional as expert and fact witness in court. With the staff at the Center for Individual and Family Counseling, she developed the SAFTE (Sexual Abuse Family Treatment and Education) Program, an intensive 6- to 9-month treatment program for all nonoffending family members, including siblings and extended family, that provided individual, group, and family treatment. She is currently in private practice and works with the Providence/St. Peter Hospital Sexual Assault Clinic in Olympia, Washington, developing and organizing sexual abuse therapy groups and supervising graduate-level interns. She also loves parenting her son and daughter and managing the singing group the Righteous Mothers—four funny, philosophical folk-rock musicians.

Carel Camerer, MA, LMT, has a background as an educator and trainer and has worked with children and families since 1980. She began therapeutic intervention work with abused, traumatized children and nonoffending adults in 1983. She cofounded the Center for Individual and Family Counseling and has led interstate as well as national trainings and workshops on identification and treatment of child sexual assault as well as group therapy as treatment for child sexual abuse. With a passion for the complexity and diversity found throughout all of nature and humankind, she weaves together the principles of two congenial therapeutic partners: Oriental medicine and psychology. Her extensive studies of *Jin Shin Jyutsu* and Chinese Five-Element Theory dramatically affect her unique treatment style and mind-body work. In her current private practice, she treats sexually abused children and adult survivors as well as individuals with stress management issues, anxiety disorder, psychosomatic and autoimmune disease. She also teaches "Wellness Wise" classes to the staff at Providence/St. Peter Hospital and *Jin Shin Jyutsu* classes privately in the community. Her practice has grown to include women and couples with fertility and adoption issues, adoptive children, and preadolescent girls coming of age. Her integrated method of practice helps people heal at the subtle level of spirit, which positively influences mental, emotional, and physical health.

Lynn Damiano, MA, is a state-certified psychotherapist in private practice in Olympia, Washington, and adjunct Associate Professor at St. Martin's College in the Master's of Psychology Program. She began working with chemically dependent adolescents and their families in 1984 and developed one of the first adolescent chemical dependency intensive outpatient programs in the state. During that time, she pioneered efforts to bring early identification and assessment practices into county high schools and middle schools. This early experience laid a foundation for the later cocreative development of the SAFTE (Sexual Abuse Family Treatment and Education) Program at the Center for Individual and Family Counseling, where she became a partner and co-owner in 1988. The current focus of her practice includes group work with women survivors of sexual abuse. Her "Adult Daughters of Not So Functional Families" group has been offered twice a year since 1989 as a powerfully transformative complement to individual therapy. She also treats couples in traditional and alternative marriages and partnerships who are experiencing difficulty or growing pains. She regularly presents workshops, consultation, and supervision groups on a unique assessment and treatment method she developed over years of practice and study called Intra Psychic Mapping (© 1994). This method combines object relations, developmental, and dialectic theories into a powerful and practical tool for exploring behavior and motivation, understanding defensive patterns, and creating change at the core level of personality.

We would love to hear from you!

Do you have any feedback for us on exercises in this book that you have tried?

We may be doing a sequel to this book, so we are also interested to know if you have additional exercises that you have found to be especially effective. If you do, please describe them for us. If we use them in the next book, we want to be sure to give you credit, so remember to include your name.

Please send responses to

Lynn Grotsky
2419 Carpenter Road
Lacey, WA 98503
e-mail: rtmom@aol.com

Or if you have questions and interest in the application of mind/body work for the treatment of psychosomatic symptoms of sexual abuse, curiosity about how to adapt our exercises to adult survivor groups, or have specific questions regarding the treatment of 3-6 year olds, please send inquiries and thoughts to:

Carel Camerer
2222 A State Ave NE
Olympia, WA 98506
e-mail: MtnMammas@aol.com

And if you like to wax pyschological about sexual abuse theory or related issues such as treatment protocols for sexual abuse and chemical dependency (in primary or secondary victims), or "family dynamics associated with sibling abuse" and "blaming the victim," or would like information about "Intrapsychic Mapping" as a tool for assessing and treating sexual abuse and family patterns, please send us your questions, musings, and experience to:

Lynn Damiano
2222 A State Ave NE Suite A
Olympia, WA 98506
e-mail: MtnMammas@aol.com